ECONOMIC HISTORY OF CUBA

Julio Le Riverend

ECONOMIC HISTORY OF CUBA

ENSAYO

Book Institute / Havana, 1967

Original title in Spanish:

HISTORIA ECONOMICA DE CUBA

Editora del Consejo Nacional de Universidades, La Habana, 1965

Translation/María Juana Cazabón and Homero León

Design/Tony Evora

INDEX

Part I

EUROPE AND THE DISCOVERY OF AMERICA

Part II

THE CONQUEST

Part III

FOUNDATIONS OF COLONIAL ECONOMY (1510-1659)

PART V

THE CUBAN ECONOMY DURING THE IMPERIALIST ERA (1886 - 1958)

PART VI

THE REVOLUTION

Part I

EUROPE AND THE DISCOVERY OF AMERICA

Chapter I

BACKGROUND

1.1. *The discovery of America*

1.1.1. Complex nature of this event: it summarizes the European evolution during the so-called Later Middle Ages. 1.1.2. Its significance: Europe discovers itself, since its own capacity for expansion is put to the test; the finding of the unknown continent has decisive repercussions upon science and thought. Special reference to the breaking up of Biblical tradition. Colonialist racism. 1.1.3. Economic importance of the discovery: the role of America in the development of European capitalism. 1.1.4. Capitalist accumulation and American wealth.

1.2. *General social and economic conditions in Europe at the end of the fifteenth century*

1.2.1. Political formation; rise of the monarchical organization. Unitarian tendencies: special reference to this process in Spain. 1.2.2. The dissolution of the feudal system: the commutation of payments in goods and the spread of commercial or merchant economy; ruin of the feudal lords. 1.2.3. Development and consolidation of the cities; commercial and industrial expansion; appearance and role of the bourgeoisie. 1.2.4. Technical transformations.

1.1. *The discovery of America*

1.1.1. The discovery of America constitutes a very complex event, for it summarizes the political, social and economic evolution of the Later Middle Ages, and synthesizes the scientific and pre-scientific currents that came into conflict at the end of the fifteenth century. The discovery of America brings into play the most varied elements of society at that time; and, especially, those which characterize rising commercial capitalism.

Among the elements which should be brought out are the following:

a) Financial resources, both state and private, characteristic of merchant capitalism in its process of development, as can be seen in the participation of Luis de Santangel and Juanoto Berardi in the provision of funds for the preparation of Columbus' first voyage;

b) Political will of the Catholic Sovereigns, who struggled against feudal individualism and were then carrying on a general effort towards the consolidation of absolute monarchy in Spain;

c) Geographical and maritime knowledge in the Atlantic stage of European commerce and navigation, a stage which started in the fourteenth century. Columbus himself is a symbolic example of the shifting of commercial and maritime activities towards the Atlantic;

d) Depredatory impulse of men who were outside the social framework of feudalism; that is, of the city bourgeoisie who aggressively engaged in lucrative ventures. Of this we find an exponent in Columbus, son of an artisan and an artisan himself; and

e) Hunger for gold in the most advanced countries of Europe, because of the scarcity of the precious metal which they needed more each day to settle the traditionally wanting commercial balance with the Far East and to satisfy internal commercial growth.

1.1.2. The discovery of America has repercussions and brings about results of primary importance towards the interpretation of the modern world.

In the first place, Europe discovers itself in coming upon a different human race, which will serve to test its increasing capacity for domination and for the exploitation of natural and human resources overseas.

Along this road, rising capitalism hastens and reaffirms its consolidation. The profit-seeking commercial bourgeoisie typical of the Later Middle Ages relied, from then on, upon the grand-scale exploitation of colonial economies. It is not by chance that in very important commercial towns such as Augsburg, Ravensburg, and Nuremberg, where some of the most outstanding commercial groups of this time had their headquarters, a great amount of interest for America was apparent; the Venetians showed a similar interest. The immediate joining of these merchants and their interests in the process of penetration in America is a fact apparent from the earliest times (Germans in South America, Rio de la Plata, and Brazil; the Justiniani in the Hispaniola sugar industry; the colonizing enterprise of the Welsers in Venezuela; and the Germans in the Cuban copper mines). This interest is reflected by the numerous editions of the letters of Americo Vespucio. [1]

In the second place, bourgeois humanism, characteristic of the Renaissance, found in America arguments of great importance for the breaking up of the socio-historical framework established in Biblical tradition: the American Indians have no clearly defined place in the Bible. Arguments on their origin constitute an interesting aspect of the importance of the discovery of America, since they do not appear to be descended from Japhet nor Sem nor Cam. The doctrinal efforts to force the interpretation so that the American Indians be somehow included within Biblical tradition are an excellent example of how the discovery of America made obvious the limitations of the Bible. The problem of original sin constitutes a most special aspect; the Indians, who were completely naked, could not be descendants of the primitive couple (Adam and Eve), because after original sin all their descendants should wear clothes.[2] Consequently, a part of humanity had been discovered that did not fit within the Biblical framework.

In the third place, the problems of colonization contributed to declare the racist concepts as an instrument of domination over backward peoples and lands, which the European wishes and needs to exploit in order to satisfy the demands of the merchant groups who finance the conquest and colonization.

1.1.3. Beyond doubt, the economic repercussions of the discovery are fundamental.

Europe needed raw materials and manufactured goods which, in part, it had been obtaining for some time in the Far East through the Arabs. This need was so strong that Columbus in this first voyage all but fancied seeing oriental products in the Antilles. America not only provided Europe with gold and silver; but, since 1520, it exported cane sugar, an article on increasing demand in Europe which could not be found in what we may call its traditional sources of supply. (See Chapter II). The theory that colonial economy should "complement" European economy grew in strength, leading down, in the seventeenth century, to the first capitalist theory of overseas domination, which is known by the generic name of mercantilism (within mercantilism, colonial derivations receive the name of "colonial pact").

The influence of America contributed to accelerate the process of feudal dissolution, since the "revolution of world commerce" inspired and strengthened the beginnings of industrial capitalism. It is not by mere chance that England, the first American colonial power, was, as well, the first country to be precisely organized after the industrial capitalist manner.

On the other hand, the exploitation of the natural and human resources of America was one of the material historical bases for the colonialist expansion of the capitalist countries (especially England and France).

1.1.4. In order to bring about all these consequences, it was necessary that there should have been in Europe a certain level of capitalist development. The two types of capital predominant in the Middle Ages (usurious and commercial) had reached a concentration that allowed for the unchaining of the process of accumulation; a process which, as is known, consists in the dispossession of artisans and farmers and in their conversion into wage-earners.[3]

The neat division of work in the cities during the Middle Ages had undergone changes during the fourteenth and fifteenth centuries. The merchant who walked about the market-places buying and selling articles of diverse regions became a commercial entrepreneur who supplied the artisan with raw materials and payed him for his work. Some of these merchants bought the equipment and made it available to artisans, officials, and apprentices, who for this reason became true wage-earners.

Among the artisans as well, there took place a process of concentration. The guilds lost their primitive flexibility, and numerous officials and apprentices, during the fifteenth and sixteenth centuries, could not acquire the condition of masters with their own establishments. The more powerful artisans became veritable industrial capitalists who paid wages to numerous officials and apprentices. These two transformations, that of the merchant and that of the artisan, signified that the means of production were no longer within everyone's reach, but only within the reach of a few who monopolized them.

On the other hand, the dissolution of the feudal system liberated thousands of peasants from payments and serfdom; and the lands were turned to commercial crops or pastures, for the benefit of the new landholding class that sprang either from the feudal class or from new elements who acquired the lands with usurious, commercial, or industrial capital.

The commercial entrepreneurs and the landholders received huge benefits from colonial exploitation, for they either invested in expeditions, established privileged commercial companies, or produced for exportation.

1.2. *General social and economic conditions in Europe at the end of the fifteenth century*

1.2.1. When America was discovered in 1492, the feudal system of production and of social relations was breaking up. During the thirteenth and fourteenth centuries, the feudal lords had to struggle against the kings, who became stronger with the support of the socio-economic elements in the cities, that is to say, of the bourgeoisie. The feudal barons had maintained a permanent state of war during three centuries, fighting among themselves for domination over productive lands and masses of serfs, and devastating and extortioning rural and urban areas of population. In the fourteenth and fifteenth centuries there was no longer a clear distinction between the "rights" of the feudal lord and the abuses of the rural bandits. The case of Spain itself serves as an excellent illustration of this, for the Catholic Sovereigns had to carry out a most energetic campaign against the Estremenian and Galician chieftains.

The feudal regime weakened itself as a result of the Crusades, which started in 1095. The enormous expenses brought about by these expeditions forced the barons to obtain loans, compromising their property in the hands of moneylenders, whether lay or ecclesiastical (monastic orders, orders of knighthood, etc.): for this same reason they needed to sell privileges to the cities and the merchants. The "immense mystic lottery" which are the Crusades, as Gonzalo de Reparaz wrote,[4] opened the way to the extinction in no small measure of many feudal families and their riches in landholdings. Because of the Crusades, as well as because of the weakening of the feudal system of production, thousands of serfs became free from their duties and their debts.

On the other hand, the struggles among the great feudal lords in the thirteenth and fourteenth centuries contributed still more to their weakening: the Hundred Years' War, quarrels and wars between kings and the Pope, War of the Roses in England, war between the French sovereigns and the Dukes of Burgundy, etc.

In France and England, the bourgeoisie and the peasants participated actively in this process. It would suffice to remember the attitude of the city of Paris, under the leadership of Stephen Marcel in the middle of the fourteenth century, and its union with the peasant *jacqueries.*[5]

Peasant uprisings occurred in all the countries and lasted for nearly two centuries. They were defeated, but they contributed greatly to break up the feudal regime, and helped to establish absolute monarchy, supported by the bourgeoisie.

The kings were opposed to feudal dispersion and individualism. They were feudal lords who, as they attained power, tended to unify the country, to centralize justice, to protect the security of trade, to guarantee rural life, to normalize the tax system. In Spain this tendency appeared from the thirteenth century, as a result of the progressive concentration of power in the hands of the Kings of Aragon, on one hand, and of the Kings of Leon and Castile, on the other — kingdoms which, at the time of the discovery of America, were united by the marriage of Ferdinand of Aragon and Isabella of Castile (the Catholic Sovereigns). The Catholic Sovereigns intended to concentrate justice in their own hands, struggled against feudal chieftains, and created a true "people's party" (the Holy Brotherhood) which represented the union of the monarchy and the bourgeoisie against the abuses of the rural bandits. This process was reversed by the policy established by Charles V, who relied upon the feudal classes and groups (the nobility and the high clergy), bringing about the uprising of the Castilian communities, whose defeat opened the process called the "Spanish decadence."[6]

The fifteenth century was the time when monarchies acquired their first power, which means, on the other hand, that the bourgeoisie had for the first time achieved the creation of internal conditions favorable to its development. In all of western Europe there was an increase of commerce and a great industrial impulse, symbolized by the expansion of trade in the Atlantic and the rise to mercantile and industrial predominance of cities such as Lisbon, Antwerp, and London. The Roman Church itself was undergoing a process of gradual decrease in the power of the monastic orders and of the bishops — a power which was being transferred to the Pope.

1.2.2. In the process of dissolution of the feudal regime, the basis of the manorial system of domination changed. The feudal system, in what we may call its pure state, was based upon the direct exploitation of the labor of the serf, who was obliged to make payments that tied him to the land, on one hand, and to the lord, on the other. But, with the penetration of commercial economy in the lordly manors, there came about a transformation. The feudal lords, because of the Crusades, of their internal struggles, and of the strengthening of the cities, were progressively coming to depend more and more upon monetary economy: they needed money for their expenses, their retinues, and their enterprises for political domination. The feudal lord would then rather exchange the old payments, the personal labor of the serf, and the rents payable in goods into monetary loans.[7] This commutation of payments changed the feudal lord into a modern landowner, who was interested above all in the income brought in by the land. The progressive submission of the feudal lords to commercial monetary economy allowed groups of serfs and cities to materially buy certain advantages, thus opening the way to the development of the modern landholding class. This process was not unique in the European countries, nor did it happen simultaneously.

This transformation strengthened the revenue system of the monarchies, which charged under the form of taxes what the feudal lord used to extract from the laborers. The support of the armies was now the duty of the monarchy. The lord no longer lived in his manor, but left to participate in court life; others settled in cities in the vicinity of their lands.

1.2.3. The system born from the dissolution of feudalism found its best expression in the development of the cities. The origin of the cities is a widely discussed question, but it is well to point out, as Marx did, that there is no break of continuity between the ancient Roman cities and some medieval cities. The question of origin would be posed only concerning a group of cities which appeared after the fall of the

Roman Empire. Whatever their origin may be, it is true that cities appeared and grew as an anti-feudal force. On one hand, their population was made up of men who somehow had freed themselves from the closed feudal pattern (because land was scarce where they lived, because they were running away from one region to another, or because they had bought their freedom). This process was hastened as a result of the shifting about of people which took place during the Crusades. [8]

The city dweller as a rule had no land, although some cities, as a corporation, held feudal power over the surrounding country. City life was based on commerce and industry, and its main social groups were made up of merchants and artisans.

The city wished to grow, to increase its population, because this added to its strength; hence the principle established by the statement "city air grants freedom," which meant that any man who lived for a time in the urban community was freed from duties, payments, and feudal ties. Merchants and artisans were organized in guilds, and city organization reflected the structure of the guilds. In many cities there came about a process of "aristocratization" and concentration of riches and power, as a reflection of what was happening inside the guilds themselves and inside professional organizations. The master artisans, in small groups, came to monopolize the practice of the professions, while officials and apprentices found increasing obstacles in the way of setting up their own establishments.

This process of "aristocratization" linked the urban bourgeoisie with the monarchy and with the nobility and the landowners. Popular uprisings appeared, rural or urban, and the compulsory working conditions of the dispossessed became worse. The bourgeoisie, whose very existence presupposed the "proletarization" of the urban masses, withdrew from them. Without giving up its anti-feudal attitude, it took sides with the monarchy, and, wherever possible, with the nobility as well, sharing in their power.

1.2.4. The expansion and transformation of the industrial organization was carried out along with technical discoveries which served to increase the productive capacity of equipment and to obtain a larger surplus from salaried labor. Thus the bourgeoisie could accelerate the process of accumulation. This should not lead to the belief that the Middle Ages were a stage in which no technical innovations were introduced; we materialists can accept neither the idyllic, reactionary view of the Middle Ages, nor the catastrophic view resulting from bourgeois democratism in the last century.

Among the most important innovations we must mention the use of the collar-type harness, which permits us to obtain maximum advantage from the traction of horses and mules, and which spread throughout Europe since the thirteenth century, allowing a greater amount of goods to be carried along the roads.

The scarcity of slaves and of population in general decreased the employment of man-driven mills and, in their place, there spread the use of the hydraulic mill, which attained a considerable development in the Middle Ages.

Finally, navigation was perfected by the application of the rudder to the sternpost of the ship, replacing the movable oar which served as rudder; this permitted sailing against the wind. This instrumental advance was the basis for the development of ocean navigation. [9]

BIBLIOGRAPHY

1. LEVILLER, ROBERT. "Mundus Novus"; origen de la fama de Vespucio. *Inter-American Review of Bibliography;* October-December, 1959.
2. ATKINSON GEOFFREY. *Les nouveaux horizons de la rennaissance Francaise,* Paris, 1935.
3. MARX, KARL. *Capital,* 3 vol. Mexico, 1959, volume I.
4. REPARAZ, GONZALO DE. *Historia de la Colonización,* 2 vol. Madrid.
5. RIBAD, ANDRE. *Historia de Francia,* Mexico, 1941.
6. MARX, KARL, and ENGELS, FRIEDRICH. *La Revolución Española.* Moscow, s.f.
7. DOPSCH, ALFONSO. *Economía Natural y Economía Monetaria,* Mexico, 1943.
8. PIRENNE, HENRI. *Historia Económica y Social de la Edad Media,* Mexico.
9. LILLEY, SAM. 3. *Hombres, Máquinas e Historia,* Buenos Aires, 1957.

Chapter II

ECONOMIC BACKGROUND OF THE DISCOVERY AND THE COLONIZATION

2.1. *Economic and military expansion*

2.1.1. Colonizations and colonialist movements in European history. 2.1.2. The colonization of continental Europe since the eleventh century. 2.1.3. Overseas expansion after the Crusades: Asia Minor; the East; the Mediterranean Islands. Importance of these colonizations from the viewpoint of economic domination. 2.1.4. The coming out into the Atlantic; the Madeira, Cape Verde, and Canary Islands; the African coast.

2.2. *Commercial impulse*

2.2.1. Traffic from commercial centers of the Mediterranean to those of the North Sea. 2.2.2. Industrial and commercial development. Appearance of the great markets; the case of sugar and wool. First encounter with the need for sources of raw materials. 2.2.3. The influence of the fall of Constantinople.

2.1. *Economic and military expansion*

2.1.1. The phenomenon of the foundation of colonies was not a new one in European history when the conquest and colonization of America began. In its earliest origins colonization is joined to the emigration of peoples: masses of persons that move and occupy new spaces, from which they drive out former occupants, for various reasons (exhaustion of natural resources; demographic pressures; conquest of riches created by other peoples; etc.). However, colonization is no such thing unless it is linked to the exploitation of the land, of agriculture —in general, of natural resources. This is why the process of colonization acquired a special meaning during the Middle Ages. And it changed into the exploiting domination over natural and human resources in the modern age. It is not a question of the fact of domination being something new: Phoenicians, Greeks, Carthaginians, and Romans, in their systems of colonization, showed that close ties exist between the process of emigration and economic and political interests. [1] Of course, it should be noted that such a tie was more clearly evident in the final stage of the Roman Empire, in which the mother country was a center for the absorption of riches found in the conquered and colonized lands, rather than a fatherland.

In truth, the Middle Ages began as a gigantic process of colonization which historians, following the historical and graphic tradition of Rome, that is, of the Roman imperial interests, call the barbarian invasions. After the barbarians came other peoples —Normans, Vikings, and Arabs— forming as a whole a veritable wave which lasted from the year 100 to the year 1000 of our era. The mass emigration of peoples changed into true colonization starting in the fifth century, that is, after the fall of the last Roman Empire.

2.1.2. Europe entered a process of colonization which itself flowed into one of self-colonization. First, the invaders and the peoples who dwelled in the different sections of the Empire mixed together. The great feudal domains took shape, keeping the former inhabitants who would give rise to the class of serfs; this former population was made up solely of the defeated, or of a mixture of the defeated and the victors. The first major result reflecting this colonization, of which a new economic, political, and social organization was slowly emerging, was the Carolingian Empire or Empire of Charlemagne.

This short-lived empire having dissolved, while on the one hand, the Norman invasions started, on the other hand, religious orders established monasteries which contributed to open new lands for cultivation, accordingly, helped to colonize. Charlemagne himself organized the system for the colonization of the frontiers in the marques or zones of contact with peoples who tried to penetrate into the fertile lands of Central Europe. In the south, the Arabs colonized in Sicily and in Spain.

During the twelfth, thirteenth, and fourteenth centuries, the growing population overflowed from the spaces used so far, and rushed into all free land. Woody, marshy, or poor lands were taken over by the lords, or by the monasteries, or by groups of independent farmers, as happened in France, in the Netherlands, and in Germany. [2] In Spain the process of colonization in these centuries was carried out as an apparent result of the re-conquest.

Certain legal institutions reflected this huge process of colonization, as was the case of *presura* or *aprisio,* that is, the right to occupy unexploited land for cultivation. The development of commercial economy made no small contribution to the hastening of this process, since then all the feudal lords and even the free agricultural communities were interested in attaching value to unused land, in order to send increasing amounts of agricultural products and industrial products of agricultural origin into the market. Moreover, transportation facilities and the possibility of using roads gave a new turn to the cultivation of the land.

Indeed, there went on in Europe an unceasing process of colonization which, properly speaking, prolonged itself in America under the imprint of the rising commercial and industrial capitalism.

2.1.3. The Crusades themselves implied a process of colonization. Thousands, hundreds of thousands of men left towards the Holy Land: they settled in Jerusalem and in other lands, where they formed the Latin kingdoms; they occupied Mediterranean islands; they plundered and colonized; they moved feudalism to these lands. Since they were unable to hold them without the aid of the Italian cities, they granted exceptional privileges to Genoese and Venetians, and depended on them to a large extent from the commercial and financial viewpoint.

All in all, as Gonzalo de Reparaz says, the Crusades embodied a vast "colonial attempt under the guise of mysticism." Naturally, the fruits of this primitive colonialism were reaped by the great Italian centers of rising commercial capitalism, as was revealed, on the occasion of the Fourth Crusade, in the conquest of Constantinople in benefit of the Venetians. This situation lasted until the Genoese as well obtained predominance in this great market place.

European commerce with the East, that is, with the nearest Asiatic regions, expanded after the Crusades, and did not decline upon the disappearance of the Latin kingdoms and princedoms which were formed there under their protection. Venice organized its commerce and navigation, and succeeded in gaining economic rule over Cyprus, Crete, and other islands. In these lands the Venetians established a powerful economic and political organization based on colonization by means of a small number of families from the mother country, who controlled commerce and, to a great extent, the productive lands. The Venetian colonial system took advantage of certain feudalistic elements in order to secure an aristocracy which would support the domination of the mother country.

We must admit that these colonizations had a new meaning, revealing themselves as a series of events linked to certain very precise economic interests. The case of the development of the sugar crop on the islands submitted to Venetian rule is an example; it conformed wholly to a definite commercial policy, and foretold, as a consequence of the increasing need of sugar in Europe, what eventually would happen in the Atlantic stage of the first capitalist development. [3]

2.1.4. When, in the fourteenth century, European commerce went out into the Atlantic, because of the development of the lands bordering the North Sea, a new phase started in capitalist commercial economy. Ocean navigation, for the time being, solved the problem of transportation of bulky goods whose freight would have been expensive if moved overland; the advances in navigation (Chapter I, 2.4.) favored this possibility. Venice and Genoa then traded actively with Portugal, Flanders, and England. The land routes branched out, connecting along different roads the Mediterranean with the north of Germany, Flanders, the north of France, and England.

While commerce flourished in the Near East —that is, in the regions to the east of the Mediterranean Sea— there emerged since the thirteenth century an active trade in the western Mediterranean. Barcelona and Marseilles, Pisa and Genoa had established contact among themselves and with the Barbary and other points located in the north of Africa and in the south of Spain. Navigation on the Atlantic was destined to favor the development of the new colonial-commercial powers. The Portuguese and the Spaniards, among whom expansive commercial capitalism emerged, we might say prematurely, launched out into the ocean and re-discovered and conquered the Madeira, Canary, and Cape Verde Islands, colonizing them; the Portuguese, on the other hand, pounced upon Africa and sailed along its coasts since the middle of the fifteenth century.

From that time on, and throughout the fifteenth century, colonization clearly conformed to economic objectives. There was grabbing of productive land, exploitation of the natives, and establishment of an economic organization intended to solve the problems faced by capitalist development in the mother country. Let us note, by the way, that in these Atlantic islands, where the colonization later to be continued in America was being tested, we find the industry and trade of enslaved Africans, from the very beginning.

2.2. *Commercial impulse*

2.2.1. The changes described represent a shifting of European trade centers from the Mediterranean to the Atlantic. The formation of great commercial and industrial centers in England, Flanders, Germany, and the Baltic region tended to create there a certain unity which repeated the process of development that had unfolded in the Mediterranean during previous centuries.

In northern Europe, cities such as Bruges and London, Bremen and Lubeck came to be new commercial emporiums that rivaled the great cities.

In Italy itself the maritime cities witnessed the rise of the banking power of Florence, which came to develop its sea trade too late. In spite of all these changes, the interests of Venice were not substantially affected, because Egypt was still an excellent middleman in the supply of the Far East products that Europe demanded. Eastern Mediterranean trade would hold out until the middle of the sixteenth century; and, of course, trade in the western part (Italy, southern France, Spain and north Africa) would not only continue, but would increase under the favorable influence of the capitalist type of general development.

2.2.2. The rise of great commercial and industrial cities in northern Europe and the persistence of commercial activity in the Mediterranean combined to create an important European market. The ties between zones became closer, as happened, for example, between Flanders, England, and Spain concerning wool trade and textile production.

Articles moved in all directions. Merchants travelled along European ports and inland fairs from Novgorod to Medina del Campo, from

Ravensburg to Malaga, from Marseilles to Ypres.[4] In the midst of this international trade, there emerged the bill of exchange, banking, trade laws, the institution of consuls, economic elements which industrial and financial capitalism inherited, and would employ, with variations, up to our days.

International markets emerged, especially for basic products such as wool, sugar, and spices. The rising commercial capitalism traded products to as large an extent as possible, and moved them all about Europe, with a view to the advantages obtained by the merchant and the producer. This is why there already appeared in Europe the process of a standstill in the economic development of certain zones in benefit of others. The struggle for predominance or control of these products was clearly outlined, as was proved by the first English capitalist class, which, since the fourteenth century, intended to keep for itself the national wool trade. In this aspect the administrations of the monasteries, who were large producers of this textile fiber, were particularly outstanding. This initial struggle for the control of trade may also be seen in the Canary Islands, over which Flemish and British commercial interests contended; as to the former, the commercial interest of Antwerp in the sugar trade was at stake. These contradictions appeared at the end of the fifteenth and the beginning of the sixteenth century, in relation to the first evidence of the need to control raw materials and basic consumers' goods, which was an event typical of capitalist development. The more advanced countries took possession of the lands that produced these articles. And, as more developing countries emerged, successive commercial predominance of certain cities reflected the great fluctuations in this international struggle for economic supremacy.

The importance of Lisbon at the beginning of the sixteenth century represented Portuguese colonial power; as that of Antwerp and Amsterdam at the end of the sixteenth and during the first half of the seventeenth centuries symbolized the capitalist commercial development in the Netherlands (Holland, properly speaking); and, later, the supremacy of London in the eighteenth century meant that England was the predominant capitalist country.

2.2.3. While these changes occurred in the North, others were going on in the Mediterranean. The Turks were progressively taking over the former Arab Empire; in the first place, they ruled in Egypt and Asia Minor. However, they did not close the door to trade with the

Venetians and Genoese: on the other hand, Venetian trade did not lack other routes (across southern Russia) allowing it to obtain Asiatic products.

In 1493 the Turks attacked and conquered Constantinople. This event has traditionally been considered as an immediate cause of the removal of European trade to the Atlantic; but it must be kept in mind that the Turks did not close their trade with the Europeans. Far from this, they reaffirmed the privileges and agreements which the latter had with the former rulers in all of the Near East. As an English historian has noted, the prices of oriental products in Europe underwent no remarkable change after 1453, which goes to prove that these products were not scarce. [5]

In 1502 the Venetian merchants who arrived at Near East ports in search of spices and other Far East products found nothing to buy. At that time an event had taken place that would do away with the riches of Genoa and Venice: the Portuguese, sailing southward on the Atlantic, along the coasts of Africa, had sailed around this continent and arrived in the Far East with their ships. There they had bought, without middlemen, the products in which the European consumers were interested, and which Venetians and Genoese traditionally bought in the Near East. This event —the direct trade of Europeans in Asia— rather than the presence of the Turks in the Near East, was the decisive cause of the decadence of the Italian cities on the Mediterranean, where the highest development of primitive capitalist commerce had been achieved.

BIBLIOGRAPHY

1. Reparaz, Gonzalo de *Op. Cit.*
2. Pirenne, Henri. *Op. Cit.*
3. Le Riverend, Julio. "Historia del Azúcar antes del Descubrimiento de América". *Revista Bimestre Cubana,* January-June, 1947.
4. Day. Clive. *Historia del Comercio.* 2 vol. Mexico. s.f.
5. Lybier, A. H. "The Ottoman Turks and the Routes of Oriental Trade." *The English Historical Review,* Oct. 1915.

CHAPTER III

COLUMBUS, THE ECONOMY OF HIS TIME AND THE DISCOVERY OF AMERICA

3.1. *The life of Columbus*

3.1.1. Brief reference to the questions it has aroused. The sign of Columbus; from forger to saint; from ignoramus to wise man. Limited importance of these questions.

3.2. *Symbolism of Columbus*

3.2.1. Columbus' native land of Genoa, or its commercial expansion: experience of the Discoverer as a seaman in the Mediterranean. 3.2.2. How Columbus' move toward the Atlantic can be explained. 3.2.3. Experience of the Discoverer as a seaman; his knowledge of economic activities basic to the history of America.

3.3. *The negotiations: the Santa Fe Agreements*

3.3.1. Financial support to Columbus' expedition. 3.3.2. Traditional mercantile spirit of the Santa Fe Agreements. Benefits of the enterprise.

3.4. *Columbus before America*

3.4.1. How Columbus' objectives are reflected in his *Diary.* "Easy" wealth. The natives as a market and as a suitable people to dominate. 3.4.2. The motive behind the falsehood of the discovery of Asia. 3.4.3. Struggle between royal power and Columbus.

3.1. *The life of Columbus*

3.1.1. Around Christopher Columbus a veritable web of hypotheses and suppositions has been woven, along with some historical data that try to explain the "mysteries" of his life. Since the very sixteenth century, there have been historians and pro-Columbus and anti-Columbus characters who, in party-like organizations, have made the printing presses run dry with all sorts of opinions, criteria, conclusions, and judgements on the personality of the Discoverer. This it to say, naturally, that his is a personality of the greatest importance, aside from the more or less subjective opinions expressed about it. Some hold him as a saint and a Catholic, while others believe him to be a converted Jew, none too sincere. An old argument on his wisdom places him, at the same time, among the greatest geniuses of humanity, surrounded by contemporaries all but lacking in the most elementary culture, and as a mere practical seaman, as there were many in his time. Let us not mention that the argument is extensive in other aspects, such as the higher or lower social status of his family, his age, and his temperament. Thanks to traditional historical criticism, Columbus has been a privileged human being: he was born at least in ten different places, and his remains lay at the same time in three tombs.

Evidently, there is a historiography that delights in transforming a series of secondary questions into great affairs; the historiographical question is created because it is convenient to the interests of the historian to deal with these minor questions while the essential issues are neglected.

This historiography creates the Columbus that each historian, according to the preferences established by his interests, regards as most representative. Unfriendliness and international differences promote works that, with the pretext of Columbus, exalt the Spain of the Catholic Sovereigns, or lower it; prejudice and rascist interpretations encourage hypotheses on Columbus' origin; reasons of confessional propaganda hand us a saintly Columbus, worthy of beatification. There are historians who pose as liberal when, lying within the plane of the "non-temporal" moral truths, they tell us of a Columbus that is ambitious or vain.

Although it would be preferable that Columbus' biography, like those of other historical characters, were perfectly cleared up, a large number of all the questions that have encouraged these arguments lack any substancial interest toward the interpreting of his character in the fundamental events of his life.

Columbus, a man of his time, that is, a man of a class or social group that resulted from a definite socio-economic evolution; a man who acts within the world of great modern transformations that open the way for industrial capitalism; Columbus, historical being, at once concrete and symbolic, without forced disguise, without "softening" frills does not easily emerge amidst the historiographic forest through which he has had the fortune of passing since the sixteenth century.

3.2. *Symbolism of Columbus*

3.2.1. Columbus was born in Genoa around 1451. Son of a wool weaver, it seems he attempted for several years to follow his father's trade, at a time when artisans were losing their independent lives, falling under the exploitation of the commercial entrepreneurs or of the great, enriched artisans. His country was still, and had been since the thirteenth century, one of the most powerful commercial centers in the Mediterranean; and was also, along with Venice, one of the European areas where the capitalist processes of social stratification and of accumulation first appeared; accordingly, neither chance nor his "genial" natural disposition were the forces that moved him toward sea trade, but the circumstances of his time. Sea trade and navigation were the convenient ways out for young city men at that time, when they wished to flee from the pressures resulting from the elimination of the feudal structure and the foundation of the capitalist organization. It was a form of liberation and of joining the army of new social forces that moved Europe towards progress.

At a certain time in his life, perhaps around 1465-70, he began to sail in the service of great sea merchants: the Di Negros and the Centuriones. He traveled throughout the eastern Mediterranean, which was typical of the times, as we have seen in Chapter II. Thus he acquired his first experience in the great school of navigation and commerce formed by trade with the Near East, that is, with the lands subject to the Arabs (Egypt and Asia Minor) and with the Byzantine Empire. This commerce was of pure exchange, that is, without settlers, and it was carried out by means of small establishments or agencies which foreign merchants set up in important trading cities: a relatively complex navigation, though undoubtedly simpler than ocean navigation. During several years he alternately departed from and arrived at Genoa: between 1470 and 1476 he visited the eastern Mediterranean islands, especially Chios, which was the object of exploitation on the part of great Genoese families such as the Justiniani. [1]

3.2.2. One day Columbus appeared on the Atlantic. The events leading up to this change of scenery remain in darkness. This makes it no less symbolic that the most famous seaman of the last part of the fifteenth century should have been led away from the Mediterranean toward the ocean, as if carried off by the current of economic transformations that also drove the center of European commercial activity out of the Mediterranean Sea to the Atlantic Ocean. This move of Columbus' appears to have been linked with political events of his time, for the Centuriones were in the service of the House of Anjou, who at that moment contended with the Aragonese for domination in Italy. It seems that he sailed from Genoa to the western Mediterranean; and, going out into the Atlantic, he reached the Netherlands and England. This was a route of intensive traffic at the time.

It is said that he was shipwrecked in an unfortunate encounter with enemy ships, and that Columbus had to swim his way to the Portuguese shore —an episode characteristic of a time when merchants and sailors struggled fiercely, under any banner, to snatch away each other's business and make off with political predominance, businessmen merging with pirates and bandits.

3.2.3. Portugal was a maritime and commercial center of the greatest importance, and this not only because it constituted an intermediate stop between the Mediterranean and the North Atlantic, but because its own development had carried Portuguese trade toward the south of the ocean, following the profile of the African continental coast. Columbus linked himself to this new face of commercial capitalism, born at the time when the "world market revolution" was about to take place.

In Portugal Columbus was accredited as a cartographer, a profession that, in such an environment, brought prestige and good income. He met Felipa Muñiz de Perestrello, married her, and joined a family of certain standing. This was a very important event, for the lady was a daughter of Bartolomé Perestrello —of Italian origin, by the way—

grandee of Porto Santo Island since 1446. The Perestrello family held political power in the Portuguese islands and considerable property; conspicuously, a sugar mill in Funchal.

Along these roads Columbus came into contact with new activities —ocean navigation, African slave trade, sugar production— all of which played a decisive role in the discovery and colonization of America. In all, with these experiences, Columbus was on his way to his great enterprise, since he not only enrolled anew in the aggressive host of merchants and seamen who eagerly sought new business and new natural and human resources to exploit, but also inherited and took advantage of other men's experience. As a whole, he knew the world of the time, which was progressively expanding; and he knew what cosmographers and practical people thought about it. It must not be forgotten that among the Portuguese seamen and sailors lay the sources whence emerged Columbus' idea of crossing the ocean to reach Asia. It was not a new idea; nor, consequently, was it original; nor did Columbus see it as a scientific purpose, even though, as happens with all practical conceptions, there existed within it an underlying scientific basis. The roundness of the earth was a widespread idea, though not officially accepted by the Church, which then maintained its traditional cultural monopoly.

Pro-Columbus historians do not accept the version that Columbus learned about voyages on the Atlantic, and they dismiss the question by regarding as false everything said in this respect. They attribute the forging of stories that diminish the glory of their hero to the envy of his contemporaries, or to the ambitions of Ferdinand V of Aragon, or to personal intrigues. It is possible that the Huelvan sailor named Alonso Sanchez, who died in Columbus' house and told him of the accidental discovery of America, did not actually exist. According to certain chroniclers since the sixteenth century, it is possible that Columbus would have known nothing about the voyage of Johanes Scolnus (whom some identify with Columbus); however, it is true that Columbus knew all there was to know about the existence of lands on the other side of the sea (more or less legendary lands, shown in maps of the time such as Martin Behaim's). And this suffices to make us conceive well-founded doubts as to Columbus' being an enlightened man, who "invented" geography, who extracted it from pure mental labor, and who upheld ideas unknown to his contemporaries. The legends then told about ocean lands and their uninhabitability were not only a check to knowledge and navigation, but also a stimulus for them; at the same time, Portuguese seamen were proving, year by year since 1450, that there were no such uninhabitable lands. [2]

Facing the interests of Columbus and of Spain, there emerged the interests for domination of other groups, such as the English and Portuguese traders, and legends that favored their own ends; this fact is far from new in the history of capitalism to our day; but to let all this contribute in making of Columbus something substantially different from the type of men who were then in charge of opening a new stage in human history is inadmissible.

3.3. *The negotiations: the Santa Fe Agreements*

3.3.1. We do not actually know how there grew within Columbus the plan of reaching Asia by crossing the Atlantic Ocean toward the west. It is said that the cosmographer Toscanelli influenced the appearance of this thought; but this has been rebutted by some historians with solid arguments. The fact is that around 1484 Columbus offered his project of a transatlantic voyage to King John of Portugal. This fits in with his residence in Portugal and his links with the great flow of sea expeditions organized there during the fifteenth century. King John, for some reason not sufficiently known, did not accept the idea; it has been claimed that he sent out into the ocean a secret expedition, which gave up the project in fear and disparaged the plan on its return. We should, perhaps, keep in view the fact that there already existed in Portugal a powerful conjugation of national interests linked to the southern sea route, that followed the profile of the African coasts. On the other hand, during those years the Pope, through Bulls, had granted the Portuguese full sovereignty over the lands lying in that direction, which made them view the possibility of reaching Asia along this route, losing interest in other projects.

About this time Columbus had to flee from Portugal, because of debts, as some historians would have it, or for other reasons, perhaps not removed from the feudalesque conspiracy of Ferdinand de Braganza (1483); and he left for Spain where he found the protection of the Duke of Medinacelli, who set him on the way to the royal court.

The Catholic Sovereigns (Ferdinand of Aragon and Isabella of Castile) did not immediately accept Columbus' project. Some historians believe that they were bent upon the elimination of Arab rule, which was then reduced to the Kingdom of Granada; and that they were struggling against the feudal highway robbers in Galicia and Extremadura, and for these reasons did not at once favor the plan. However, Columbus did not depart from Spain; he remained as another courtier, following the Sovereigns, who helped him to make a living; and so the years went by until, after the liberation of Granada, the Sovereigns seemed to be in a disposition favorable to the development of projects for outside expansion. There remains no doubt that Spain, as a country closely tied to the Atlantic, was in the best of conditions to compete with Portuguese outside expansion, in line with the great transformations of the period.

After the fall of Granada, Columbus' project was considered. Some historians maintain that it was turned down at a meeting convened by the Sovereigns, due to the ignorance of the people consulted; but actually, there is no specific proof of the reasons behind such a refusal. It is acceptable to suppose that the persons who made up the council, who occupied important posts at court or in the service of the Sovereigns, or held important ecclesiastical or cultural positions, did not argue over theological or scientific questions; at most, under the disguise of ideological topics, financial and political aspects were debated, for it is known that, from the beginning, Columbus made demands which must have appeared disproportionate to his contemporaries. In the face of this new refusal, Columbus gave up the idea of remaining in Spain, although he decided to await another effort of the La Rabida monks in defense of his aspirations. Friar Juan Perez renewed his pleas before the Queen. The fact that the Friar Confessor to the Queen supported Columbus means that the reasons behind the refusal were not confessional or technical, but rather of a practical nature. Spain encountered the growing Portuguese power on the Atlantic; and, according to the Papal Bulls, there remained no other way but to cross the ocean straight across if it wished to attain the riches of Asia. At this stage, the decision on the affair fell into the hands of very practical men, possibly not at all concerned over theological or scientific matters; men such as Luis de Santangel, actuary of the Aragonese court and an important moneylender, who provided the necessary sum to prepare the expedition; Alonso de Quintanilla, another noteworthy courtier; Juan de Coloma, and others whom Manuel Serrano Sanz mentions and whose importance he emphasizes. [3]

The decision and the financing were backed up by bourgeois elements in the service of the sovereigns —a most important fact, not only from the general viewpoint of the meaning of the Catholic Sovereigns' policy, but because Columbus project seemed to hold a special importance for these men, and that is why they joined in its defense.

3.3.2. Columbus asked the monarchs for great concessions, as a reward for the discovery of a new sea route. He demanded a share in the profits of eventual trade with the "discovered" lands; the title of Admiral of the Ocean Sea; personal trading privileges in the lands with which Spain would come into contact. Apparently the Sovereigns obtained no advantages whatsoever. Nevertheless, the Santa Fe Agreements were signed (April 12, 1492) wherein Columbus got all he had asked for. In all, the Agreements constitute a contract between the Sovereigns and Columbus to the purpose of dividing the profits of the enterprise for the benefit of both parties. The contents of these agreements reveal it as a commercial enterprise; it speaks of nothing but barter or trade, since it was expected to reach Asia. No colonizing enterprise whatever is mentioned.

3.4. *Columbus before America*

3.4.1. The expedition departed, stopping at the Canary Islands to repair and supply some of the ships. The incidents of the discovery, which took place on October 12, 1492, are very well known. Columbus with his ships arrived at a small island in the Bahamas, coming for the first time into contact with an unknown world that lay between Europe and Asia. Days later, on October 27, he stopped at the island of Cuba for the first time. Through a partly literal version of Friar Bartolome de las Casas, we are acquainted with Columbus' logbook. This document would suffice to establish clearly the very unscientific and wordly concerns of Christopher Columbus. [4]

In his log, Columbus showed great concern about finding gold, which, as we know, all of Europe needed for its commercial transactions. He went so far as to hint at the possibility of exploiting the labor of the natives as a mild people, fit to be dominated. He was so interested in oriental products that he all but fancied to see them in the lands he had just discovered. [5]

Like a good capitalist merchant, he obtained products from the natives and always gave them something in return, pointing out the little value, by Spanish standards, of the things he gave away.

It was the spirit of profit that reigned within his personality, over and above the so-called saint and the possibly non-existent scientist.

3.4.2. Columbus returned to America in 1494 with a very important expedition. He took it upon himself to grant serious significance to his discovery, although he insisted on having reached Asia. On his second voyage he stopped at Cuba once again, this time on the southern coast, along which he traveled almost to its end, as far as the Isle of Pines. All of a sudden, Columbus considered it necessary to declare that Cuba was not an island, drawing up a record to this effect before the actuary of the expedition of June 12, 1494. All witnesses stated that the land in question was not an island, although one of them, Miguel de Cuneo, an Italian who seems to have joined the expedition out of curiosity, later confessed that they were all of the opposite opinion. Actually, the punishment threatened by Columbus for those who dared contradict him —that is, a fine of 10,000 maravedis and mutilation of the tongue— was sufficient to meet with absolute silence. The record has been opposed as counterfeit, and this is possible; but we must not forget it was convenient to the interests of Columbus to have arrived in Asia; for, thus, the Santa Fe Agreements, which he regarded as the source of his rights to the material enjoyment of his successful voyages, remained intact.

3.4.3. Columbus made two more voyages to America without stopping at Cuba. Since the second voyage, problems began as his interests came into conflict with those of the Sovereigns and of other groups of the time. Around these differences, which, after all, were material differences, a whole debate has been entwined in which pro-Columbus and anti-Columbus historians distribute among the characters of the period every sort of praise and abuse, as each of them sees fit.

The fact is that Columbus discovered an unexpected continent and that the profits and monopoly of exploitation of that continent granted to Columbus by the Santa Fe Agreements could not but worry the Sovereigns. The primitive commercial enterprise had become an enormous enterprise for the exploitation of natural and human resources which could not be left in the hands of one man alone, but, quite to the contrary, must be transferred to the hands of groups and of dominant political interests in Spain, among whom, in the first place, we must mention royal power.

BIBLIOGRAPHY

1. Alvarez Pedroso, Armando. *Cristóbal Colón, biografía del descubridor,* Havana, 1944.

Vignaud, Henri. *Estudes critiques sur la vie de Colomb avant ses découvertes,* Paris, 1905.

2. Cronau, Rodolfo. *América, Historia de su Descubrimiento*; vol. I., Barcelona.

3. Serrano Sanz, Manuel. *Orígenes de la Dominación Española en América.* Madrid, 1918.

4. Colón, Cristóbal. *Diario del Primer Viaje,* Havana, *National Commission* of UNESCO, 1962.

5. Iglesias, Ramón. *El hombre Colón y otros ensayos.* Mexico, 1944.

Morrison, Samuel Eliot. *Admiral of the Ocean Sea. A Life of Christopher Columbus,* 2 vols. Boston, 1942.

Spotorno, Giambattista. *Códice Diplomático de Cristóbal Colón,* Havana, 1887.

Part II

THE CONQUEST

CHAPTER IV

DOMINATION OVER THE TERRITORY

4.1. *The plan for the conquest of Cuba and its motivations*

4.1.1. The mysteries of Cuba. Slave trade in the American Mediterranean and the position of Cuba. 4.1.2. Secret voyages through the Caribbean and the Antilles. The position of Hispaniola; arrival of immigrants and opposing group interests. 4.1.3. Appointment of Diego Velázquez.

4.2. *Outline of the Conquest*

4.2.1. Components of the army; Velázquez and his captains. 4.2.2. The invasion; its incidents. 4.2.3. The founding of cities; characteristics; function; strategic position; relation to the economy.

4.3. *Significance of the Conquest*

4.3.1. Destruction of native economy. 4.3.2. Cuba as a steppingstone to new conquests.

4.1. *The plan for the conquest of Cuba and its motivations*

4.1.1. Up to the moment when the conquest of Cuba began (1510), the island was surrounded by "mysteries," insofar as what lay inside it was truly unknown. The origin of this mystery can be traced back to the impression made on the Spaniards by Columbus' second voyage, during which they visited the southern coast of Cuba, an apparently inhospitable land, full of swamps and bordered by keys and sand banks that hindered navigation — all this in contrast to the northern coast, which displayed a vigorous nature. There was a contradiction between an apparent richness and a no less apparent poverty. On the other hand, we already know that, in his second voyage, Columbus decided to declare that Cuba was not an island (Chapter III, 3.4.2.).

Nonetheless, Juan de la Cosa, in his map of 1500, presented Cuba as an island; but this knowledge of the true geographical condition of the country remained partially secret, since the threat of fine and persecution on the Discoverer's part lay heavy over all. There must have been many secret voyages, carried out against the privileges zealously maintained by Columbus; and one of them, attributed to Alonso de Ojeda or to Vicente Yañez Pinzón along with Juan de la Cosa must have been carried out around 1498, and served to prove that Cuba was an island.

Besides this, hardly had the Spaniards settled ir the Antilles when numerous clandestine or occasional voyages were undertaken with the purpose of stealing Indians and plundering the riches of the territory. On the other hand, conquerors came to Cuba pursuing runaway natives from Haiti (Hispaniola). Naturally, Cuba became known as far as its coasts were concerned, but no one knew what lay in the interior: whether or not there was any gold, whether or not the Indians were gentle, whether or not they had commercially available products in immediate supply, etc. These mysteries had to be solved.

Since 1504, the King was interested in having Cuba become adequately known; but Knight Commander Ovando, governor of Hispaniola (Santo Domingo - Haiti), carried out no projects to this end.

4.1.2. Well into the sixteenth century, there is knowledge of a secret voyage undertaken by one Sancho Camacho, who seems to have been in Cuba by order of Commander Ovando, a voyage whose results are unknown. [1]

The settlers established in Hispaniola went through a difficult situation in the first years of colonization, which is clearly reflected in Friar Bartolome de las Casas' *History.* After the conflicts of Columbus with some of the Spaniards who had settled there, Bobadilla's temporary government was characterized by the beginning of a colonizing policy; Spaniards were granted the so-called tenancies of land and the right to exploit groups of Indian laborers. It seems logical that the beneficiaries of these advantages should have neglected Cuba, for they had plenty to do and to gain in Hispaniola. However, old quarrels remained between both groups, whom we might describe as partisans of Columbus' interests, on the one hand; and partisans of the King's interests, or royalists, on the other. Besides this, by virtue of royal legal decrees of 1495 and 1497 that encouraged emigration, those who arrived with the purpose of becoming tenants increased in number. Nevertheless, it can be stated that new settlers attained less profit, since their predecessors had distributed all the wealth among themselves. [2]

An oligarchy, typical of the beginning of American colonization, came into shape here. The "rear guard" settlers pressed for riches, and, since riches were denied them, were in disposition to undertake adventures in other lands, upon the promise of spoils. Such a thing happened when the conquest of Cuba was announced in Hispaniola; the same thing happened in Cuba when the expeditions for the conquest of Mexico were organized.

In 1509, Commander Ovando was relieved of command and substituted by Diego Columbus, son of the Discoverer, to whom the King did not wish to return all the privileges that the Santa Fe Agreements had given his father; to make up for this, he had united him in wedlock to Doña Maria Toledo, a member of the distinguished family of the Duke of Alba, and had appointed him Admiral and Governor. With the arrival of Diego Columbus, old antagonisms undoubtedly grew more bitter. Among the officials appointed by the King we find Treasurer Miguel de Pasamontes, a man of great authority, for he represented the interests of the State, already opposed to those of the Columbus family.

The King needed to know what was going on in Cuba, since up to that time the colonizing enterprise had rendered no remarkable profit; that is why he insisted that the "mysteries" should be discovered. In 1508, Ovando appointed Sebastian de Ocampo to sail around Cuba, and he carried out the voyage, returning to Hispaniola. Actually, the purpose was not to find out whether Cuba was an island, but to learn of its conditions. Ocampo made known the harbors that he regarded as worthy of high esteem (Jagua, on the south; and Puerto Carenas, that is, the future Havana, on the north). It was indispensable to complete this information by entering the island, and this is why orders were given for a fully organized conquering expedition.

4.1.3. Diego Columbus decided to appoint his Uncle Bartolome head of the expedition; but the King ordered the latter to present himself immediately at the royal court. It is obvious that the King did not wish the Columbus family to go on increasing its rights to enjoy great benefits in America. If Bartolome Columbus had conquered Cuba, this feat would have strengthened the family claims to maintain the privileges granted the Discoverer in the Santa Fe Agreements.

Diego Columbus then saw fit to appoint Diego Velázquez, a tenant "richer than any other," who had arrived in Hispaniola on Columbus' second voyage and had been outstanding in crushing Indian resistance in the section of Xaragua, under the orders of Commander Ovando. He had taken part in the founding of several cities, and he owned many plantations in Xaragua, whose ports were close to Cuba. Las Casas says that "he was prudent, though held to be slow in understanding."

4.2. *Outline of the Conquest*

4.2.1. The conquering armies were organized under a leader appointed by the King or, as was the case here, by Admiral Diego Columbus, who had the faculty to do so. They constituted veritable private enterprises and drew up contracts or agreements by which the King and the army shared the profits of the conquest. Each member of the army received advantages according to his economic and military contribution, or merely enrolled for a salary.

About 300 men joined Velázquez. Some contributed capital and goods to equip the expedition; others contributed only their personal services. Naturally, there were many relatives of Velázquez'. Among other expeditionaries, we should mention Hernan Cortes, Juan de Grijalba, Francisco Hernandez de Cordoba, Garcia de Holguin, Father Bartolome de las Casas, and others who appear among the founders of Cuban cities. Francisco de Morales came as second-in-command. Somewhat later, they were joined by Panfilo de Narvaez and several others from Jamaica.

4.2.2. The exact date of arrival of the conquerors in Cuba is not known. According to Artiles, the army left Salvatierra de la Sabana near the end of 1509 or the beginning of 1510. Their place of arrival is also debated upon; for, while some historians say that they landed on the north of what is now the Province of Oriente —to be precise, in the vicinity of Baracoa, where Indian Chief Hatuey wandered at the time — others, such as Fernando Portuondo, are of the opinion that they landed on the south. Nevertheless, both opinions coincide on one point: in any case, Velázquez and his men arrived in the region near Maisi, in the Eastern end of Cuba. [3]

The fact that this zone was the headquarters of Hatuey, an Indian who had fled from Santo Domingo upon the abuses of the conquerors, led Velázquez to found the city of Nuestra Señora de la Asunción de Baracoa, where he built a fortress that served as a base for military operations against unsubmitted Indians. The Spaniards' superior armament and the lack of unified action on the part of all the Indians caused Hatuey to be defeated and burnt alive as a rebel.

Once this resistance was overcome, the rest was not difficult; that is why the conquest of Cuba is a merely economic event, with no greatness whatever.

Velázquez swiftly organized the conquest. When his second in command, Francisco de Morales, mistreated the Indians in the zone of Maniabon, he had him arrested and sent back to Santo Domingo. Thus he did away with a co-worker who did not like him, while at the same time he maintained his authority over the enterprise. [4]

The conquest was organized by means of three groups. One group, aboard a ship, would follow the coastline on the north, keeping in contact with a second group who would start by land toward the west. A third group and Velázquez himself would sail along the southern coast.

The land group was commanded by Panfilo de Narvaez, accompanied by Father Las Casas. He started out from Bayamo, where the first massacre of Indians took place. In his advance through the territory, he terrorized the Indians, once again attacking them with ferocious cruelty in the place called Caonao. They learned of the presence of shipwrecked Spaniards, and succeeded in finding two of them —women, at that— from whom they learned that the Indians had killed the others and that there remained one survivor among them.

While in the zone of Sabaneque (north of Las Villas), they learned of the existence of gold to the south; and, leaving a group of men behind, the others went on toward the west until they reached what is now the Province of Pinar del Rio. In Havana they were joined by a shipwrecked Spaniard, García Mexia.

When the heads of the expedition met at Jagua, Velázquez ordered that sixty men should remain in Havana and that Narváez, aboard the brig, should continue to the western end (Guaniguanico and Guanahacabibes), as he eventually did. With this, the occupation of the territory was consummated.

4.2.3. As they crossed through the territory, the conquerors founded the first cities. After Baracoa, Velázquez himself founded San Salvador de Bayamo. While Narvaez founded San Cristóbal, south of what is now Havana, Velázquez founded Sancti-Spíritus and Trinidad. Some time later they founded Puerto Príncipe, now Camagüey, and, last of all, Santiago de Cuba in 1515.

These cities have lasted; but the reasons considered by the conquerors in founding them are not exactly based on the wonderful geographical conditions of their sites. More urgent reasons originated these urban centers. In the first place, Bayamo, as well as Puerto Príncipe, Sancti-Spíritus, and Trinidad, were located in zones of abundant native population; although the finding of gold in the rivers that flow toward the south (Arimao, Agabama, etc.) may have influenced the founding of the last two. Accordingly, those cities were a garrison and, at the same time, the place for gathering together the profits from the wealth produced by the Indians. Santiago de Cuba, as well as San Cristóbal, south of Havana, was founded for its position on the Caribbean Sea, where many expeditions were being undertaken; to Velázquez, the King particularly entrusted one of these (that of Pedrarias Davila to Castilla del Oro, that is, Central America), so that it should be aided from Cuba. All Spanish activities before 1520 were carried out to the south of Cuba; to the north, lands and the immensity of the ocean were only vaguely known to lie. Cities on the southern coast became necessary, for since the early days commercial traffic was organized through the Caribbean Sea with Central America and Jamaica.

4.3. *Significance of the Conquest*

4.3.1. The conquest of Cuba has a manifold significance. The destruction of native organizations is undoubtedly the most important. The Cuban Indians were unable to endure the pressure of the Spanish material civilization, nor could they adapt themselves to the labor system that was immediately imposed upon them; they were practically exterminated and their culture reduced to dust. Naturally, the Spaniards absorbed some of the native creations into their colonial organization; this is particularly true and important as to agriculture and food. However, the rapid extinction of the Indians during the sixteenth century considerably decreased the possibility of any deep racial and cultural mixture.

4.3.2. On the other hand, since Velázquez' arrival Cuba began to play the role of bridge or supply base. As it became a land of refuge for the dissatisfied, not only did it relax the profound strain of conflicting interests at Hispaniola, but became as well the outpost for invading farther off lands. The expeditions for the discovery and conquest of Mexico were oragnized in, and departed from, Cuba, as later did those that supported the entrance into the south of what is now the United States.

BIBLIOGRAPHY

1. Chacón y Calvo José María. *Cedulario Cubano* (Los orígenes de la colonización) I. (1493-1512). Pages XXII and XXIV.
2. Casas, Bartolomé de las. *Historia de las Indias,* Book III, Chap. XXI.
3. Artiles, Genaro. *Primer Congreso Nacional de Historia.* Trabajos presentados. Havana, 1943.
4. Guerra, Ramiro. *Historia de Cuba*; vol. I., Havana, 1921.

MATANZA DE INDIOS EN CAONAO.

CHAPTER V

THE INDIANS AND THE CONQUEST

5.1. *The Indians and their economic organization*

5.1.1. Indigenous groups; their background and general characteristics. 5.1.2. The Tainos: their agriculture and industry.

5.2. *The doctrinal argument over the conquest*

5.2.1. Result of the conflict between both cultures. Rights of the Indians. 5.2.2. General view of the doctrine on just wars. The interests lying behind that doctrinal argument. Las Casas. 5.2.3. The doctrine on just wars as the theoretical basis for colonization.

5.3. *Reflection of this argument in Cuba*

5.3.1. It is not reflected at all: the Indians are dispossessed and subjected to labor. The ideas of Bernardino de Manzaneda.

5.1. *The Indians and their economic organization*

5.1.1. The economy —the general development of native society on the arrival of the Europeans in Cuba— was not of a uniform nature.

Through the information of chroniclers, as well as through archeological evidence, we know there were three indigenous cultures. The most advanced were the Tainos, whose fundamental characteristic was agriculture; the *Ciboneyes,* hunters and fishermen, were less advanced; last of all, the *Guanahatabeyes* were mere pickers of fruit. Of late, the possibility has been suggested of establishing an even lower level which would belong to the archaic culture of an unknown people, or of one that left no historical imprint on their identity, as the others did.

Certainly, there is still much to be done in Cuba, archeologically speaking, for field work has not been carried out according to a plan nor with adequate systematic continuity. The light shed by archeological findings, to this day, has not decisively contributed to complete the picture of indigenous civilization delivered by chroniclers and historians and other sixteenth century sources, along with comparative studies of the other Antilles and South America, zones where the presence of the same type of Indians as in Cuba has been detected. However, the information at our disposal permits us to arrive at some important conclusions.

It seems that Cuba was occupied and conquered twice before the arrival of the Europeans in America. Originally inhabited by the most backward people, the *Guanahatabeyes,* it was later occupied by the *Ciboneyes* and the Tainos. The *Guanahatabeyes* might have come, perhaps, from the south of the United States, for certain similarities have been noted in their dress with those of some peoples from that area. The *Guanahatabeyes* built no houses; they lived in caves or within natural shelters, and, upon the arrival of the Europeans, they had gathered in the western end of Cuba (Peninsula of Guanahacabibes). They were cavern Indians, according to Pichardo Moya.[1]

From the direction of South America, whence they came, along the Antilles, from island to island, arrived the *Ciboneyes,* truly advanced collectors (hunters and fishermen) who occupied the whole territory and inhabited seaside towns by the rivers. Finally came the Tainos, also from the remaining Antilles. When the Europeans arrived, the *Ciboneyes* occupied the Cuban territory from Oriente to Pinar del Rio; but in Oriente and in part of what is now Camagüey they were subject to the Tainos, of a more advanced culture, who had subdued them. *Ciboneyes* and Tainos were, respectively, inhabitants of the coast and the highlands, as Pichardo Moya explains.

However, we should not dismiss the idea that the Tainos were entering the territory west of Camagüey, although not permanently establishing there. Nor should we eliminate the possibility that a part of the *Ciboneyes* were more primitive farmers than the Tainos; that is to say, that they were beginning to advance beyond the earliest stage of their socio-economic organization. It must not be forgotten that these peoples arrived in waves, and some of the later ones might have had a higher organization than the previous waves of the same people. When Columbus discovered America a new people were making their entrance into the Antilles: the Caribs, inhabitants of the Lesser Antilles, began to attack Puerto Rico in order to subdue the Tainos who were established there.

5.1.2. The Tainos had succeeded in creating an economic organization in which the cultivation and elaboration of yucca played a major role. They were gathered in villages of no great population, under chiefs whose posts were, perhaps, hereditary; they had social differences based on the division of labor, and they benefited from the work of the subdued *Ciboneyes,* whom they calley *naborías.* Therefore, they had abandoned the primitive classless organization, that is, the one without division of labor. Their instruments were made of stone and wood, and their pottery was simple.

The Tainos had developed agricultural techniques for a series of crops. One of them was known from the southern zone of Brazil-Paraguay (Tupí-Guaraní zone), where it was possibly first cultivated, and it spread toward the north, keeping pace with the movement of peoples that originated in that region: it is yucca (or *mandioca,* South American name). Tobacco and cotton, as well as corn, were an important part of Taino economy. As we see, all these plants were added to the common stock of capitalist economy, as a result of the discovery.

The Tainos had common cultivated fields. By means of a mere stick or *coa* or *jan* they opened a hole in the ground and inside they dropped the seed or shoot of the plant being sown; nature did the rest. But they had discovered what modern agricultural technique would call cultivation in beds. The Tainos piled the earth around the plant they had sown and in this way formed *montones* which the Spaniards, because of their appearance, called *conucos* (or little cones). Thus they concentrated the nourishing power of the plowable soil around the seed.

After the yucca, whose period of development was long, had been harvested, they started the manufacture of cassava, which the Spaniards graphically denominated "bread of the earth."

The variety they cultivated was sour yucca, which contains an element poisonous for man. To make it edible, the poison necessarily had to be extracted, and to this end they had invented a most clever system. They grated the yucca on a *guayo,* and the mass that resulted was placed inside a *sibucán,* a kind of bag strainer or tubular container made of woven plant leaves. They tied the *sibucán* to a tree branch, and along the free end they threw their weight and pulled; the *sibucán* would stretch and, in so doing, pressed upon the mass of grated yucca so that the poisonous juice drained off. When the mass had been sufficiently strained, it was removed from the *sibucán,* prepared in the shape of a flat cake, and baked over hot stones or *burenes.* Cassava bread was the food which the Tainos combined with all others, and this is why it was said to be the equivalent of European wheat bread. It had the quality of keeping for a long time without spoiling, unless it got wet, making it especially good for storage purposes. [2]

5.2. *The doctrinal discussion over the conquest*

5.2.1. The conflict of European economy and war implements with Indian economy and equipment resulted in the destruction of the latter. On the other hand, the Spaniards dispersed the Indians, tearing them away from their villages and cultivated fields toward faraway places, to *estancias* or mines; or else they employed them as luggage carriers. The Spaniard, conqueror or settler, took no account of the ties between the Indian and the land. He did not put to himself the question of whether or not the Indian had a right to the land; therefore, he took the land, and he also took the Indian. Naturally, all the conquerors and colonizers proceeded likewise: their domination was based on the expropriation of the natives and on their forced subjection to labor; but how was this phenomenon explained in sixteenth century Spain?

5.2.2. Here we must give a summary of the legal doctrine of the time on "just wars"; that is, on one hand, the "right" of the Spaniards to rule in America, and, on the other, the human and social nature of the Indian.

According to medieval legal doctrine, as put into practice during the re-conquest of Spain, there existed two groups of peoples: the *infidels* and the *gentiles.* Infidels were those peoples who, having known the gospel of Christ, did not accept it; therefore, they were people who had come into historical existence following the life of Christ or, at the very least, during his lifetime. Gentiles were those people who, having existed before, had not had the opportunity to know the gospel, such as the Greeks, the Egyptians, etc. The infidels who, knowing Christianity (it was supposed to have been preached throughout the world) did not follow it, could be "justly" attacked by the Christians and dispossessed of all their goods and enslaved. Their goods went into the hands of the Christian aggressors. All this implies that, under the name of Christ and by decision of his representative, that is, the Pope, the property and land ot the infidel (also of the gentile) went into the hands of the Christian, obtained by a "just war." [3]

When the Spaniards arrived in America, they did not argue about theology nor about legal science; they took possession of all resources, as though the Indians had been infidels and not gentiles. From 1510 onward, the problems began to appear. Some doctrinarians "discovered" that the Indians were gentiles, because they never knew the gospel; and, accordingly, the only truly solid right of the European to enter their territories was that of preaching. Then, if after having the gospel preached to them the Indians refused to embrace Christianity, they could be forced to do so by means of a "just war." If they were not infidels, their rights had to be respected as the rights of human beings. Of course, there were doctrinarians who carried the European point of view to such lengths as to deny the human condition of the Indians, insisting that they were serfs or slaves by nature.

But this argument, which went on through the sixteenth and (with decreasing emphasis) into the seventeenth centuries (and which also appears in doctrinal discussions in Portugal, in France, and even in the English colonies themselves) did not serve to improve the lot of the Indians to any substantial degree. The conquerors and the settlers defended themselves, bribing those who upheld the doctrines most favorable to them. And, since colonial societies were constituted upon oligarchic bases, the most powerful economic group never respected the human condition of the Indian nor his rights. Indian legislation reflects in some measure the doctrinal guidelines that favored the Indian; but it was never duly carried out. [4]

One of the most outstanding men inside this doctrinal struggle was Father Bartolomé de las Casas, a secular priest who entered the Dominican Order because within the medieval theological and legal tradition it represented a dotrinal position more favorable to the Indian. It is good to remark that there must be no confusion on one basic point: Las Casas did not oppose Indian labor for the profit of the

European, but he intented this to be within a system that would allow freedom to the Indian. If we could use words more precisely, we would say that this idea tended to create a wage system of labor, while the conqueror and the settler wished to keep the Indian under a system of forced labor similar to slavery and to feudal serfdom.

However, all this doctrinal web should not be considered a useless historical fact. Historical facts may be basic or secondary, but they are all useful for getting to know a certain economic, political, and social organization. In this case, behind the doctrinal argument, that is, under the cloak of the ideas of those who favored the liberty of the Indians, and of those who favored enslaving them, lies the true conflict among the interests of groups and institutions. The Church, divided in her interests, wished to keep the Indian under the rule of the preachers; but, at the same time, as a Church, did not oppose the power of the colonial oligarchy. This oligarchy wished to maintain its privileges, exploiting without limit the natural human resources. The King, the Spanish State, wished to maintain the Indians as vassals to increase his own strength. At the same time, he was distrustful of the excessive power gained by the oligarchies; but he did not come into conflict with them, because the oligarchs and the privileged European, as opposed to the Indian, constituted the support of the colonial regime. For these reasons, the study of these doctrines should be carried out regarding their links with colonial reality.

5.2.3. From the viewpoint of this reality, that is, of the motives, possibilities, and results of the conquest, this great doctrinal argument embodies the first *theory* of *colonization;* namely, the joining of ideas and interests that try to explain and justify the domination of faraway, backward peoples and lands by foreign economic and political groups. As a result of the period, it was all surrounded by a mass of theological considerations. A century later the first purely capitalist theory of colonization would appear, shaped by the current of mercantilism; its aspects of overseas domination received the name of *colonial* pact. [1]

5.3. *Reflection of this argument in Cuba*

5.3.1. Even though, since 1500, there are legal documents that declare the freedom of the Indian, the conquerors established in Cuba a slave-like system of labor and took over the lands, fi~st of all those already cultivated by the Indians; that is, they regarded the Indians as mere infidels. If at all, the problem was incidentally mentioned in 1518, in a memorial of Friar Gerónimo Bernardino de Manzaneda, who said as follows:

> ..."since all that land was previously the property of Indian chiefs, if to each one were given the seat and lands of his ancestor, all the islands would belong to such; and for Your Highness there would remain not a span of land in them; which would be no small inconvenience; it is my opinion that Your Highness should see that each one be given his own, if in justice nothing else can be done."[5]

As we can see, Manzaneda believed that the Indians were the owners of their lands, but that, if their rights were respected, there would be nothing to give the conquerors.

In fact, the earliest documents in relation to Cuba do not reflect that the ideas debated, whence emerged the Burgos legislation of 1512, had any particular resonance. Naturally, the conquerors and the first settlers in Cuba knew of the argument; but, like all the other conquerors, they only demanded the continuance of the system of distributing Indians, and even of its becoming a permanent institution instead of a temporary one.

On the other hand, Velázquez distributed lands among the members of the conquering army, starting the speedy process of land grabbing, whose evolution, characteristics, and resulting forms of agrarian structure we shall see in the next chapter.

BIBLIOGRAPHY

1. Pichardo Moya, Felipe. *Caverna, costa y meseta.* Havana, 1945.
2. Reynoso, Alvaro. *Agricultura de los indígenas de Cuba y Haití.* Paris, 1881.
3. Zavala, Silvio. *Las instituciones jurídicas en la conquista de América.* Madrid, 1935.
4. Hank, Lewis. *La lucha por la justicia en la conquista de América,* Madrid, 1959.
5. Academia de la Historia de Cuba. *Papeles existentes en el archivo general de las Indias.* Vol. I., Havana, MCMXXXI, page 54.

Part III

FOUNDATIONS OF COLONIAL ECONOMY (1510-1659)

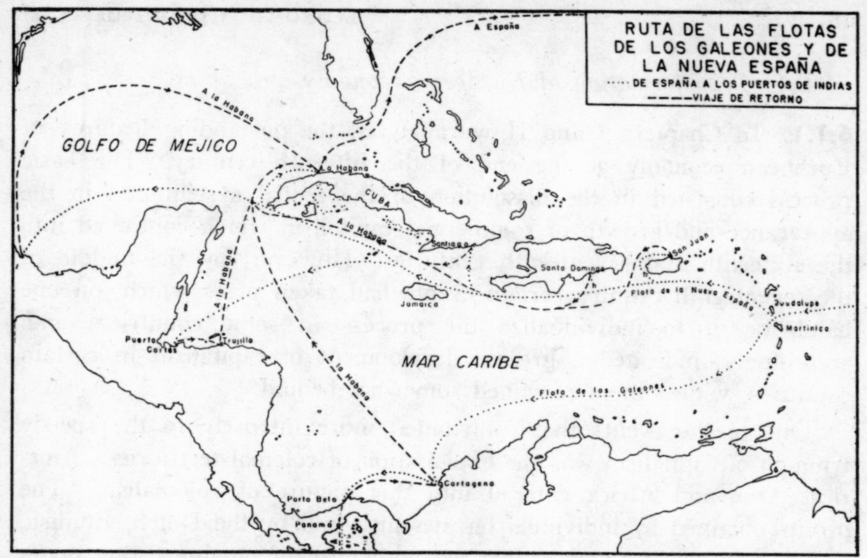

CHAPTER VI

EUROPE AND AMERICA DURING THE SIXTEENTH AND SEVENTEENTH CENTURIES

6.1. *Transformation of European economy*

6.1.1. European economic development and colonial expansion. The case of English capitalism. 6.1.2. Mercantilism; national economic unity. 6.1.3. The spread of trading companies. 6.1.4. Appearance of colonial wars.

6.2. *Crisis of Spanish economy*

6.2.1. Discussion of the problem in general: psychological and racial theses. 6.2.2. Influence of America in that crisis: inflation and emigration. 6.2.3. The policy of domination in Europe. Regional diversity and impoverishment of the Spanish people. Ulterior development.

6.3. *America*

6.3.1. The century of stabilization. 6.3.2. Mining and cattle-raising vs. agriculture. The two Americas: feudal ranches and plantations. Import economy. 6.3.3. Slavery and its varied forms and intensity. 6.3.4. Appearance of the English, French, and Dutch: brief survey of their colonies. 6.3.5. Foreign trade.

6.1. *Transformation of European economy*

6.1.1. In Chapters I and II we analyzed the oustanding features of European economy at the end of the fifteenth century. The basic process consisted in the dissolution of the feudal system and in the appearance and growth of commercial capitalism which continued into the sixteenth and seventeenth centuries. However, by the middle of the seventeenth century certain events had taken place which, on one hand, began to individualize the process in some countries; and, accordingly, indicated a greater development of capitalism in certain countries, while others remained somewhat behind.

One of the events that contributed more intensely to the speedy triumph of capitalism was the exploitation of colonial territories. America, Asia, and Africa entered into this picture of colonialism. The profits obtained by individual businessmen and by the Dutch, English, and French trading companies; the possibility of obtaining raw materials, such as cotton; the slave-based production of "tropical" products, such as tobacco, sugar, indigo, vanilla, cacao, demanded by Europeans; the use of colonial articles to increase the slave trade in Africa: these are all aspects of this decisive influence of colonialism in the rapid development of capitalism. [1]

European capitalism appeared and developed through a process of accumulation characterized by the dispossession of the peoples: farmers and peasants lost their lands, and city artisans lost the opportunity to get established by themselves, with their own working tools. The great mass of European peoples, progressively dispossessed of their independent means of livelihood (lands or tools) had to live by their work as wage-earners. Colonization, as well, implied a process of dispossession: the Indians lost their lands, the colonial oligarchies monopolized riches, the African slave was the object of maximum exploitation. Commercial accumulation was accelerated.

Spain and Portugal, which launched into colonial domination in the sixteenth century, were victims of the immaturity of their capitalist elements. On one hand, a good-sized portion of their urban population (bourgeois) and of the landless nobility, impoverished by the ruin of the feudal lords who protected it, emigrated to the colonies, there becoming landowners or unproductive elements (adventurers, soldiers, clergymen); on the other hand, colonial wealth (precious metals) brought about economic processes which the industrial structure was in no condition to use advantageously; on the contrary, industry collapsed. The other European countries (namely, the Netherlands, England,

and France), during the sixteenth century, advanced in their own process of accumulation, began their industrial organization and used to advantage the precious metals coming from America to favor the formation of a business class who invested its profits in industrial activities. Besides, the increase in land rentals helped the former feudal lords to become capitalist landholders, substituting one class for another.

Holland, that is, that part of the Netherlands which became independent from Spain at the end of the sixteenth and the beginning of the seventeenth centuries, succeeded in developing a commercial power that predominated during nearly all of the seventeenth century; but it had to give way in the face of English and French industrial development. Amsterdam was already an important trade center in northern Europe by the sixteenth century; now, in the seventeenth it would become the great international market place for Asiatic and American products and a first-class banking center. It suffices to point out that a great part of its riches were due to sugar refining, and that Holland, having hardly begun its capitalist race, took by assault and conquered sugar-growing northern Brazil. But facing Dutch trade rose British and French interests: the English with the Navigation Law (1651-1660) and the French with Colbert's protectionism toward the end of the seventeenth century.

England advanced ahead of all countries along the road of capitalism. The process of land enclosure, to turn farmlands into pastures for wool-bearing cattle which provided raw material for the textile industry, ended toward 1620. Almost one half of the lands previously under feudal regulations fell into the hands of capitalist landholders; farmers and peasants were dispossessed and forced to work for wages or suffered persecution as "vagabonds." In the cities the old artisan guilds fell into the hands of a small group of enriched masters; the mass of apprentices and officials, who could not achieve masterhood or who could not launch on their own, organized into fraternities. In every branch, the great merchants were set apart from the artisans. These great merchants specialized in the handling of industrial products and succeeded in progressively subduing the artisan. Thus emerged the commercial entrepreneur that distributed the raw material among numerous artisans who delivered to him the manufactured product. In some cases this merchant provided the poor artisan with his working tools (looms, etc.), so the artisans, to a greater or lesser degree, became true wage-earners under the commercial entrepreneurs.

This destroyed the power of the guilds. On the other hand, these industrial activities were carried on outside the large traditional cities, moving to others more conveniently located for international commercial traffic (such as Liverpool) or to rural areas. Before the seventeenth century, the system of concentrating hundreds of artisan weavers in one building had already been tested; thus emerged the great capitalist industry that would develop in the eighteenth century, especially after 1760, as a result of the mechanical inventions which characterized the so-called Industrial Revolution. [2]

6.1.2. This internal development of an industrial nature served as a firm basis for commercial expansion. It should not be suprising to have the *mercantilist* economic theory emerge in England after the beginning of the seventeenth century. No more would it be said, as in the *metallist* theory, that the country possessing larger metal reserves —silver and gold— should be the richest and most powerful. Now the theory would declare that the richest and most powerful country should be the one which sells (exports) more than it buys (imports). Hence, protectionism in the face of foreign competition, in the mother country as much as in the colonies, a policy which tended to secure the greatest and increasing profits for the dominant commercial groups. Mercantilism, as a theory of capitalism in its manufacturing stage, spread all over Europe. In some countries, such as France, it was, besides, a theory and a policy directed against the remnants of feudal individualism (interior and inter-provincial customs, group privileges, tolls, etc.) that hindered commerce and industry within the country. This political significance of mercantilism revealed itself particulary in *Colbertism* or French mercantilism, which was the result of the governing policy of Minister Colbert (1662-1683). In order to face foreign competition and, in turn, in order to compete, the "Colbertist" State fostered those industries that private initiative did not create, thus helping to hasten the process toward the victory of industrial capitalism in France. [3]

The mercantilist theory was also a theory of colonialism. The so-called "colonial pact" meant that the colonies produced certain articles which the mother country needed, receiving from the latter all that the subsistence of the colonial population required. Naturally, this "pact" would not allow the colonies to develop a production which the mother country did not need or already possessed.

6.1.3. This colonial exclusivism was common to all expansionist European groups. And it embodied the theoretical aspect that tried to justify not only the deliberate underdevelopment of the colonies, but also the first great wars waged over the distribution of the colonies—the "colonial" wars of the eighteenth century.

During the sixteenth century the Spanish and Portuguese colonies suffered repeated attacks coming from commercial groups of other countries; but the interests of capitalist trade had not succeeded in persuading states to regard the struggle for colonies as their own struggle, and to act accordingly. This is the reason why many of those aggressions took place on the private initiative of businessmen, seamen, and adventurers. The increasing link of those interests with monarchic power toward the end of the sixteenth and, most of all, during the seventeenth centuries would bring about an important change with the appearance of a *national* policy of colonial expansion in England and in France. Mercantilism, as a protectionist economic theory, was also a doctrine that regarded war as a major instrument of the interests of each commercial group: war of tariffs; war of diplomatic maneuvers on the weaker kingdoms, such as Spain and Portugal; war of blood, of pure and simple plunder. Trade justified the great navies; great navies justified the expansion of trade by force.[4]

Colonial wars would truly appear during the eighteenth century, and not only during periods of war, but also during periods of peace in Europe.

6.1.4. To a large extent, colonial expansion and the subsequent wars appeared as the handiwork of the trading companies that, since the middle of the sixteenth century, revealed themselves to be societies of stock or shares. The Dutch, English, and French established companies which obtained the privilege to trade with and, occasionally, to colonize certain regions of America, Africa, and Asia. These companies were the ones which waged the wars, which reached agreements with rulers and native peoples, which governed territories and made decisions about them. The French and English slave-trading companies obtained the monopoly of slave trade in Spanish America before and after the treaties of Utrecht, respectively. Even Spanish companies were established, such as the Royal Company of Havana (1740), of which we shall speak later on.

6.2. *Crisis of Spanish economy*

6.2.1. Within the European pattern shaken by the aspirations of the different monarchies, the most important political event since the middle of the sixteenth and up to the end of the seventeenth centuries was undoubtedly the Spanish "decadence." The fact that Spain was the beneficiary of the discovery, as well as its political and military influence in the Netherlands and in Italy, granted the Spanish Sovereigns an extraordinary supremacy. The fame and power of the empire over which "the sun never set" is still proverbial and embodies the longings of regressive groups.

There remains no doubt that Spain and Portugal emerged ahead of time as economic and political powers as the result of being the crossroads between the Mediterranean and northern Europe, and between all of Europe and Africa. However, this period ended in the last part of the sixteenth century. The Spaniards of that time were conscious of this process, and the time that elapsed from that moment, up to the first half of the eighteenth century, has been known since then as the period of "decadence." The topic of this "decadence" has been one of the most widely discussed in general European historiography. It has also furnished an excellent pretext for the entrance into America and into Spain itself of the worst manifestations of reactionary historiography that turn the discussion of the question toward psychological or racial interpretations: Spain languishes because the Spaniards are fanatical or lazy (which is extended, through "biological inheritance", to Latin Americans). Meanwhile, the success of the other European states is due to the wonderful "moral" conditions of their subjects.

6.2.2. Spanish "decadence" emerged toward the end of the sixteenth century, and became evident as a speedy sinking process during all of the seventeenth century. In order that this should happen, it was necessary for very deep social processes to take place. We may essentially define this combination of causes and effects of the "decadence" as a standstill in the process of capitalist development, whose circumstances we shall summarize.

In the first place we must remember that, in 1521, Charles V defeated the Spanish bourgeois elements at Villalar, thus reaffirming the King's alliance with the high clergy and the high nobility. It was in such a way that the progressive, anti-feudal forces who had victoriously cooperated with the Catholic Sovereigns lost political importance.

But this explanation would not suffice. The Spanish bourgeois forces lost strength as a class, and this was due to a complex web of causes well known in history. First of all, we must point out the weakening of the bourgeois groups as a result of the expulsion of the Jews (at the end of the fifteenth century); of the emigration of bourgeois groups to America, where they became great landholders; of the expulsion of the Moors, farmers and artisans (at the beginning of the seventeenth century). This was a bourgeoisie that slowly bled to death during one and a half centuries. But we must be careful not to believe that the cause of all this persecution was "fanaticism." The Jews were persecuted for their riches, as had already happened and would happen again in other European countries; those emigrating to America were offered an easy opportunity for enrichment; the Moors were expelled for fear of a new Arab "re-conquest." Besides, the Spanish State progressively became an instrument to repress the new classes, an end to which the Inquisition served as the executing arm. The Inquisition never clashed with the kings, and this gave its actions an eminently political and non-religious character. Repression was directed against the bourgeois forces, the same that in England, France, and Germany were carrying forward the new ideas about commerce, loans, and capitalist-type labor. It is easy to note that the lowest point of economic and political "decadence" coincided with the moment of greatest inquisitional activity.

Let us point out that America sent into Spain a flood of wealth in precious metals. The inflation benefited mainly the landholders and the merchants; sixteenth century artisan industry, fundamentally based on manual labor, was undoubtedly ruined. This industry could not take advantage of inflation because the benefits of this process could not be absorbed by an organization based on manual labor. High land rentals impoverished the people and enriched the court nobility. In order for this phenomenon to bring about a strengthening of the commercial or industrial capitalist forces, it would have been necessary for the process of dissolution of the feudal system to have advanced sufficiently, producing a decisive mass of wage-earners whose employment would have allowed for the transformation of the high prices caused by inflation into capitalist profit (surplus value).

Within the circumstances, it is logical that the non-productive ways of life should have acquired great prestige. The mass entry into the secular clergy and into religious orders was an event that came as a solution of the crisis for large sectors of the bourgeoisie and the impoverished lesser nobility, and it had very little to do with legitimate religiousness. This increase of unproductive groups became, in itself, a cause for the hastening of decadence. As much can be said of begging, whose widespread diffusion in those times is proverbial.

Even more important was the process of formation of a renter bourgeoisie who invested commercial capital in loans to the King in exchange for rentals or perpetual *jures* or rentable lands.

Spanish economy, therefore, became a parasitic organization. The commercial groups who monopolized trade with America did not have their own production, and, accordingly, obtained in Europe most of the industrial articles required in America. They ended up by becoming a group of mere middlemen whose goal was to make purely speculative profits with colonial commerce. All this progressive submission of Spanish economy to European economy was possible because, as Spain languished, capitalist productive forces in England and France developed, during the seventeenth and the first half of the eighteenth centuries, in the form of applying machinery to production and of massive organization of the workers in factories.

However, Spain did not keep completely apart from the general evolution that went on around it. The same abundant literature on the decadence and, especially, the ideas of men such as Cellorigo and Moncada prove that within it lay historical forces which fostered the continuation of the capitalist process halted in the sixteenth century.[5]

6.2.3. That war-mongering policy of domination in European zones, which had begun to appear before the discovery, when the sovereigns of Aragon contended with the French princes of the House of Anjou for supremacy in southern Italy, has been pointed out as a cause contributing to decadence. Such a policy spread when the crowns of Spain and Germany met on the head of Charles V. On the other hand, Spain was launched out into the struggle against Turkish expansion in the Mediterranean. Out of all this emerged an interminable series of wars and disturbances, such as the religious reform, which forced the Spanish people to carry out vigorous efforts and to spend their resources. At the end of the sixteenth century the Netherlands rose against Spanish domination and, after a war of extermination, succeeded in having Spain recognize the independence of Holland. The struggle for predominance in Europe and for the American colonies brought Spain face to face with England, who achieved its first great naval victories. Men and resources provided by America and Spain were spent in those enterprises, whose maintenance the progressive deterioration of economy in the mother country prevented.

On the other hand — precisely because, since the middle of the sixteenth century, it still showed marked feudal characteristics — Spain was divided into "kingdoms" or provinces, whose legislation, customs, administration, and economy were kept up, fostering the isolation or the separation among the territorial components of the mother country. The centralizing and unifying impulse, typical of capitalist absolute monarchies was lost; and for this reason the causes of the general weakening of Spanish development remained. Let us remember that the monopoly of American commerce was granted to Seville, injuring the remaining areas of the country; this example shows to what extent regional individualism and the lack of unity affect the maintenance of a pre-capitalist economic structure.

As the result of stagnation and of the loss of resources, the country became impoverished.

6.3. *America*

6.3.1. During the seventeenth century, America entered a stage of stabilization: then the bases of its economic and social organization were defined. This definition brought about a neat separation among groups of colonies. On the other hand, the French and English colonies, which sharpened that colonial difference, began to take shape in the same century.

6.3.2. Within the Spanish colonies two groups stood out especially: colonies based on mining and ranches; colonies founded on the planting of tropical crops. In a general way, the former included high areas, mountains or plateaus (Mexico, Colombia, Peru), where the climate favored the presence of Europeans and where, besides, Indian population was abundant; the others were insular or coastal areas, of a climate that was hard on Europeans — especially at a time of no great hygienic progress — and of scarce or very backward native population: examples of this are the Antilles and the area around the Caribbean. The former made up the great viceroyships; the latter had governments of lesser institutional development.

In the viceroyships the dominant classes were the miners and landholders who exploited the labor of the Indian peon or half-breed in forms remindful of medieval serfdom. In the other colonies the great crops were based almost exclusively on the mass employment of African slaves; there was also a landed oligarchy here; but it was essentially absenteeist and, besides, shared its power with the importing merchants.

Naturally, African slavery existed in all the territories, but with varied intensity. In general, the life of the slave depended essentially on the more or less intensive nature of production.

Stabilization, that is, the fixing of dominant groups, institutional development, and systematic exploitation of resources appeared first in the continental colonies; while the others, depending on great export products, would not start to achieve major development until the eighteenth century. This caused Spanish colonial power to be based on the riches of the viceroyships during the second half of the sixteenth, all of the seventeenth, and the first half of the eighteenth centuries. Thus, Mexico had a certain superior function in the Caribbean and Central America, and Peru ruled as far as Rio de la Plata.

These more developed colonies exported precious metals and some basic products; but they had a certain level of industrial production and could produce a number of articles similar to those imported from Europe (oil, wine, for example). Accordingly, their trade was more varied. The remaining colonies exported one or two products (sugar, cacao, cotton), and imported all of the others to fill their needs.[6]

6.3.3. Foreign colonies presented certain characteristics, with perhaps the exception of the so-called New England, in the north of the present United States, where contemporary English society was reproduced faithfully enough, consequently presenting a more advanced commercial, maritime, and manufacturing development. But the colonies, from the south of what is now the State of Virginia to the Guianas, were properly slave-plantation colonies to an even greater degree than the similar Spanish colonies. As much can be said of the territories under French rule, except Canada, where the essential strength was the fur trade, and the agricultural exploitation of the more temperate areas on the St. Lawrence River.[7]

6.3.4. Since the end of the sixteenth century, foreigners had been coming to America; but it was not until the second half of the seventeenth century that they consolidated their colonies. This was part of the struggle for the colonies, which underwent several stages until the eighteenth century: piracy; storming of territories (Jamaica in 1654 by the English, Brazil by the Dutch); and colonial domination by means of wars and treaties (the Peace of Ryswick, 1697; of Utrecht, 1713; of Paris, 1763).

6.3.5. The obtaining of colonies in all of America aided the English and the French in their economic penetration which, on the other hand, had benefited by the limited productive capacity of Spain. However, Spanish monopoly was not broken until the second half of the eighteenth century; and, actually, the colonial commercial system was liberalized only as far as the less developed territories were concerned; not the viceroyships, which were jealously guarded for their great wealth.

BIBLIOGRAPHY

1. Williams, Eric. *Capitalism and Slavery,* Chapel Hill, 1944.
2. Marx, Karl. *Capital,* vol. cit.
3. Hecksher, Eli F. *La época mercantilista,* México, 1943.
4. Silberner, Edmundo. *La guerra en el pensamiento económico,* Madrid, 1954.
5. Carrera Pujols, Jaime. *Historia de la economía española,* 5 vols. Barcelona. Especially vols. I and II.
6. Bagu, Sergio. *Economía de la sociedad colonial,* Buenos Aires, 1949.
7. Reparaz, Gonzalo de. *Op. cit.*

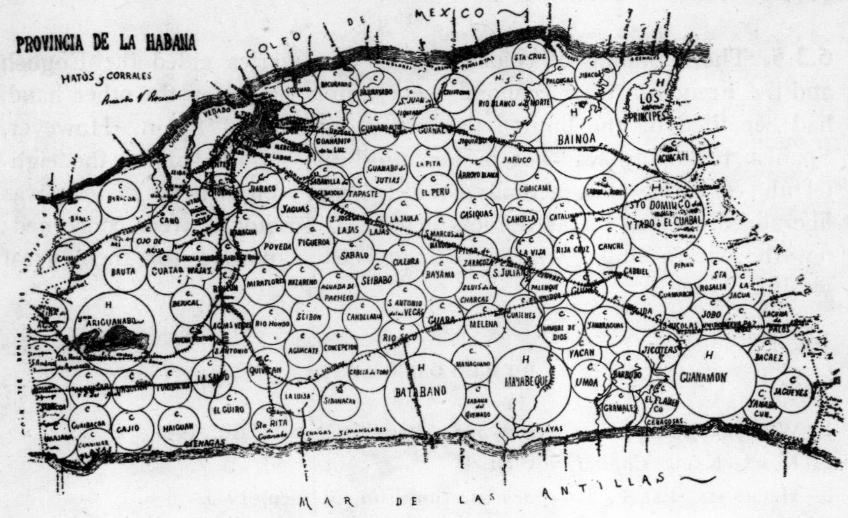

CHAPTER VII

APPROPRIATION OF THE LAND AND AGRARIAN STRUCTURE

7.1. *The "lordly" impulse*

7.1.1. Role of the land in Europe, as an element for domination. Transformation of this role in America. 7.1.2. Colonial social relations. 7.1.3. The problem of survival and the first forms of agrarian colonization; tenancies and *estancias*.

7.2. *The mechanism of appropriation*

7.2.1. The right of the strongest. Medieval *presura* and occupation. 7.2.2. Land grants; institutionalization. 7.2.3. Municipal oligarchies and land grants. Latifundium and *minifundium*.

7.3. *Ranches and corrals*

7.3.1. The struggle between the "lordly" impulse and common rights. 7.3.2. Source of the circular ranches. From exclusive use of pastures to ownership of the land.

7.1. *The "lordly" impulse*

7.1.1. In Europe land was a symbol of power. Even when feudal economy was transformed along with social relations, bringing about a progressive predominance of commerce and industry, there lingered on, as a modern remnant of that system, the thought that he who possessed lands was powerful and outstanding. Consequently, there was an impulse toward the possession of lands above all within the mass of the lesser nobility (the Spanish *hidalgos*) and, in general, within all the groups whom the dispossession resulting from the dissolution of the feudal system had transformed into a mass of men without trade or income.

This means that the conquerors and colonizers arrived in Cuba with the outline for a social, economic, and political organization. Accordingly, they intended to reproduce in these lands the social relations reigning in Europe, as if they had been a piece of machinery which could be loaded on a ship and set up in the colonies with no great effort. [1]

7.1.2. In order to implant the European form of social relations, they had to find in America the necessary elements. To reproduce the feudal system, they must find serfs; but in these lands there were only Indians who had their own social relations, not in any way similar to European feudalism. And to reproduce capitalist landholding, they must exploit commercial or industrial resources; but the Indians did not offer this type of production, and the exploitation of European products brought over from Europe needed to be organized, or else Europe must be made to enjoy articles typical of native economy.

Therefore, the Spaniard had to adjust his social relations and his economic organization to the conditions found in America. He grabbed the land; by so doing the European minority who obtained it acquired economic, social, and political power; but, lacking serfs, the solution was to subject the Indian to a labor system similar to slavery. He took the land away from the Indian and forced him to work for the European. Although it was not an identical process, the conquest in America brought about a phenomenon of dispossession similar to that which characterized the appearance of capitalism, whose first impulse is based on the dispossession of peasant and artisan masses. This similarity explains why legal doctrines should have ranged from the application of a purely slave system to that of a purely wage system (see Chapter V, 5.2). Thus they forced the Indian to work "after the European manner"; they forced him to produce native or European articles on a commercial scale. Commercial capitalism, then in its stage of development, demanded that America supply products for the European market; that is why sugar was already exported in 1520, and even before this American articles were being commercialized.

7.1.3. However, since Columbus' enterprise denoted a commercial nature up to 1497, the State (the King) gave no thought to the necessity of providing land for those who came to America. The first settlers of Hispaniola (Santo Domingo-Haiti) suffered great hunger, and depended on food given by the Indians or taken from them. There was great discontent among them; they asked for lands, and got the so-called tenancies, that is, very small farms with native crops, especially cassava. [2] Those tenancies coincided with the distribution of Indians for labor, and "tenancies with Indians" emerged.

When Velázquez arrived in Cuba with his army, he distributed tenancies to "help the conquerors live." They were made up of cultivated lands with "yucca mounds"; that is, Indian lands which Indians would cultivate for the benefit of the Spaniards. These were the early times, when the conquerors could not survive unless they lived on the produce of the land. Since the Spaniard knew the qualities of cassava, an important trade was immediately organized on this article with the other colonies and, above all, with trading ships and expeditions that needed a substitute for wheat bread. And this is how, out of native agriculture and industry, there emerged the first commercial exploitation in Cuba.

The lands so distributed were exploited in the form of *estancias* (farm-ranches). That is, as a mixed estate, agricultural and cattle-raising, where the first crops brought over from Europe and hog raising were combined with major native crops.

The *estancias* were scattered around those areas where Indians lived, and the Spaniards scattered with them, for in the *estancias* there were managers or European stewards who watched the Indians. On the other hand, many of the conquerors who did not get tenancies, because they did not wish to live in the villages founded by Velázquez and his army, wandered about the *estancias.* It was these men who enrolled to follow adventure, when Hernán Cortés' expedition to Mexico was organized, in search of other regions where they might find lands and working Indians.

As we can see, the first thing the conquerors did was to grab the lands and subdue the Indians. Upon these bases, colonial economy and society began to take shape.

7.2. *The mechanism of appropriation*

7.2.1. The fact that Velázquez gave out lands does not mean that the settler made them rightfully his own. Actually, the predominating process in America until the middle of the sixteenth century was precisely the appropriation of land as a matter of fact, with no respect for even the doctrine itself or for the laws of the period. Consequently, if we say that the source of agrarian ownership in America is based on violence and fraud, we are not judging according to our opinion, but on the testimony of numerous laws in which royal power accuses the colonial oligarchy of taking lands "on its own and for its own", respecting not the property of the Indians; nor of the urban communities (public and communal lands); nor of the State (royal lands).

Naturally, the settlers tried to justify this appropriation. An old medieval agrarian institution that spread all over Europe, called *presura* or *aprisio*, permitted the occupation of bare or uncultivated lands. The difference lies in the fact that in Europe it actually worked to foster the settlement of many free peasant communities; while in America it worked for the exclusive benefit of the formation of a great landholding oligarchy. [3]

7.2.2. When royal power was strengthened in America, land grants were regulated. All lands that did not belong to Indians, to cities, or to individuals were supposed to be public property, that is, of the King, royal lands. This represented the doctrinal development of medieval legal ideas of which absolute monarchy took advantage to strengthen royal power before feudalism. In consequence, the King had the power to distribute royal lands to be exploited by settlers; therefore, in land grants, as in *presura*, we find the obligation to make the land yield fruit.

Velázquez granted the first lands without due authority to do so; but in 1520 the King confirmed this fact. Since there was no authority in Cuba who possessed such a power, the municipal government or *cabildo* (city council) of the cities took it upon itself to grant the lands, although it was not expressly empowered for so doing. The council could distribute those lands that were part of the cities' own property; while the city *egidos* should be common or used by all inhabitants. Towards 1530 land grants started to become regulated. After that the Cuban city councils began to grant latifundia for cattle raising. This is not to say that, very often, prominent settlers did not appropriate lands without asking the council.

For the municipal concession to have full force, it was necessary that the King should *confirm* the grant; but this was almost never done, being a slow and costly process. As a result, most of the land grants in Cuba during the sixteenth and seventeenth centuries lacked the legal requisites established by royal power. So it was upon force and illegality that the bases of Cuban agrarian property were laid in the sixteenth century.[4]

The first grant for a cattle-raising latifundium of which there is knowledge dates back to 1532, when the city council of Sancti-Spíritus granted Fernando Gómez the farm of Manicaragua, with a three-league radius.[5] Since then the city councils would not cease granting land. It was said at the time that, in order not to injure another settler, the petitioner should be given land to the extension of one or two leagues in radius "all around" the place where he offered to raise cattle, or where he had already done so. He was obliged to "populate" the land with cattle, if he had not already done so; and if he refused to do it, he was threatened with a repeal of the grant, which would then be at the disposal of some other petitioner.

7.2.3. But what is the sense and the efficiency of all this? In order to answer this question, we must refer to the evolution of colonial economy between 1520 and 1550. When the Indians started to disappear and the establishment of new colonies, such as Nueva España (Mexico) and Peru, diminished the importance of the cassava trade, the settlers tenanted in Cuba left for other regions in search of lands where riches would be greater and easier to obtain. The population of the cities founded by Velázquez decreased to a minimum; naturally, these few who stayed behind not only monopolized the labor of the remaining Indians, but they also controlled political power in the municipal governments. All the resources concentrated in their hands, and they became an oligarchy.

Since there were not many Indians, nor enough African slaves, and cassava or other products could not be exported, there remained but one possibility of exploiting the land: the cattle industry. This required few people; but, besides —and this is most important of all— the cattle brought over by the Spaniards had developed by itself: it wandered about the plains as *cimarrón* (runaway), without an owner. The people set out to round up this ownerless cattle, as a community right. The oligarchy took advantage of the opportunity, and by agreement of the council distributed the territory among themselves as cattle-raising latifundia, one and two leagues in radius. Once the grant had been given, or even before, the beneficiary would place a small group of herdsmen (Indians, half-breeds, Africans, etc.) in the land, to round up the runaway cattle. This cattle could then be branded with the beneficiary's own brand. As we can see, the primitive oligarchy did not buy the land, for they grabbed it; nor did they raise cattle, for they stole it; nor did they work, for they had poor men who did it for wages: an excellent business. And, since they ruled the council, they could do as they pleased; sometimes they did not populate the land with cattle, nor cultivate it, either. Nonetheless, their grants were not repealed. Of course, there were also *minifundia* (uneconomically small landholdings), but they were not typical of colonial economy.

7.3. *Ranches and corrals*

7.3.1. The one-league-sized latifundia were the *corrales* (corrals) for minor or porcine cattle; the two-league-sized ones were the *hatos* (extensive ranches) for major cattle. There were various names, but these predominated historically. The "all around" land concessions were the source of corrals and extensive ranches of circular shape and boundaries.

When a grant was given, this did not mean that the beneficiary acquired the property, since for this it should have been necessary to obtain confirmation from the King; but even in this case the King, according to the legal doctrine of the time, reserved for himself the right of eminent domain over exploitable lands.

Actually, the only concession was the right to use the pastures on the land, excluding all the rest of the colonial population. However, the landholding beneficiary was not content with that. He also forbade rounding up runaway cattle within the one or two league radius; that is, the great landholdings were based on the exclusion of the people from certain rights, rights confirmed during the Middle Ages as *common,* that is, belonging to all the inhabitants of an urban or rural center. The effort of the landholding oligarchy to defeat the rights of the common people were to a large extent reflected in the records of the Havana City Council.

On the other hand, the Council ordered that Indians, halfbreeds, and free Negroes might not round up cattle on their own, but in the service of others, that is, for wages. They were thus forced to give up their rights, placing themselves at the disposal of the great landholders. But, in actual practice, the poor European population was also dispossessed, or had no access to the land. Two or three families in each city monopolized the land and the State and municipal institutions.

This is not to say that the poor people had absolutely no possibility of obtaining land. Many immigrants left the city and settled on royal lands, cultivating them; other asked for grants and were given "pieces of land to cultivate *conucos*" (tiny farms) or land for clearing of brambles and opening for cultivation; but these were only the very few. Besides, the pace was set by the latifundia and the servile work of the Indian and the African. To have no slaves —and there were many citizens who did not have any— meant belonging to a very low social category, close to that of the slave, in fact; it also meant the impossibility of acquiring notorious wealth. Many European immigrants were forced to work for wages.

7.3.2. When another cattleman or inhabitant was forbidden to exploit the land within a radius of one or two leagues "all around," a circular limit was being set. Around 1750 the agrarian situation became difficult, for, as we shall see in Chapter X, the oligarchy itself had abused its power, bringing about confusion in the land grants. On the other hand, since royal power then began an offensive against oligarchies who took lands "on their own and for their own," several "surveyors" or inspectors arrived in Cuba. One of them, Alonso de Cáceres, drew up the municipal ordinances of Havana, which were immediately enforced without the approval of the King. The ordinances reaffirmed the grant system practiced so far; but, besides, they encouraged the demarcation of the great landholdings. Thus, starting in 1580, the first circular boundaries were laid out, some of them remaining to this day, as revealed in air photographs taken by the Cuban Institute of Cartography and Land Census (*Instituto Cubano de Cartografía y Catastro*).

When these boundaries were established in the land, what had been a mere permission for the use of pastures became full-fledged property, property not recognized by contemporary legal doctrine (for at the beginning of the seventeenth century there were documents that so declared, in the name of the King), nor constituted according to the procedures established by the laws then in force. And, even though we cannot believe that the fulfillment of those laws justified the dispossession of the Indian and of the poor colonial population, their unfulfillment entirely discloses the vices which lie at the source of the colonial agrarian structure in its formation.

The fact is that, by the end of the sixteenth century, the landholding oligarchy had consolidated, and that the greater and better part of the Cuban land had fallen into the hands of a small number of settlers. And during the seventeenth century, until 1659, there was no substantial change in status, although the increasing scarcity of free lands was already limiting the formation of latifundia.

BIBLIOGRAPHY

1. MARX, KARL. *Capital, vol. cit.*
2. LE RIVEREND, JULIO. "Vecindades y estancias. En los albores de la organización agraria colonial"; *Islas,* Santa Clara, No. 7 and 8 (1961).
3. COSTA, JOAQUÍN. *Colectivismo agrario en España,* Madrid, 1915.
4. OTS Y CARDEQUI, JOSÉ M. *España en América. El régimen de la tierra en la América Colonial,* Mexico, 1959.
5. GONZÁLEZ, MANUEL DIONISIO. *Memorias históricas de la Villa de Santa Clara,* 1858.
6. *Actas capitulares del Ayuntamiento de La Habana.* 3 vols. Havana, 1939-1941.

CHAPTER VIII

EXPLOITATION OF THE LAND: AGRICULTURE AND CATTLE RAISING

8.1. *Early period*

8.1.1. Agriculture for survival. The conqueror: he needed to have others produce what his hunger required. 8.1.2. Agricultural continuity through the subjection of the Indians. 8.1.3. Cassava, native survival.

8.2. *New sources of wealth*

8.2.1. Plant species imported; their variety and limited importance in the sixteenth century. 8.2.2. Advantages of cattle-raising; its organization.

8.3. *Outline of cattle colonization*

2.3.1. The cattle-raising impulses and its route through the interior.

8.4. *Outline of agrarian colonization*

8.4.1. Penetration into the interior. City agrarian belt. 8.4.2. Spread of tobacco and its cultivation. 8.4.3. Spread of the cane crop.

8.5. *Agrarian development and struggles*

8.5.1. Survival agriculture and "saturation" of grants: Judge Cáceres "reform" (1574). 8.5.2. Subdivision of early latifundia. Alliance between cattle-raising latifundia and commercial agriculture. 8.5.3. Tobacco planters against cattle-raising landholders until Governor Salamanca's decree (1659). Repercussions of the spread of crops over early latifundia.

8.1. *Early period*

8.1.1. First of all, that is, when the conquerors arrived in an American region, they needed to have other men produce what their hunger and their lust for profits demanded. The conquerors and early settlers did not come to exploit the land by themselves and, even if it had been so, in many cases this required that the crops they knew about should be availàble in America or, in any case, that they should be familiar with Indian crops. All this implied a period of learning or of experience concerning the natural resources of America. But the social factor was much more important. Actually, the conquerors and colonizers had not come to establish new social relations in America, that is, different from the ones existing in Europe. Consequently, they came to subdue the natives, to exploit their labor, as the dominant classes on the other side of the Atlantic exploited the labor of the majority; peasants, artisans, etc.

For the time being, an effort was made to transform Indian agriculture into an occupation destined to guarantee the survival of the settler. We have already mentioned the hungry condition of the Hispaniola settlers (Santo Domingo-Haiti) before 1500, vividly described by Friar Bartolome de las Casas in his *History of the Indies*. As a matter of fact, such agrarian survival resources were monopolized by some of the settlers, who had received some of the distributed Indians, to organize the first great commercial business enterprise in American history: they sold products to the settlers who had no Indians or lands and, besides, to the ships that traded around the Caribbean or that returned to Europe. This explains the primitive importance of the cassava or "bread of the earth" trade in Jamaica, in Hispaniola, in Cuba, and in the small island of Cubagua (Lesser Antilles).

8.1.2. This early impulse towards lucrative survival agriculture implied a continuation of the native exploitation of certain products. It also implied the continuation of native technical tradition, for it was the Indians who cultivated the land. For the time being, the only European contribution was the demand for more intensive work, for a higher production from the native laborer — a most important factor in the physical extinction of the inhabitants of America.

This picture of the early years was reproduced in Cuba from the moment of arrival of Diego Velázquez and his army. In the early "tenancies" with Indians, which the settlers received as spoils, native work, native technique, and native products predominated.

The Spaniards exploited these "tenancies" in the form of *estancias* (farm-ranches). The *estancia* represented an intensive manner of making the land produce. In the *estancia,* to begin with, there was porcine cattle and some heads of bovine cattle. European and foreign crops were also introduced there: wheat, cane, rice, vegetables, etc., although this happened only several years after the conquest.

In the *estancias* there were Indians; somewhat later there were also African slaves, and there were always Europeans who were the "owners" of the *estancia,* or mere stewards or managers, or they might also be sharecroppers who managed the exploitation for the absentee "owner." So we see that a few years after the conquest of Cuba there was in the *estancias* a veritable display of all the social and productive relations of which the Spanish dominant groups made use in order to profit from American riches. Velázquez established several *estancias* after his arrival in Cuba, as he explained in his 1514 *Letter of Report.*

The *estancia* was not originally a large-scale system of land exploitation. It was always rather a *minifundium,* and in its historical evolution it maintained just such a nature as a mixed exploitation (agrarian and cattle-raising), in which crops were predominant. Naturally, they contained a variety of crops, though the possibility of exporting or selling the harvest tended to make them into single-crop exploitations.

In the early times, *estancias* spread all over the territory; but, when the process of extinction of the Indian speeded up and the first uprisings occurred (1528-1532) they tended to gather around the cities. Besides, being small-sized farms that contributed to the maintainance of the urban population, they were located as close as possible to the market.

8.1.3. In fact, Indian labor in these early times guaranteed the transformation of cassava into an important commercial product, later eliminated by the importance of wheat flour, whether coming from Spain or, after 1590, from Mexico.

8.2. *New sources of wealth*

8.2.1. Diego Velázquez brought into Cuba those species of domestic animals of economic value: oxen and cows, goats, horses, asses, sheep, and domestic fowl. He took the specimens from his farms in Hispaniola and from the "royal farms," where these animals were bred. The geographical environment was favorable; that is why, very few years later, they are said to have multiplied remarkably. These animals settled comfortably on the plains or natural pastures and in the low hills, where they easily found food as runaway cattle.

8.2.2. The plant species possibly did not arrive so soon. We do not know exactly when wheat, rice, cane, bananas, and other vegetables of great economic value were brought in, but they were cultivated, to a greater or lesser degree, since the sixteenth century. Cane arrived in 1494, with the Discoverer's second voyage; rice, around 1512; and bananas in 1516 according to Oviendo. From Hispaniola they came to Cuba and from Cuba to the continent, especially Mexico. Of course, it is possible that cane should have arrived from Hispaniola before the others, around 1510-1520. To a large extent, these species spread by themselves, for their cultivation required the labor of African slaves or European farmers. Naturally, the Indian was forced to learn the cultivation of these crops, but his extinction demanded that African slaves or Europeans should carry the burden of non-native, that, is, European agriculture.

The bases for a colonial economy, subordinated and "complementary," were constituted by the commercial products, both native and European, especially the latter, since they already had an open market in Spain. On the other hand, the European population naturally tended to demand products which it was in the habit of using in its own country; nevertheless, it did not refuse the native products, above all during the early days of colonization.

8.3. *Outline of cattle colonization*

8.3.1. When cattle-raising within latifundia became widespread through the process described in Chapter VII, there started a speedy colonizing movement towards the interior; this followed an early stage when the settlers belonging to the municipal oligarchies chose to have their lands near the coasts, because of the difficulties for internal communications. Extensive ranches and corrals appeared, first of all, in areas near the cities; but they quickly had to move farther away from them, thus becoming an effective instrument for colonization or for economic and demographic expansion. Each large ranch and each corral had in its center or *sitio* a few buildings (houses or *bohíos* — Indian huts) and some crops for the sustenance of those who worked there, free men and slaves; sometimes they included a shelter for travellers in transit from one city to another.

The *sitios* in ranches and corrals were located near sources of drinking water —springs, lagoons, rivers, and streams— because they provided places for watering cattle; but this need was greater in raising major cattle (bovine) than minor cattle. Of course, these latifundia had greater need of natural pasture lands (*sabanas* and plains) than of rivers. The woodland or forest area was appropriate for porcine cattle which fed on wild fruit, especially guavas. But generally, in the sixteenth and even in the seventeenth century, all large ranches had sections of woodland reserved for the extension of pastures when the original site had been intensively used and denoted considerable loss of nutrient power; that is, as we say in Cuba, when the land had *tired out* through natural wear and as a result of the permanence of cattle.

Naturally, cattle-raising latifundia became widespread faster in the western region (now the Provinces of Pinar del Río, Havana, and Matanzas); it also spread in the region of the great Central plains (now Camagüey), in such a way that, by the end of the sixteenth century, all usable land in the aforementioned areas might be said to have been entirely distributed among the cattle-raising latifundia. The municipal oligarchies did not lose any time in their lust for land-grabbing.

Undoubtedly, there were areas where the process for the predominance of primitive latifundia was slower, as happened in the present Province of Oriente and in certain zones of Las Villas. On the other hand, in the western region itself the process of "saturation" of latifundia was not uniform.

The exploitation of those large ranches and corrals was extensive. It required small labor force; and this explains why cattle-raising latifundia became decisively important when the Indians disappeared as an economic factor, that is, around 1550. A few herdsmen, whether Indians, African slaves, or half-breeds, sufficed for looking after the cattle. After all, there was no cattle breeding, nor any care. The beneficiary of a land grant in the sixteenth century did not improve his flock; he simply grabbed the runaway cattle found in the plains, where he chose the *sitio* for his ranch. From that time on, his men, slaves and wage-earners, would merely round up the cattle once or twice a year to mark the new heads with the brand of the landholder. This rodeo occasionally served to separate the cattle from different holdings which mixed in one ranch. [1]

The "lord of the ranch" was not interested in selling fresh meat, because, on one hand, it had to be sold for a fixed price at the municipal butcher's; and on the other, the demand was limited by the small urban population, except in Havana, where the permanence of hundreds of travellers journeying between Spain and Mexico demanded a more abundant supply. The great landholder was more interested in the hide of the cattle, a major export article after 1560. Consequently, his men set out to round up or hunt the cattle, for which purpose they used the so-called *punta de montería* or *desjarretadora,* a kind of blade that allowed the tendons of one hind leg to be cut; the cattle then fell to the ground, where it was killed and its hide taken off; the rest was all lost. We know that around 1560-1580 there were years in which sixty thousand hides were exported; this can give us the measure of the enormous amount of meat lost in the plains. This barbarous manner of exploiting wealth was common to the remaining colonies, and it lasted in Cuba at least until the nineteenth century.

8.4. *Outline of agrarian colonization*

8.4.1. Agricultural exploitation remained close to the cities, growing into sort of agrarian belts, especially, while the *minifundia* were diversified, estancia-type farms. When agriculture was commercialized, that is, when large scale exportation of agricultural products began at the end of the sixteenth century, the farms devoted to cultivation tended to move away from the cities. At first, there was a real struggle for the control of the best lands near seaport town; coastal lands were contended for as well; finally, agriculture expanded towards the interior.

8.4.2. The farm specializing in tobacco growing generally moved inside the territory following the course of the rivers. Natural tobacco fields are lands of sandy soil formed by the rivers along their course, and they are characterized for their fertility. Planters settled in these natural tobacco fields, seeking the best rivers. The tobacco planter generally cultivated the land himself, occasionally aided by a slave.

Europeans knew the cultivation of tobacco in the primitive *estancias* where the laborers were mainly Indians; but, in this aspect, the most outstanding immigrants were the islanders from the Canary Islands, who arrived in Cuba from the second half of the sixteenth century. They were persistent and hard-working farmers who searched for lands and scattered throughout the territory of the country. They settled royal lands; but they also entered the large ranches, coming into conflict with the cattle-raising landholders.[2]

8.4.3. The cane plantation did not become widespread in the same manner. In the first place, many of the early *estancias* near the cities specialized, turning into cane fields; in the second place, cane fields quickly multiplied within the cattle-raising latifundia, because the landholders themselves, as a result of their wealth, could double as sugar planters; and, accordingly, there was no economic or social conflict between both agrarian exploitations. However, the cane plantation and the sugar mill tended to remain near the cities or on the coasts, for sugar, being heavy, needed short-distance transportation and ease of communications. As we shall see in Chapter X, at the end of the sixteenth century there were cane plantations around Havana and Bayamo. And towards 1650, that is, in the years when the first period of Cuban economic history closes, cane plantations had spread considerably through other areas of the country.

8.5. *Agrarian development and struggles*

8.5.1. Around 1570 there appeared in the region of Havana a phenomenon of "saturation" of the usable land. On the one hand, the oligarchy had appropriated great extensions forming ranches and corrals. This proliferation of latifundia brought about many quarrels and created great confusion, injuring the oligarchy itself; on the other hand it smothered those crops which could not spread out, even though the urban population needed greater supplies as it increased. Order had to be established.

Besides, the power of the State (the interest of the King) then started an offensive against the excesses of the oligarchies, who had helped themselves on a grand scale, grabbing all the available land. As a consequence of this, there arrived in Cuba Alonso de Cáceres, a judge from the Santo Domingo court, who drew up a set of municipal ordinances where he regulated land grants and tried to safeguard the existence of the small agricultural farms, necessary for the food supply of the urban center. In establishing these regulations, Judge Cáceres did not diminish the power of the oligarchies, but confirmed the traditional system of land grants.

8.5.2. But the struggle for the land did not end. It became more bitter as agricultural needs increased. The subdivision of the early latifundia embodied a first aspect of this struggle. Inside the ranch and the corral, minor crops developed as the population increased, and also commercial crops such as cane. Cattle raising began to lose land, and to certain areas, like Havana, cattle had to be brought from far-off ranches (located in Sancti-Spiritus, Puerto Principe, and even Bayamo). But this subdivision of the early latifundia did not represent any social conflict, since these forms of agrarian exploitation favored the landholder. In fact, there was an alliance or a coincidence between cattle raising and commercial cane agriculture.

8.5.3. Conditions in the tobacco plantation were different enough. At the end of the sixteenth and the beginning of the seventeenth centuries, there were numerous plantations along the rivers near Havana and in the south of Las Villas. The cattle-raising ranchers tried to expel the tobacco planters from their lands. They accused the planters of taking the water supply away from the cattle, of setting woodlands on fire, of taking up land for a crop which did not serve as food for the people. At the beginning of the seventeenth century the Havana City Council forbade opening new tobacco plantations near the city; and along the first half of the seventeenth century, prohibitions were constantly issued that tended to injure the interests of the tobacco planters in some way. The latter defended themselves by lawsuits or by killing the cattle which trespassed in their plantations. This opposition and interest strife was general in nature. In the middle of the seventeenth century it became acute in the southern part of Las Villas, where there were many plantations along the banks of the Arimao, Agabama, and Caracusey rivers.[3] The tobacco planters were forced to sue the cattle-raising ranchers and the Trinidad City Council. Governor Salamanca, in his capacity as legal authority, solved the conflict by means of a decree (October, 1659) in which he decided that the planters might remain on the lands they held, because the State was interested not only in the vigilance they kept over fields and seacoasts, but also in tax revenues and trade based on tobacco.

Naturally, the aforementioned decree did not prevent the struggle from going on. Up to the very nineteenth century, the tobacco planters had to fight for their lands; first, against the great landholders, and, later, against the sugar-mill owners.

BIBLIOGRAPHY

1. Le Riverend, Julio. *La Habana* (*Biografía de una provincia*). Havana, 1960; espec. Chaps. II, III, IV, VI, and VII.
2. Ortiz, Fernando. *Contrapunteo cubano del tabaco y el azúcar,* Havana, 1940.
3. Rivero Muñiz, José. *Apuntes para la historia del tabaco en Cuba,* Havana, May, 1959.
4. Le Riverend, Julio. "Documentos para la historia económica y social de Cuba." *Boletín del Archivo Nacional,* Vols. LIII, LIV, 1956 (Governor Salamanca's decree is transcribed).

CHAPTER IX

LABOR EXPLOITATION

9.1. *The Indians and their work*

9.1.1. First form of exploitation of the Indian: distribution with "delay". Transformation of the distribution into a commission-enterprise. 9.1.2. Liberators against exploiters. 9.1.3. Historical significance of this struggle.

9.2. *Negro slavery*

9.2.1. Background. General slavery as a condition for colonization. 9.2.2. Development of slavery in the sixteenth century. "High production", motive for Negro slavery. 9.2.3. Commercial agriculture and slavery; mining and slavery. 9.2.4. Condition of the urban slave.

9.3. *Labor in the cities*

9.3.1. Urban social organization. The artisans. 9.3.2. Apprenticeship contracts. Coexistence of labor systems. Importance of the Negro in Urban economy. 9.3.3. "Vagrants" and compulsory labor. 9.3.4. Immigrants: their incorporation into labor.

9.1. *The Indians and their work*

9.1.1. The conquerors and settlers in Hispaniola (Santo Domingo-Haiti) acted since the early years as if the Indians were convenient subjects for slavery. The Discoverer himself, in 1495, sent shiploads of Indians to be sold as slaves in Spain. For the time being, no decision was reached on the question, and Columbus would continue giving Indian laborers to the Spaniards who settled there. Bobadilla also distributed Indians, along with the first "tenancies." It was not resolved until 1500 that the Indians were free; and, as a logical consequence, in 1503 the order came to pay them wages, while Governor Ovando permitted a new distribution. This manner of wage labor would receive the name of "delay". In 1509 it was ordained that the Indians should work so they could be more easily christianized; and, accordingly, Diego Columbus was empowered to distribute them for this purpose, thus joining the civilizing and religious pretext with the exploitation of Indian labor.

The State had at that time a new economic interest. It wanted the free Indians to become vassals of the King, thus strengthening the monarchy; but it hoped the mining industry would produce high income, and for this reason it was ordained that miners be given preference in the distribution of laborers. Furthermore, in 1511 it was commanded that settlers with Indian laborers should employ one-third of them in the mines; abuses increased. It is not a coincidence that in the same year Friar Anton Montesinos, a Dominican established in Santo Domingo, should preach a sermon against the abuses and avarice of the settlers, opening a long debate on the liberty of the Indians.

When this incident took place, Diego Velázquez had arrived in Cuba. He brought an experience concerning Indian labor; he knew, because he was one of the richest settlers in Hispaniola, that the slave or semi-slave labor system established by the Spaniards was tremendously harmful to the Spaniards themselves. The Indians, submitted to intensive labor, which was against their organization and productive tradition, were physically destroyed or ran away to become *cimarrones* (maroons) or rebelled, fighting fiercely in spite of the difference in armament. Consequently, Velázquez distributed the Indians with a "delay" of one month: once the month's work was over, the settler had to let them return home, paying them wages. [1]

This was consistent with the Burgos legislation (December, 1512) that declared the freedom of the Indians; the need of christianizing them; their obligation to work, so the conquerors might contribute to "Europeanize" them; and the principle that they should be paid, though not in money. And in 1513 there appeared a new regulation by which the Indian was made to work for wages during nine months.

But the settlers in Cuba, as well as in Hispaniola, were not satisfied with this solution. With such a system they were not certain of always having laborers at their disposal, because the Indians were quickly disappearing or running away or rebelling. From 1515 it was apparent that the conquerors in Cuba desired a permanent distribution. They said that the free Indian did not want to work "after the European manner" (that is, he did not want to become the typical capitalist beast of burden), nor did he want to become a Christian — pretexts that covered up the need of safeguarding the labor force necessary to the continuous and increasing profit system which existed in Europe and was being brought to America. But royal power maintained periodic distributions. In 1522 Velázquez was authorized to distribute Indians, as long as no one received more than two hundred. Naturally, Velázquez favored his relatives and friends who lived in Cuba, as well as influential persons in Spain who served him in his struggle against Hernan Cortes. New elements then emerged within the distribution system. "Delay" disappeared, and the Indians were permanently employed. Many settlers who had few Indians joined them with those of other settlers to form a "society" in the nature of a true enterprise. However, the permanent assignment of Indians or commission, generally practiced in the rest of the continent, was characterized by the Indian's obligation to pay tribute to the commissioner.[2]

By that time, gold mining had begun (1520). Its disastrous effects upon the life of the Indians were deeply felt, as had already happened in Hispaniola. The settlers knew that the high productive yield they demanded of the Indians was the cause of their decrease in number; but they declared it to be the result of the fact that the periodic distribution of Indians brought about, on the commissioner's part, an absolute lack of interest in keeping them alive. They suggested that the distributions be perpetual, as well as the commisions; and that African slaves be imported besides. Since the system was not altered, the new distributions made by Gonzalo de Guzman, Provisional Governor upon the death of Velázquez, did nothing but increase discontent and fraud among the settlers, and wretchedness among the Indians.

9.1.2. The problem became general in America. The "party" of the champions of Indian liberty, then headed by Las Casas, waged great battles against distributions and commissions. The King decided to try a new method to christianize the Indians, so that, once "Europeanized", they would work to the liking of the ruling settlers. Friar Pedro Mexia de Trillo proposed an "experience" to that end: the undistributed Indians should be given to a European to educate, until it were decided that they could live in freedom, like the Spaniards. This "experience plan" was to be practiced in Cuba; this caused a protest from the settlers who had Indians and from Governor Gonzalo de Guzman himself. From 1526 to 1532 the "experience" developed amidst the hostility of all who favored forced labor, including Bishop Miguel Ramirez. Naturally, it was a failure, not only because it was difficult, in a short time, to change the Indian into a beast of burden "after the European manner," but because the plan was carried out in such a way that led to failure.

Towards 1530 the Indians had disappeared in large numbers. This coincided with a decrease in the production of the gold mines. There were already hundreds of African slaves in the mines and in the *estancias*. Even though petitions were still made for a regulation of Indian distributions which would favor the interests of the oligarchy formed during the conquest, the question lost interest as the native laborer decreased in economic value as a decisive element in colonial organization. The fact that, before 1540, gold mining rendered scarcely any profit contributed not a little to this loss of interest. As lucrative commercial enterprises there remained only cassava production and cattle raising, which had not yet acquired any special importance.

In those years, Las Casas' "party" won great influence in the court of Charles V. The interests of the monarchical State came into conflict with those of the American oligarchies; for royal power, though allied to them (they were its chief support in holding the colonies), had no desire for the reproduction of a feudal system against which kings had had to struggle since the fourteenth century. The thesis of Indian liberty was then returned upon. From this turnabout emerged the new laws of 1542, forbidding the Indians to be commissioned anew when the existing commissions ended (law number 35).

The protests acquired the nature of veritable uprisings; for the King's representative, Blasco Nuñez de Vela, was beheaded in Peru, a country agitated by civil wars and the Pizarros' ambitions of independence. On this occasion the oligarchies showed to what extent their interests were opposed to those of the monarchical State.

In Cuba, as well, there were protests, headed by Bishop Ramirez, who wrote letters to the King describing the "sadness" and "poverty" of the exploiting settlers, due to the lack of Indians. He threatened with the entire depopulation of the island. Governor Juanes Davila, who had married a widow commissioner, allied himself to the interests of the oligarchy and did not enforce the new laws.

Royal power gave in. After all, if the oligarchy was its ally in the defense of the empire against the remaining European states which threatened it, and represented a "garrison" in the face of rebellious Indians and African slaves, Charles V could not openly clash with the oligarchs, no matter what his misgivings concerning their fidelity might be. Thus, in 1545, law number 35 forbidding the renewal of the commissions was repealed; and the law which liberated the Indians from an abusive commissioner was also annulled. Commissions were kept up, though altered.

In Cuba the principle established by the new laws was not repealed. After all, the oligarchy was not so powerful as in other colonies, nor the Indians so numerous as to be kept under forced labor. But exceptionally, towards 1550 there was in Cuba no distribution exceeding the amount of 50 Indians. In 1550 a new governor, Gonzalo Perez de Angulo, declared those laws to be in full force.

Then appeared the "reductions." In the second half of the sixteenth century, it was ordered that the Indians be grouped in villages, so they should begin to assimilate the European way of life. These villages or settlements were the "reductions," which since 1550 would be used as instruments for the submission of nomadic or rebellious Indians, especially by the missionaries, among whom the Jesuits in Paraguay were outstanding. Accordingly, it was not by mere coincidence that, after the enforcement of the new laws, there appeared in Cuba Indian "villages" such as Guanabacoa, Caney, and, perhaps, Jiguani. Naturally, this is not to say that there were no Indians in the cities, mixed with the Spanish population; or that there were no Spaniards or half-breeds mixed with the Indians in their "villages." [3]

Although visibly disappearing, the Indian went on being a laborer of certain importance; by mid-century he became a herdsman, learning to use the *punta de montería* and to ride horseback; he went on practicing agriculture in the *estancias* where the Spaniard and the African learned to cultivate and use native plants; he worked for wages or as a sharecropper. Existing social conditions, after more than half a century of colonization, brought upon him the need to work: he had been deprived of his land, and had no opportunity to obtain municipal grants. One choice alone remained before him: to work in the same manner as the dispossessed worked in Europe.

9.1.3. What is the significance, what is the historical perspective in all this process of formation of a forced labor system for the Indian?

When speaking of Las Casas, historians often present a hazy character of vague ideas, divorced from the social reality of the times. To historically define the struggle between the commissioners and Las Casas as a true social event does not detract from the latter's greatness; on the contrary, it places him as an element of progress, as a herald of a more advanced economic and social organization than the one the commissioners established with the support of the monarchical State.

In order to place both positions, we must turn back to the conditions in Spain in 1492-1550. During those years, there were two types of social and productive relations in the mother country — those typical of the decaying feudal system, and the capitalist ones, which struggled to spread and predominate. We have already pointed out in Chapter I that all of western Europe was then undergoing a period of economic and social transition. It was so that the struggle between these two systems in Spain was transferred to America. The role of the State, of royal power, was none other than to make the most of this opposition for strengthening the monarchy; and this is why its policy regarding Indians changed according to whether it was more convenient to support the oligarchies or to weaken them. All in all, Emperor Charles V did this in Spain until the uprising of the "communities" allowed him to join the feudalistic groups (the nobility and the high clergy).

The commissioner tried to transform the Indian into a serf or slave—forms of social relations which coexisted within the feudal framework, although agrarian serfdom predominated. From this viewpoint, the conquerors and the oligarchic settlers tried to reproduce in America a type of social relation that existed in Spain. They succeeded in so doing; however, they did not exactly duplicate the pattern, for productive and social relations cannot be exported, but require the creation of general conditions which permit their reproduction.

Those in favor of liberty did not deny the necessity of having the Indian work; accordingly, the free Indian would necessarily have to work, and would have the right to an emolument, as established in the Burgos legislation of 1512. Those who favored this system wished that labor in America be organized upon the basis of a social relation which existed in Spain, the bourgeois-wage-earner relations. And, since it was not possible, either, to reproduce it mechanically, the wage labor system resulting from this effort was strongly imbued with feudal characteristics, as the compromise which it was. We can observe this in the organization of the Mexican *quatequil* and the Peruvian *mita,* in which a compulsory nature predominated over wages.

All this means that the commissioners represented an element of reversion of the historical process, and the "liberators," one of advance; for there is no doubt that the capitalist organization then meant progress for humanity. Las Casas and his tenacious struggle then gain a significance which brings them closer to us, who are under the obligation to evaluate him adequately, rejecting historiographic judgments which place him before us as an absurd being who opposed "reality" or who madly advanced beyond his time.[4]

Consequently, the legal and theological doctrines that served as a theoretical instrument for the discussion of the property and labor system in America (Chapter V) are not a mere verbal adventure, but a disguise for profound struggles among economic and social forces.

9.2. *Negro slavery*

9.2.1. When we spoke of the organization of forced labor for the Indians, we pointed out that slavery had not altogether disappeared from European society during the highest peak of feudalism; this is, that African slavery in America is a historical *continuity.* Christian slavery in Europe and the slave trade established with the Arabs is a proof of this continuity —a continuity which acquired a faster and deeper rhythm even before the discovery of America, that is, at the end of the fourteenth and all during the fifteenth centuries, due to the fact that the Europeans came out into the Atlantic, especially the Portuguese.[5]

The conquest of the Madeira, Cape Verde, and Canary Islands not only brought about a process of commercial colonization in which sugar production played a major promoting role, but it fostered the enslaving of the natives of those islands (such as, for example, the Canary *guanches*) and encouraged the African slave trade already begun by the Arabs. (See Chapter II).

In consequence, not only these islands, but also southern Portugal and Spain experienced a sudden increase of trade in slaves "bought" or stolen in the Atlantic coast of Africa.

America certainly stimulated and increased this infamous traffic to an unequaled degree. This meant that slavery could be a convenient instrument for the exploitation of human labor in all the stages of social development, including that of industrial capitalism. Until the social process created in each colony a "reserve industrial army" (a numerous and improverished working class), Indian, Negro, and even white slavery might have been the ideal of the dominant groups.

It would be naive to link slavery with racial interest. The European, Christian white man was enslaved in Europe and America, and so was the Indian, like the African. The racial theory is a disguise intended to deprive colonization of the universally brutal nature it has to our days. For the groups who profited from other men's labor, any slave was good enough; his condition as such was essential, not his race.

In the same way, it would be naive to charge this or that historical character with the fatherhood of African slavery in America. No one had to suggest it, it existed from the first moment as a result of the continuity we mentioned before.

9.2.2. It is possible that the first African slaves arrived from Spain after Columbus' second voyage (1494). From that date on, licenses were granted to individuals for bringing them. Many officials and authorities received permission to bring some slaves to Hispaniola (Santo Domingo-Haiti): two, three, or more, whom they sold on arrival. In 1501 the entrance of Moorish slaves was forbidden, while that of African slaves born in Catholic countries was permitted. And, undoubtedly because of the number existing in 1503, Ovando asked for the complete prohibition of the trade, for, in previous years, the Negroes had shown an open tendency towards rebellion and conspiracy with the Indians.

But the interests of the State, as happened with the Indians, stimulated this trade, for in 1505 the Catholic Sovereigns sent Negro slaves to work in the mines. For this reason, when Diego Velázquez arrived in Cuba, or shortly afterwards, slaves began to be imported. We know that in 1515 the city solicitors asked permission for some to be brought over from Hispaniola.

Towards 1520, due to the first signs of Indian extinction, the efforts to obtain Negro slaves were redoubled, though not by occasional licences, but in great shipments. Thus, it is possible that the one hundred and forty-five slaves brought from Cape Verde in 1526 could have been the first "load" that arrived in Cuba.

Others would come, perhaps part of the thousand authorized by the King in 1527, so that there was an abundance of them from 1530 onwards. It had been many years since the settlers had discovered the higher productive yield of the Africans' labor: according to contemporary witnesses they produced more than two Indians. And that is why we see their incorporation into mining and agriculture. In a visit to the *estancias*, in 1538, one could note the presence of Africans, along with the Indians. It may be said that towards 1540-1550 there might have been about one thousand slaves. It is true that around those years not only had the Crown granted the first treaties or general contracts for importing slaves into America, but smuggling had also begun.

The first attempts to establish the sugar industry coincided with the emphatic petition for importing Africans. And we do not lack information on the arrival of somewhat heavy "loads" in 1571 and 1604; these illustrated a trade which was increasing in spite of its irregularity, to the point that, in 1630, there is knowledge of the arrival of three hundred slaves.

So much did the amount increase, that, at the beginning of the seventeenth century, they were considered dangerous for their possible aid to the Dutch enemies who had practically blockaded the Island. Their dangerous nature had already been proved by numerous cases of *cimarronería* (marooning) which brought about the organization of searching parties to hunt for runaway slaves.[6]

9.2.3. The process of growth of the slave population was intimately linked to the organization of a cane *plantation* economy. Cane cultivation and sugar production demanded hundreds of slaves, and, as the exports of this product increased, the intensification of labor brought about a greater number of deaths among Africans, hastened their extenuation, and forced a speedier replacement of the exterminated ones. No less significant was the employment of numerous slaves in the El Cobre mines.

9.2.4. But, of course, there were slaves devoted to other labors. There was a considerable number in the cities, joining in artisan industries, in the construction of buildings and forts, in the loading and unloading of ships, in domestic service. Many of them lived in houses separate from their masters and obtained their own earnings which allowed them to liberate themselves or to pay the price of their manumission. Of these it was said that their money came from what they stole from their masters; possibly, this accusation sprang from the proposition that everything earned by the slave belonged to his master. The fact is that not only direct exploitation of labor existed, but also the "renting" of the slave; the latter was a recourse for those who owned only one or two. There are known cases of the renting of young girl slaves whose price doubled when a fleet was anchored in the Havana harbor.

Many slaves bought their freedom or were declared free by their masters through testamentary provision. Others, generally children, were freed by their masters, disgusted at having their offspring as well becoming slaves. But these facts cannot, as some historians will have it, lead us to the conclusion that slavery in Cuba was a "mild" system, or "milder" than in other colonies. Those who uphold this often start from the idea that the slave, as the master's property, was cared for by the latter; this is true, although we must not forget that the cost of the slave was a value closely related to his productive yield. The master was much more interested in a short, useful life, based on very high productive yield through intensification of labor, than in a long, useful life with low yield. Proof of this is that the sugar-mill owners were always concerned with exploiting the slave more and more.

9.3. *Labor in the cities*

9.3.1. In the cities there was free labor since the early days. Conquest and colonization are characterized by the founding of cities, or urban centers, wich are necessary for reasons of outside communications or to serve as garrisons in areas chosen for their abundant native population, for their closeness to the mines, or for other causes. In the early days, especially in colonies with a scant number of Europeans, these cities were made up, above all, of an unproductive population: oligarchs, clergymen, soldiers, sailors, through-travellers who required numberless products, articles, and services of an industrial nature. Neither the Indians nor the African slaves rapidly learned the respective techniques, nor did the slave-type organization itself favor this learning; this would take place only later, because the European artisans and wage-earners did not come to work at their own trades, but to try to get rich through the methods characteristic of the colonial system: land-grabbing, mining, slave-owning, commerce.

But, since the unproductive population demanded this industrial type of labor, and there were progressively more and more Europeans who had no opportunity of getting rich easily (because the oligarchy monopolized all natural resources and effective political power in the colony) many artisans established themselves in Cuba to exercise their trade, and many elements of the dispossessed population had to work for wages.

Naturally, the number of artisans and wage-earners never represented an important factor in the colonial economic and social organization. It did not lose its essentially slave nature, that is, that the capitalist-type elements were secondary and, besides, could not develop greatly during more than three centuries.

In all Cuban cities there were artisans and wage-earners, though this was more evident in Havana. Numerous industrial trades were represented in the city: shoemakers, silversmiths, calkers, shipwrights, bakers, tailors, etc. They worked in their own shops, subject to the traditional rules. No medieval-type artisan guilds were organized in Cuba; brotherhoods were set up, and there was group participation of artisans on all public holidays. To our knowledge, not until the seventeenth century were there *alcaldes examinadores* (official examiners) charged with giving approval to the exercise of the trade to those apprentices and officials who wished to establish on their own.

9.3.2. These artisans hired apprentices, who were generally adolescent, orphan, and poor. The apprenticeship contract obliged the young man to serve for five years in the house and shop of the artisan, doing everything he was told to do. The master must give him lodging, food, and clothing, and teach him all the secrets of the trade. If the young man ran away before the five-year period was over, he had to serve once more from the beginning.

It is true that some artisans owned African slaves and that these learned the trades, but it should generally be supposed that this was not the common case. The slave who learned a trade did not in time cease to be a slave; he only increased his market value.

There were other types of wage-earners since the early days. Indians, free Negroes, and Europeans hired themselves to work for wages, in the service of a merchant or a landlord. In this last case, they served as stewards or overseers on the farms. However, in agricultural and cattle-raising work the sharecropping contract seems to have predominated over wages.

9.3.3. Sections of those elements who lay outside the oligarchic society —poor whites, free Negroes, half-breeds— found an open road in the exercise of minor urban commerce or in free occupations which were not subject to strong group regulations. Many free Negro women were laundresses or waitresses. Whites and Negroes and half-breeds practiced ambulant commerce, making up the group of the so-called *regatones* (bargainers) constantly persecuted by the municipal regulations. These occupations all had their source in the need to supply the transient population from ships, the garrisons, the elements from unproductive classes, and those who depended upon them. Finally, many elements from this dispossessed population made a practice of rounding up cattle to sell the meat and make use of the remaining by-products.

Against these occupations and against those who practiced them, the oligarchic city council issued prohibitions tending to have them work for wages in the benefit of commercial entrepreneurs, or landlords. This was the case of the round-up prohibition: poor people were forbidden to practice it unless for wages, that is, for the account of an enterprising master.

9.3.4. Among those who joined the labor force there were not only the "regular" immigrants (that is, Spaniards and foreigners with residence permits), but all who arrived, whatever their nationality might be. This explains the presence of French, Dutch, and English prisoners carrying on trade and minor commercial activities during the first two centuries of colonial history.

BIBLIOGRAPHY

1. Guerra. Ramiro. *Op cit.*
2. Zavala Silvio, A. *La encomienda indiana,* Madrid, 1935.
3. Hanke, Lewis. *La lucha por la justicia en la conquista de América,* Madrid, 1959.
4. Le Riverend, Julio. "Los problemas históricos de la conquista de América." *Islas,* Santa Clara, Vol. V, No. 2, January-June, 1963.
5. Verlinden, Charles. "Les influences medievales dans la colonisation de l'Amerique," *Revista de Historia de América,* México, Nos. 2 and 3, June and September, 1938.
6. Ortiz, Fernando. *Los negros esclavos,* Havana, 1916.

CHAPTER X

CHANGES IN THE PRIMITIVE AGRARIAN STRUCTURE

10.1. *Interior colonization*

10.1.1. The progressive occupation of the Cuban territory presents several stages. In the first place, coastal towns were founded, and *estancias* scattered throughout the territory hugging the coasts (sixteenth century, until 1550-60); later, they started to penetrate the interior and, besides, the State was not pleased at the gathering of citizens near the coasts, since this propitiated smuggling with foreigners. This second stage characterized the whole seventeenth century.

Actually, the main economic exploitations had gathered near the coasts, so that towards 1600 there was no space along them to distribute; it then became necessary to penetrate the fertile interior. Tobacco plantations, sugar mills and cattle-raising ranches would always try to be located in places of easy communication, in order to have a short route for transporting products. Cattle-raising, rather than agriculture, was the one which finally had to penetrate in search of very extensive natural pasture lands. This process was much more definite in the western zone (Matanzas, Havana, and Pinar del Rio) than in the central and eastern zones, where the enormous extension of fertile lands located on the northern coast and to the center remained little-colonized until the end of the eighteenth century. Between 1570 and 1630 all the lands in the interior of the western region were distributed and soon filled up with ranches and corrals.

Naturally, in the second half of the seventeenth century, the occupation of the territory had generally already taken place, except in the eastern zone; and it was the process of agrarian and cattle-raising dispersion and subdivision of the early latifundia that was just then beginning. At that time, the spaces held by cattle-raising latifundia were slowly starting to fill up with agrarian holdings.

On the other hand, around cities and accessible areas there was a "saturation" of agrarian exploitations and a struggle for the best lands. Let us remember that tobacco plantations near Havana had been forbidden since the beginning of the seventeenth century.

Cattle-raising spread in the form of *sitios* within the latifundia. Each *sitio* was generally linked to a hydrological phenomenon —spring, stream, river, pond, etc. — that provided a watering place for cattle. The *sitios* became more numerous as latifundia were divided among several "owners."

Agriculture spread, whether under commercial forms (tobacco, cane, and cacao plantations) or under forms of mere subsistence; the latter were a product of the food needs of the cattle-raising group (overseers, herdsmen, cowhands), and was consequently a kind of agriculture which tended to grow as the population in the cattle-raising latifundia increased.

10.1.2. Of course, the spread of cattle-raising contributed to colonization, but it dispersed the population into small groups, while agriculture concentrated the population. The colonization of the fertile interior was made evident by the fact that, by the middle of the seventeenth century, groups of peasant population sprang up in the regions of Guane, Güines, Santiago de las Vegas, Bainoa, Matanzas, Sagua la Grande, Guaracabulla (Placetas), and Holguín. This population was concentrated around first-class agricultural land, and not until later would it form a true urban conglomeration. This tendency was hastened in the eighteenth century, when the first municipal organizations were founded in Havana, since Velázquez and his men had established the first seven villages, before 1520. The fact that Matanzas and Santa Clara were founded in the last decade of the seventeenth century illustrates the beginning of this stage of "institutionalization" of population nuclei. We must bear in mind that the Havana municipalities of the eighteenth century (Bejucal, Santa María del Rosario, San Antonio de los Baños, Santiago de las Vegas, and Güines) not all emerged from natural causes; but were occasionally the result of some great landholder's land-appraisal policy, or of the convenience of placing groups to serve as garrison and authority within certain areas of numerous peasant population.

10.2. *Dissolution of large ranches*

10.2.1. We have said that following the occupation of the territory, there started the process of dissolution of the early latifundium. We must, at this point, make a clarification of a general nature: economic development was more accelerated in the western area than in the central and eastern regions, so that, in the latter, processes started with delay. While the colonizing occupation of the western territory took place before 1650, in the central area and, especially, in the east, there were zones which had not begun to be colonized until the nineteenth century. Consequently, the general process of subdivision of the primitive latifundium took place ahead of time in the west; it started in the seventeenth century and was in full swing between 1760 and 1830; meanwhile, in the central area, including the eastern part of Las Villas, subdivision did not start until 1820-1840.

Here we shall refer mainly to the western region. The cattle-raising latifundia founded in the sixteenth century were subdivided for many reasons. Let us point out, in the first place, the granting of sections to various "owners," each of whom would try to establish his own cattle *sitio,* so that very soon, along with the original *sitio,* there would appear others which subdivided the ranch or the corral. Besides, each *sitio* implied the construction of shelters and the formation of small food plantations for the cattle-raising population. Agriculture penetrated not only in this manner, but also in the form of tobacco, cane and cacao plantations (these, above all, in the middle of the seventeenth century) that reduced the cattle-raising lands and further contributed to the subdivision of latifundia. There was, besides, a reserve of woodland for timber. In order to open up new areas of the latifundia, woodlands were burnt down, forming the *quemados* (burnt lands) which would later become cattle plains or agricultural plantations. The name *Quemados* appeared in various Cuban regions in the seventeenth century as evidence of the more intensive colonization which was taking place. Each new cattle *sitio* established required a municipal licence that generally stated the number of heads for which it was being granted. Rodrigo de Bernardo y Estrada's book shows us that there were numerous petitions for new *sitios* in the western region during the second half of the seventeenth century; the zones of Bainoa and Guanamón —that is, the western strip of what is now the Province of Havana— were especially outstanding.[1]

Tobacco and cane plantations and, later, pasture lands were the main elements of the subdivision of the original latifundia. Cane plantations and pastures were forms of exploitation that interested the great cattle-raising landholder, and that was why he himself encouraged them; it was not so with tobacco plantations, which best suited the small farmer and where very little slave labor was used.

10.2.2. The early latifundium subdivision in the western region did not go through a similar process in the central area. There, the nearly absolute predominance of cattle-raising favored a hidden form of subdivision of latifundia. This form, which we speak of as covered because it kept the primitive latifundium undivided, was called *hacienda comunal* (communal ranch). Latifundia were subdivided into ideal portions (proportional to the value of the whole ranch), and not into farms or lots separated from each other. There were then said to be *communers* who had so many *pesos de propiedad* or *pesos de posesión* (shares of ownership) in the ranch. Pastures, water, and —at the beginning of this evolution— also installations, were communal; the cattle was divided in proportion to the shares of each *communer.* But, in a second stage, each *communer* asked the city council for a license to establish a cattle *sitio* within the ranch and to use his own *iron* or cattle brand; however, in this second stage, pastures and water were still common property, and the stock was distributed in proportion to the head of cattle owned by each *communer*. [2]

Since numerous portions of ranch *shares* were sold, whether through inheritance, through buying and selling, or through deeds, at the end of the century there were numerous *communers* in these ranches. *Communers* were also divided into large and small, bringing about conflicts of interest which have prevailed until the twentieth century. This type of ranch, that was not physically divided and kept its unity or type of original exploitation, was typical of eastern Las Villas and the Province of Camagüey, actually reaching as far as Las Tunas (now Oriente Province).

10.2.3. The old agrarian structure formed in the sixteenth century, even though it did not constitute an insurmountable obstacle to intensive agriculture and cattle-raising, progressively became a hindrance in the western part, as much as in the central and eastern regions of the country. In fact, the old ranches and corrals in the west were still considered as such while the city council did not declare them as having ceased to be such a ranch or such a corral. Unless it were "subdivided" it was difficult to demarcate the smaller farms; this was particularly impossible in the communal ranches and, accordingly, there was no way of keeping an agricultural plantation untouched amidst *sitios* or cattle pastures. Eighteenth century agriculture, based on great commercial crops, demanded facilities for the acquisition and exploitation of land, while, on the contrary, the old regulations rendered them difficult. Towards the middle of the eighteenth century the need was being felt for new regulations which we shall view in section 10.3.

Of course, it will always be necessary to point out that in the area closer to Havana the development of commercial agriculture brought about a hastening of the process, in such a way that, even under the traditional regulations, old sixteenth century ranches started to be "subdivided." The city council was asked to approve the "subdivision," that is, to recognize that the ranch or corral had ceased to be such a ranch or corral. This is to say, the ranch or corral in question was declared to have ceased as a cattle-raising latifundium as stated in the original grant. Before 1730 the first "subdivisions" had already taken place (Xiaraco Corral, Guanabo Corral, Bacuranao Corral) and the process would continue during the century to the point that Governor Bucarelly would try to prevent them as damaging to the State. Actually, these "subdivisions" did not injure the State, but were extraordinarily beneficial to the great landholders, since they represented a great land speculation. Most of them were sold according to census, and prices rose in such a way after 1760 that the subdivision of latifundia produced an unsuspected amount of real estate income. [3]

10.3. *Legal system*

10.3.1. We have seen (Chapter VII) the legal land system in the sixteenth century, based on land-grabbing, pure and simple, or in *grants* given by the city council. In 1574 the municipal ordinance drawn up by Alonso de Cáceres regulated grants somewhat in detail. Since they dealt with concessions for the exclusive use of pastures, these grants did not give ownership; in order that a right of ownership should be granted them, it was necessary that the King should *confirm* the grant or that the land be acquired through *composition.* This doctrine was repeatedly maintained during the seventeenth and eighteenth centuries; but in the face of the doctrine of the royal nature of the land the beneficiaries of the grants and their heirs managed the ranches as if they had been the real owners.

There were few confirmations of grants, and *composition,* though applied frequently enough, did not generally refer to latifundia, but to smaller farms.

10.3.2. *Composition* is a system of land concession progressively applied with greater frequency during the seventeenth and eighteenth centuries. When someone held land without a grant title, or when he held more than he had been given in his grant, he had to pay a sum to the public treasury; he had to *compose,* that is, to legalize his condition. *Composition* was the equivalent of a land sale. Once the *composition* had been paid, full ownership of the land existed. This system coexisted along with grants until the eighteenth century; but it was intensively applied in Oriente during the second half of the seventeenth century, due undoubtedly to the fact that most landholders did not have a grant title or anything of the kind.

The progressive use of *composition* indicated that the State was going through a hard time (let us remember this was the worst period of Spanish decadence) and a good source of income was established through land sales. The Spanish State then realized that the municipal authorities had made unsparing use of the power of granting lands; a power which, as we know, was never given the city councils. In the middle of the seventeenth century, a dispute over the expropriation of land for building the walls of Havana provided the excuse for the issuing of the royal decree on November 23, 1729, which forbade the municipal authorities to grant land; the Havana Council broke this law, and the order had to be reiterated through the royal decree of February 16, 1739. A royal decree in 1741, however, permitted the distribution of urban plots of land. The loss of such an important faculty marked the beginning of the fall of municipal power, the beginning of state centralization, and the progressive loss of power of the oligarchy formed in the sixteenth century. The prohibitory order had to be reinforced, for some city municipalities, such as Remedios, went on granting land.

Even though these royal decrees considered the process of land-grabbing as ended, it must be pointed out that, since 1700, the city councils had practically no land to distribute; if at all, they granted small or middle-sized farms, they allowed the establishment of new *sitios* within old ranches, or they granted permission to move the *sitios* from one place to another in the ranches. Zones with free lands, such as Oriente, were already using the *composition* system, rather than that of municipal grants.

Naturally, this does not mean that lands without owners, that is, *royal* lands, were lacking. There were such lands, but it was necessary to set them apart, for confusion of boundaries in the old grants and the frauds of the landholders, who took more land than corresponded to their grants, hid the existence of *royal* lands convenient for giving to those who asked for them.

That is why, when the system of sales of royal lands started to be employed at the beginning of the eighteenth century, the post of Land Judge was created to take charge of measuring, demarcating, and determining the land that should be or had been sold by the National Treasury. And that is also why, after grants were forbidden in 1729-39, the sales system established implied investigation of the royal lands. Thus, the legislation fostered denunciations of illegal possession of land, brought about endless litigations, and served to reward the wicked. That is, to the frauds of the landholders were now added all the tricks of those who wished to buy royal land. But, during the second half of the eighteenth century, the treasury obtained very good income from the sale of lands or from charges laid on lands held without a legal title.

Consequently, the struggle for the land kept on becoming more violent, since land acquired great value for the development of commercial crops. So it was that the problem of the cattle-raising and sugar-planting landholders' opposition to the spread of tobacco plantations became acute. Governor Salamanca's Decree (1659) had laid the foundations for having natural tobacco plantations —that is, riverbanks— be considered as royal lands and, accordingly, lands suitable to be given to the planters, even though the great landholders were against it. The motive for this was that, when the State established the tobacco monopoly, it became interested in maintaining the tobacco planters, thus fostering a production which, nevertheless, fell sharply due to the monopoly itself. The Tobacco Agency of 1760 (or second form of monopoly) declared in practice that tobacco plantations were *royal lands.* However, the planters' defense was not efficacious, for the tobacco authorities in charge of defending them finally abused their power. Actually, it was not until the issue of the royal decree of 1760 that the riverbanks and, in consequence, the natural tobacco plantations were declared to be royal lands. This legislation arrived only too late, for the sugar production development had already begun, which would contribute, even more than cattle-raising, to the taking away of fertile lands from the tobacco planters.

BIBLIOGRAPHY

1. Bernardo y Estrada, Rodrigo de. *Prontuario de Mercedes.* Havana, 1937.
2. Celorio, Benito. *Las haciendas comuneras,* Havana, 1914.
3. Le Riverend, Julio. *La Habana, op. cit.* Chapter VIII.

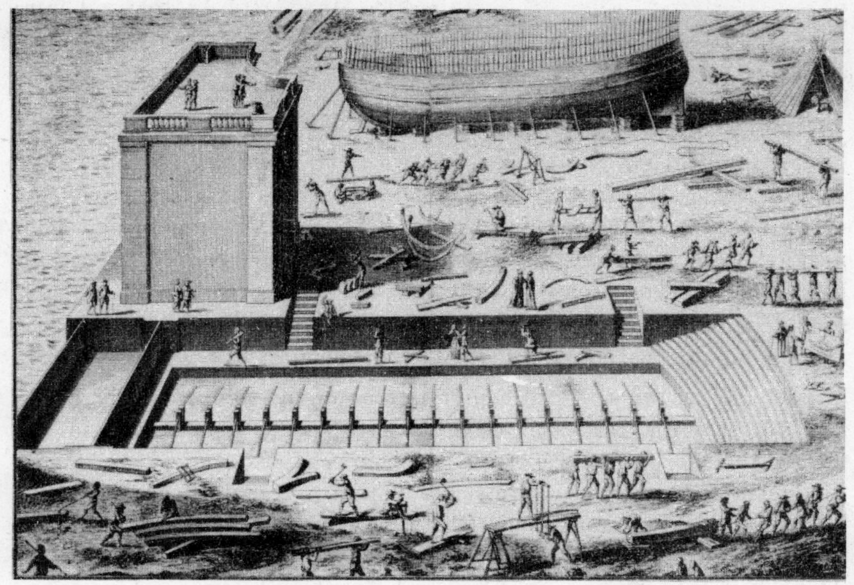

CHAPTER XI

PRIMITIVE INDUSTRIAL ORGANIZATION

11.1. *Gold mining*

11.1.1. The conquerors' "thirst for gold". 11.1.2. Characteristics of gold mining: the gold fields; sand-washing; native labor. Problems of this industry: scant production. Foundries. 11.1.3. Attraction of gold mining and its repercussions upon contemporary economy.

11.2. *Copper mining*

11.2.1. Smelting and exporting. Organization of the Santiago del Prado Mines at the end of the sixteenth century. Other mines under exploitation. 11.2.3. End of this activity. Extraction and use of copper after 1610.

11.3. *Shipbuilding*

11.3.1. Havana as a maritime station. The first ships built by Juan de Tejeda. 11.3.2. Shipbuilding and the *asentistas* in the eighteenth century. Ship repairs at the Havana harbor.

11.1. *Gold mining*

11.1.1. Traditional historians generally link gold mining with the "thirst for gold" of the conquerors, with the "avarice" of Europeans. In this sense they repeat the admonishing words of Friar Bartolomé de las Casas, and, in repeating them, imply that the conquest and colonization were not a *system* of plunder, but a mere conspiracy of ambitious and wicked men. Nevertheless, the "thirst for gold" can and should be explained in the light of European economic organization at this period, and not as an individual psychological disposition.

Actually, as we saw in Chapter II, one of the significant characteristics of western European economy during the fourteenth and fifteenth centuries was the increase in commercial exchange between the Mediterranean and the interior and northern zones of the continent. This demanded a sudden and sustained increase of the means of payment and, mainly, of precious metals to keep up this growing trade. The European gold mines had been exhausted, and it was only ocasionally that this metal could be obtained in Africa. Besides, trade with Asia presented an unfavorable balance which had to be paid off in gold. This originated in all of Europe the search for precious metals —in a word, the "thirst for gold."

From this historical reality emerged the first capitalist economic theory, which we could call *metallist* and which is summarized in the following maxim: the larger the gold reserves of a country, the richer and more powerful it will be. Later, with industrial development (seventeenth and eighteenth centuries), this metallist doctrine evolved towards mercantilism.

The "thirst for gold" is, therefore, nothing more than the individual expression of a social fact of the period. Driven by that force, kings and merchants, adventurers and artisans, everybody pounced upon colonial or less developed lands seeking gold mines. So it happened in the island of Hispaniola (Santo Domingo - Haiti) and so it happened in Cuba, one of whose "mysteries" was precisely to know whether or not it had any gold (Chapter IV). On the other hand, let us remember Columbus' great interest, in his first voyage, in knowing whether there was gold in the Antilles (Chapter III).

11.1.2. When Velázquez and his people were engaged in the conquest of Cuba, they learned that there were gold beds south of Sabaneque (now northern Las Villas) (Chapter IV). There they sent a group who started gold exploitation in the lands near the Arimao River.

Among others, Father Las Casas was granted a concession there; and it was then, as he himself explains, that he realized the injustice of the labor regime imposed on the Indians. The work of Indians in the mines was characterized by its hardship. Since the gold was mixed with the sand in the rivers or near them, the natives had to dig, carry the sand, and "wash" it in the current. To do the latter they had to remain for hours on end standing above their waist in water. Since the extraction of gold depended on the amount of sand they "washed," they were forced to work continuously during long days of labor. And since all of them were engaged in that work, there were certain areas where they did not have enough food, for there was no agricultural production.

It turned out to be that native gold was being exploited before 1520. We do not know the total amount produced, for we lack continuous information, but there is data which reflects great fluctuations. A good year would yield 100,000 pesos; but this did not happen again after 1525. Toward 1530-1540 the productive yield decreased not only because laborers were scarce, but because the richest beds had been exhausted. Nearing 1550, production was very scant and we can say that from then on it disappeared. As a whole, it has been figured that production reached an amount of some 3,000,000 pesos.

This mining was very important to the interests of the King, who received the *quinto* (one fifth) of all the gold extracted by individuals, or directly exploited the mines through managers. Settlers saw in mining an easy way of acquiring riches; but they did not hoard it, either because they sent shipments over to Spain or because they invested their gold in new conquering enterprises, as happened in the expeditions for the conquest of Mexico. At the beginning there were two gold foundries and, finally, only one in Bayamo, which worked for two periods during the year. There the miners took their gold; it was melted, shaped into bars, weighed, and the *quinto* deducted from the whole.

11.1.3. The gold fever brought about a complete neglect of native agriculture in some areas, which resulted in an acute lack of food, even for those who were at the mines. As has repeatedly been said, this caused the necessity of going to Jamaica to buy food and clothing, or of trading in cassava from the agricultural to the mining areas, a trade which was carried out by means of small cabotage vessels. Furthermore, the settlers from Jamaica, where there was no gold, were allowed to bring "their" Indians to Cuba and put them in mining. This conflict between agriculture, which was the basis for an important cassava trade, and gold mining was solved when the scant production of the gold beds brought about the abandoning of this activity. And, since that happened towards 1550, we may say it coincided with the beginning of the cattle-raising trend within primitive colonial economy.

11.2. *Copper mining*

11.2.1. Copper mining started towards 1528-1530. In those years there was talk of some mines called Cardenillo; they would later be called Santiago del Prado, and, finally, El Cobre, in what is now the Province of Oriente. This was an important event for the economy of the period, for copper was a very necessary metal due to its various industrial uses, among them the manufacture of weapons. Spain, as well as a large part of Europe, obtained its supply of minerals from eastern Germany, Austria, and Hungary. As a whole, German mining commerce and technique predominated in Europe when America was discovered.

For the time being, a Santiago de Cuba silversmith prepared samples of this copper; and it turned out to have a very high metallic content; for this reason it began to be smelted. Shortly after, a German smelter, Gaspar Lomanes, dedicated himself to this work. Finally, another German, John Tetzel (who had come from Venezuela, where he had been in the service of the Welzers, German merchants who engaged in the conquest and colonization of that region) devoted some twenty years to smelting this metal. Apparently, the conditions for a systematic exploitation were not present, although Tetzel made a trip to Europe, perhaps with the purpose of inducing German merchants and bankers to participate in this business. On the other hand, the neighbors contested among themselves and with Tetzel for the right and opportunity to exploit those rich mines.[1]

11.2.2. During those years there was no regular extraction and smelting, though part of the ore was exported to Spain. Upon Tetzel's death, the mines were granted to Portuguese merchants, until the King decided to exploit the mines directly, in the decade 1590-1600. He appointed a manager, Captain Francisco Sánchez de Moya, who was provided with slaves and implements. A foundry was set up in Havana, where the ore was taken from Oriente and from the Bacuranao area (now Tarará). This last ore was speedily exhausted. Sánchez de Moya organized a grand-scale exploitation, and laid the foundations for the mining industry in eastern Cuba. This was a period of splendor for primitive mining in Cuba. Boilers for the sugar industry were made, as well as artillery pieces, and large amounts of ore were exported to Spain.

11.2.3. However, transportation difficulties, as well as costs, prevented Cuban copper from competing with that of Europe itself; so that, towards 1610, the order was given to discontinue the smelting, and shipments to Spain practically ended. But the extractions of ore would not cease altogether. Sánchez de Moya himself had travelled all over the country in search of mines, and he had discovered that of Malezas (now Las Villas), which would be exploited during the seventeenth century, like those of Oriente.[2]

After 1610, copper was extracted for manufacturing implements for the sugar industry and, occasionally, for exportation. More than once the King allowed the early sugar-mill owners to make use of copper for the needs of their industry. However, by mid-century, copper mining was over, and it would not be attempted again until the beginning of the eighteenth century. It should be pointed out that the king's own slaves at the El Cobre mines lived practically in freedom, increased in number, and in the eighteenth century refused to return to the intensive labor regime once more imposed upon them.

11.3. *Shipbuilding*

11.3.1. Due to its position on the Gulf, Cuba was a base for navigation and commerce. Consequently, its seaport towns were, from the early days, a repair station for ships trading in the Caribbean and with Spain. There were calkers and shipwrights in Havana, as well as in Bayamo and Santiago de Cuba. The native hard woods were very appropriate for ships, and there was tar or *chapapote* for hull repairs. Cabotage traffic brought about the building of ships of small tonnage for sailing between ports in the island or to Hispaniola, Jamaica, Campeche, and, perhaps, Cartagena de Indias.

But this naval industry would receive a special impulse for political reasons, when, towards 1560, penetration into the south of the United States (Florida) was intensified under command of Pedro Menéndez de Avilés, who was at the same time appointed Governor of Cuba. Shipyards were organized, and ships were built, with tonnage in keeping with the times (400-600 tons). Later in the decade of the 80's under Governor Juan de Tejeda, shipbuilding was intensified; some of the ships then built became famous in the Spanish oceanic navy, and lasted for a great many years. But this stage ceased before the end of the century.[3]

11.3.2. In the first half of the seventeenth century this industry was resumed, and several builders were contracted; but there was no continuity. On one hand, the very decadence and consequent political weakening of Spain, and, on the other, the cost of the larger ships (for trimming, rigging, metal parts, and others used in ships had to be imported from Europe) contributed to the disappearance of the industry, which was then limited to ship repairing and small boat building. It was only in the middle of the eighteenth century that a great naval industry again existed.

BIBLIOGRAPHY

1. Henriquez Ureña, Max. "Noticia Histórica sobre Santiago de Cuba. (Siglos XVI y XVII);" *Archipiélago,* Santiago de Cuba, III, Number 18, December, 1930.
2. Wright, Irene A. *Historia documentada de San Cristóbal de La Habana* en el Siglo XVII. Havana, 1930.
3. Wright, Irene A. *Historia documentada de San Cristóbal de La Habana en el Siglo XVI,* 2 vols., Havana, 1927.

CHAPTER XII

BIRTH OF THE SUGAR INDUSTRY

12.1. *Background*

12.1.1. Outline of the sources and spread of the sugar industry. 12.1.2. The Mediterranean period. 12.1.3. The Atlantic period. Sources of plantation economy.

12.2. *"Prehistoric" period of the Cuban sugar industry*

12.2.1. Arrival of cane. 12.2.2. Sugar development in the other Antilles. Exploitation of sugar cane.

12.3. *Initial impulse*

12.3.1. Existence of the industry in 1590. State financing. 12.3.2. Idea of technique and machinery. Privileged legislation for sugar mills. Distribution and conditions of the industry in the seventeenth century.

12.1. *Background*

12.1.1. The history of cane and of the sugar industry is extremely interesting, because, for a very long time it has been linked to processes of overseas colonization and domination. We do not know the exact area where domestic sugar cane —industrial cane (*sacharum officinarum*)— originated; but there is a growing scientific trend towards the opinion that its birthplace was a Pacific island, perhaps New Guinea. From there it would jump from island to island towards Southeast Asia, where crossbreeding would take place, giving rise to diverse varieties.

The earliest reports of cane date back to approximately the year 1000 B.C., in India. A fermented drink containing cane juice as its basic ingredient was drunk at the time apart from the fact that cane has been used as a natural fruit from earliest times. From India it went into Persia (Iran) and Mesopotamia; upon the spread of Budhism it moved into China, where native varieties of cane have been found.

The industry possibly started in India; but it did not get to produce crystalline sugar. At most, some cane juice concentrate or thick molasses was produced, similar to pan sugar, which served as food or sweetening. We suppose this to have been so, because no clear testimony of crystalline sugar was recorded until the seventeenth century of our era. This testimony seems to indicate that in Iran, particularly in Gondev-Shapur (or Jondisapur), the elements of Hellenistic (Asian-Greek) culture, resulting from Alexander the Great's expeditions centuries before, were combined with those of Arab culture, which began to spread throughout Asia in that century. And out of this fusion emerged the crystalline sugar industry.

12.1.2. The fact is that the Arabs, when they began to rule the lands bordering the Mediterranean, introduced the sugar industry into Egypt, Morocco, southern Spain, and Sicily (an island south of Italy), in such a way that, by the tenth century, the sugar industry already existed in all these zones. What we might call the Mediterranean stage of the sugar industry began. In both Egypt and Spain there remains very ancient Arab treatises on agriculture which describe the cultivation of cane and the production of sugar. It was from the Arabs during the Crusades and during the existence of the European kingdoms in the Holy Land (Palestine), that the Europeans learned to use sugar and cane; and they also learned this in Sicily when the Arabs were expelled from this island.

The Venetians and Genoese, especially the former (see Chapter II), carried on intensive trade in sugar with Egypt and with other territories subject to Arab rule. It has been said, but not proven, that the Venetians discovered a primitive process for refining sugar. During the fourteenth and fifteenth centuries Europe demanded increasing quantities of sugar, for it not only served as common food but also as a preservative (manufacture of foodstuffs) competing with salt and substituting it as a preservative.

12.1.3. This is why, when trade began to move towards the Atlantic, one of the first visible results was the establishment of a sugar industry in the Madeira, Cape Verde, and Canary Islands, to which Columbus was linked (Chapter III). And, when America was discovered, cane arrived in Columbus' second voyage (1494), was planted in Hispaniola, and a few years later, towards 1520, sugar was being exported. Thus started the Atlantic stage of the sugar industry, characterized by cultivation in plantations, with slave labor force and vigorous capitalist-type features from the mercantile and financial viewpoint. Europe, developing along the road of capitalist industry, found in the Antilles and Brazil its source of sugar supply.

This far-off history of cane and sugar is very interesting, because, during the Mediterranean stage, there appeared —incipiently, of course— certain phenomena of economic colonization and of sugar plantation agriculture which would attain their maximum level in America, from the seventeenth century to our day.

12.2. *"Prehistoric" period of the Cuban sugar industry*

12.2.1. In all American regions, the sugar industry went through a dark stage prior to its development. In Cuba, as in the rest of the Antilles, this early period is not known with any degree of certainty. We know that cane arrived with the conquerors, who brought it over from Hispaniola.

A 1523 document seems to indicate that a certain industrial exploitation of cane existed in Cuba, besides the plantations; but none of this can be fully asserted. And, since there is a 1526 document that speaks of the sugar mills being built *de nuevo,* that is, for the first time, we must necessarily see in all this the reflection of a sudden interest for the sugar industry among the citizens, who were already concerned about the scarcity of Indians, the low productive yield of the mines, and the need for African slaves.

Actually, it was not until the decade 1540-1550 that the possibility of the existence of a *trapiche* (cane mill) in Santiago de Cuba was first mentioned, for African slaves were sent to tend it. It is true that towards 1551 there is mention of the "sugar present on the land", although in later records it is not mentioned again.[1]

12.2.2. What explanation could be found for these sporadic references? As opposed to Irene A. Wright's opinion, Fernando Ortiz insists that cane was processed then with a very rudimentary machine which has lasted to this day in Cuban agricultural zones, the *cuncaya*; this would explain the fact that there is no reference to *trapiches* or *ingenios* (sugar mills), but merely to sugar, which might have been only a molasses concentrate, such as pan sugar. This means that, during many years, the industry carried on a precarious existence as a rudimentary-type exploitation for internal supply and occasional exportation of molasses. Naturally, cane would be used also as a natural fruit for sucking and chewing.[2]

We know, in fact, that there were primitive cane fields from the early days. Towards 1590 there is mention of cane sown 40 years before. In the *estancias* near the cities cane was present as another crop.

While the industry was being painfully established in Cuba, sugar production in the remaining Antilles and in Brazil prospered. In the Antilles, however, it started to fall after 1560, shrinking down to an insignificant activity in Santo Domingo, as well as in Puerto Rico and Jamaica. The case of Brazil is different: the industry there, founded with active participation of Germans, Flemish, and other Europeans, progressed incessantly, becoming the first great world productive center. In other Spanish colonies, such as Mexico and Peru, the sugar industry was also established in the sixteenth century.

12.3. *Initial impulse*

12.3.1. Towards the end of the century there were several factors that cooperated in the creation of the industry in Cuba: on one hand, the fall of production in the other Antilles which, besides, were badly located in relation to maritime traffic with Spain; on the other, the decision to prohibit the founding of new sugar mills in Mexico; and, finally, the spread of the use of sugar in Europe, demanding an increasing colonial production. Of no little importance was the fact that the American colonies. with their sugar development, contributed to eliminate this production from the Madeira and Canary Islands, where the industry disappeared altogether as it did in Sicily.

The opportunity then arose before the rich Cuban sugar planters. The citizens of Havana petitioned before the Crown to provide a loan for those who wished to build *trapiches* or sugar mills, which seemed to be in operation a little after 1590. The loan was negotiated from 1596 to 1600, and it was granted in that year.

12.3.2. A total of seventeen landholders received loans. They gave as security the machinery or slaves which they had, or which they had bought to be paid for with the loan: animal-traction *trapiches* and sugar mills, a few hydraulic ones, with some sugar pans and boilers and with clay molds to *purge* the sugar (drain molasses). The loan was larger for the hydraulic mills, and smaller for the "flying wheel" mills and the *trapiches,* a detail which reveals their difference in value. The sugar mills in the eastern region were founded almost simultaneously, in Santiago de Cuba and Bayamo. [3]

These first industries enjoyed the privilege granted the sugar industry by royal decree issued in Toledo, on January 15, 1529, which declared that no part of the establishment (land, machinery, slaves) could be seized on the grounds of debts unpaid by the sugar-mill owner. This privilege served to create a special legal regime of which the owners took advantage during three centuries in order to operate with someone else's capital.

This industry, emerging with Crown financial support and with extraordinary privileges, attracted the attention of the landholding oligarchy to the extent that at least four of the sugar-mill owners who received loans belonged to this dominant group (three of them were members of the Rojas "clan").

Sugar exports to Spain started in the first decade of the seventeenth century; their basic figures are insufficiently known. The fact is that, towards 1620, there was a total number of 50 sugar mills and *trapiches,* which, at an average of 1,000 arrobas (25 lb. units) each, achieved a production of 50,000 arrobas. This production possibly increased later, for we know there were new sugar mills and exports to the amount of 80,000 arrobas towards 1670. But seventeenth century documents rather show a standstill, due to the constant complaint of the powerful citizens, according to whom the lack of slaves and the lack of transportation, plus the taxes, prevented the growth of the industry.

BIBLIOGRAPHY

1. HENRIQUEZ UREÑA, MAX. *Op. cit.*
2. ORTIZ, FERNANDO. *Contrapunteo cubano del tabaco y el azúcar.* Havana, 1940. There are two recent editions, one from the University of Las Villas and another from the National Council of Culture (Consejo Nacional de Cultura) (1963).
3. WRIGHT, IRENE, A. "El establecimiento de la industria azucarera en Cuba;" *La reforma social,* Havana, April to July, 1916.

Chapter XIII

ORGANIZATION OF COMMERCE

13.1. *The foundations of colonial commerce*

13.1.1. Reference to the European situation. Cuba as a ship supply base. 13.1.2. The need of importing. Inter-colonial trade.

13.2. *Commercial exclusivism*

13.2.1. Its sources. The House of Contracts. Restricted production policy. 13.2.2. Participation of Cuba in imperial trade. 13.2.3. The fleets. Contraband trade.

13.3. *Domestic trade*

13.3.1. Urban commerce: its various forms. Monopoly and speculation. 13.3.2. Inter-provincial trade. Havana as a middleman. 13.3.3. Minor commerce.

13.1. *The foundations of colonial commerce*

13.1.1. The general impulse experienced by European commerce during the fourteenth and fifteenth centuries brought about, as we know, an interest in Atlantic navigation, and, consequently, contributed to the discovery of America. Thus, the Santa Fe Agreements signed by the Catholic Sovereigns and Columbus in 1492 contemplated a commercial enterprise of the type most common in the early days of capitalism. However, when the conquerors arrived in America the sought-for products were nowhere to be found; on the other hand, although America seemed to be rich, they did not know how to exploit these riches commercially. For the time being, the enterprise could not be a commercial one.

In logical consequence, the first articles exported to Europe were natural and industrial products which the European consumer knew and needed: gold, hides, sugar. They were no longer dealing with the classical Asiatic products (spices, above all) which Europeans obtained, centuries back, through Venice and Genoa in the great eastern Mediterranean commercial ports; and which they had been obtaining, since 1502, from the Portuguese, once the latter had reached far-off Asia by the southern Africa route. Typical American products, such as tobacco, would begin to spread in Europe a good while later, towards the end of the sixteenth century.

Therefore, the first period lasted until 1520-30 when Europe (Spain) had much to export for the supply of conquerors and settlers, and very little to import from America. This was a period when the great colonialist interests, especially the Treasury's (the King's), complained of the expenses occasioned by America and of the meager returns in profits.

During this first period, Cuba was conquered, and its trade was carried out as part of a general plan of colonialist expansion in the Caribbean Sea and the surrounding lands. The Crown used each newly occupied land as a base for the organization of expeditions destined to penetrate farther-off zones. Since then, Cuba was a support base for Pedrarías Dávila's expedition into Central America and, somewhat later, to Grijalba's, Hernández de Córdoba's, and Cortés', for the conquest of Mexico. Towards 1530 it was Hernando de Soto's base, while Santiago de Cuba would support, on a smaller scale, those who conquered Peru. Even in the second half of the sixteenth century it served as a foothold to maintain Spanish domination in Florida.

13.1.2. This brought about, during that first period, a certain frequency in commercial exchange among the different colonies. Let us recall that there was an acute need of foodstuffs, due to which an active cassava trade was organized in the Caribbean. The Indian slave trade, which possibly preceded all the remaining aspects of colonial economic formation. was also very intensive among the different European groups settled in America before 1530. In this aspect we may point out the introduction of enslaved Panuquese Indians into Cuba, where they were exchanged for cattle, both horses and beef cattle. The first oligarchic groups in Santo Domingo and in Havana became famous at the time for the great speculation they carried on with European and American products needed in the new neighboring colonies.

It can also be observed during this first stage that Spain was not in a condition to supply the conquerors and settlers, for it lacked an adequate merchant fleet; however, those Spaniards who settled permanently in America needed to import, since their food and apparel demanded European products. Even though America, for the time being, offered some food and "cloth of the land", most of the demand was fulfilled with European products. At first, gold served to counterweigh these imports; hence its great importance for Spanish interests and for colonial oligarchies.

13.2. *Commercial exclusivism*

13.2.1. The Spanish colonial regime was characterized by a very strict monopoly, based on the King's fiscal interests and on his alliance with certain commercial groups of the mother country. This situation was essentially no different from the system implanted a century later (seventeenth century) by the English, Dutch, and French, whose main characteristic would be the more decisive role played by merchant groups of the mother country in colonial trade. As is well known, in the eighteenth century the alliance between the high bourgeoisie and royal power was consummated in Holland, as well as in England and in France; while in sixteenth and seventeenth century Spain the feudal classes, the landholders, and the renter bourgeoisie predominated.

Although the first years, up to 1530, were characterized by a certain freedom of trade, since 1503 the Crown started the monopolist policy, establishing a House of Contracts in Seville. It was not only a vigilance organization, but a "commercial house" as well. As the years went by, its nature as tax-collecting body (customs house), regulating force, and fiscal agent became apparent, and it lost, to a great extent, the character of a royal business house.

In this manner America's trade was centered upon the benefit of the King and of the Castilian and Andalusian commercial groups, especially those of Seville, port of entry and departure for all this traffic. There was then in Seville a close link of interests with great merchants of Flanders, England, and France, and there would be still more during the second half of the sixteenth and all during the seventeenth centuries. In the colonies, also, there was a similar concentration, for in each of them there generally existed only one port which was allowed to trade with Spain; this brought about a process of formation of great merchant oligarchies that would share their power with the landholding oligarchies.

The effects of this monopoly were immediately apparent, to the extent that, towards 1525, the sugar-exporting interests (Santo Domingo), protested for the lack of freedom in shipping their crops to the most favorable European markets. However, this opposition ceased, and the principle of the freedom of trade was squashed.

13.2.2. Cuba was submitted to monopoly. This submission had special features due to its geograpical situation, for it was an outpost of the Viceroyship of Mexico which was, in the northern part of the continent, the colony that carried on most intensive trade with Spain. Since 1520, the beginning of traffic between Mexico and Spain brought about the development of a trading port of the utmost importance: Havana. And, finally, towards 1540, when the fleet system started, the concentration of Cuba's commerce was indelibly marked. [1]

The fleet system was the result of various circumstances, apart from having been previously practiced by the Venetians and the Portuguese. It consisted in periodically gathering the merchant ships voyaging to America and organizing them as a convoy, under custody of warships. Thus, the available cargo tonnage was concentrated, and a better defense could be arranged before the enemy. They had a fixed route: they departed from Seville towards the Canary Islands, and thence on to America, passing south of the Greater Antilles; here part of the fleet would separate and travel on to Cartagena de Indias and Nombre de Dios, while the remaining part went on to Veracruz. On the way back they would meet at Havana, and thence leave towards the Azores and Seville. They left in April or even later, in June, to avoid the cyclonic season in the Caribbean. When this period overtook them in Havana, the ships would remain there until the following spring. This made of Havana a transit station, where, at times, there would gather thousands of sailors, soldiers, and travellers for months on end. [2]

The fleet organization left many colonies outside the major trade between America and Europe, such as Puerto Rico, Santo Domingo, Jamaica, Guatemala, whose products could not be easily exported unless single ships were chartered from Spain, or unless they could be sold in a nearby colony. Since in each colony there was only one port allowed to trade with the mother country, many cities remained isolated, as happened to Santiago de Cuba, Trinidad, and Remedios, whose commerce was limited to a scant number of very small vessels trading with Havana or with other Caribbean colonies.

The fact is that the commercial groups of the mother country were more interested in trading with Veracruz, which was the point of entry into Peru, than with the remaining colonies, much poorer than these viceroyships. But the commercial oligarchy at Seville likewise restricted this trade to the utmost, in order to increase their profit with the speculative rise of prices due to the constant scarcity of European products in the colonies.

So we see that, because of the restrictive policy of the monopolist interests, joined to the growing incapability of the Spanish monarchy to make ships available, commercial exclusivism brought about very great depressive results in America and, above all, in relatively little-populated and poor colonies like Cuba.

13.2.3. The colonies defended themselves by making the most of all the opportunities they had to trade outside the monopoly, that is, to carry on contraband with foreigners. Since the sixteenth century there were seamen, pirates, businessmen, and adventurers who settled on the coasts of Cuba for months or came into ports and harbors, such as Matanzas, to exchange European products for Cuban products (hides, for example) or for silver and gold. Frenchmen, Dutchmen, and Englishmen, successively, although sometimes there were mixed groups, held frequent contact with the inhabitants of Cuba. Towards the end of the sixteenth century there was a group settled in the area which is now Manzanillo. During the first half of the seventeenth century the Dutch were very active, though they often carried out their purposes through violent means, submitting Cuba to a veritable blockade. The so-called buccaneers and other brotherhoods of the coast began to organize later, and they succeeded in setting up permanent establishments on some islands of the Antilles, such as Santo Domingo. As a State policy for penetration in America, the English, on their part, not only occupied some of the Lesser Antilles, but landed in Jamaica in 1654 and took this island away from the Spaniards. Then started the period of colonial "wars" over the distribution of American and of Asian trade, which would characterize European history during the eighteenth century.

This Spanish monopolist policy should not be judged as an exception. All European colonialist groups began the formation of empires under this type of monopolist policy in favor of the mother country; and, in fact, in a more or less disguised form, all capitalist powers that to this day have developed colonial plans have kept for themselves, exclusively, the benefits arising from the exploitation of natural resources and of the population in submitted lands. When traditional historians affirm that the English and French surpassed the Spaniards as organizers, they affirm, at the most, that they knew how to exploit the colonies better, in a more capitalistic manner.

13.3. *Domestic trade*

13.3.1. Commerce was organized within Cuba on equally oligarchic bases. Naturally, the great cattle-raising landholders and the sugar planters negotiated on their own the sale of the exportable products of their farms (hides, sugar, molasses). There was not, properly speaking, a specialization of the export commerce. However, there were import merchants who traded with European products. They were the great merchants, linked through credit or association to the Sevillan merchants. Not only did they buy and store in Havana, but they also sold imports to merchants from other cities, such as Bayamo, Puerto Príncipe, Santiago de Cuba, etc. They were speculators, who monopolized import goods to bring about an increase in prices. They were constantly being complained about; for, besides, the small merchants also monopolized and speculated, occasionally with the manifest complicity of officials and authorities.[3]

13.3.2. There was an active enough trade in Havana and in other cities. Havana was not only the port of entry for all, or most of, the European goods that arrived with the fleets; it was also a city which needed products from far-off areas, because, at times, it contained thousands of transient travellers who were unproductive consumers. It was supplied with cattle by the central zone of the country, and with other products by Remedios. Havana received from the rest of the island products to be exported by the fleets; coastal vessels traded from one place to another when the enemy did not prevent their doing so. That is why certain exploitations, such as the sugar mills, sought the proximity of the sea, which allowed for heavy and voluminous products to be moved via coastal vessels.

There existed a great variety of tradesmen, apart from the great merchants. They were the shopkeepers registered with the municipal authorities, and the street vendors (*regatones*) whom the City Council constantly harassed. These tradesmen were often charged with altering prices, with eluding the basic occupations, and with competing with officially-registered merchants. Indeed, the *regatones* and the poor peddlers were persecuted, not the powerful monopolists; the idea was to force the common people to work for wages, and not to live on their own. All this attempted to prevent them from buying directly from the producer, except on the days and hours of public market fixed for the purpose. In this way the people bought their supplies, and the door-to-door distribution carried out by the *regatones* was rendered unnecessary. However, as the poorer population (that which lived on a day-to-day basis) increased, the *regatones* became more useful and remained a part of urban commerce; on the other hand, many cattle-raising landholders and major tradesmen used *regatones* as middlemen, and the soldiers of the garrison themselves sold products on the streets.

BIBLIOGRAPHY

1. HARING, CLARENCE H. *Comercio y navegación entre España y las Indias,* México, 1939.
2. VEITÍA LINAJE, JOSEPH DE. *Norte de la contratación de las Indias Occidentales,* Buenos Aires, 1945 (Work written in the seventeenth century, which has served as a major source to those who deal with commerce in America, such as the previously mentioned Haring himself).
3. ROJAS, MARÍA TERESA. *Indice y extractos del archivo de protocolos de La Habana,* 1578-1585; 1586-1587; 1588, 3 vols., Havana, 1957. *Actas capitulares cit.* Chap. V.

[illegible] such as the [illegible] sought the protection of the [illegible] for the [illegible] and [illegible] products to be moved via coastal [illegible].

There existed a great variety of tradesmen, apart from the great merchants. They were [illegible] registered with the [illegible] authorities, and the street vendors [illegible] whom the [illegible] constantly harassed. These tradesmen were often charged with altering prices, with [illegible] the basic [illegible], and with competing with officially registered merchants. Indeed, the [illegible] and the [illegible] peddlers were persecuted [illegible] the idea was to force the common people to work for wages and not to live on their own. [illegible] attempted to prevent them from buying directly from the producers, except on the [illegible] of public markets fixed for the purpose. In this way the people bought their supplies and [illegible] distribution carried out by the [illegible] was [illegible] unnecessary. However, as the [illegible] population [illegible] lived on a day-to-day basis increased, the [illegible] became more useful and [illegible]. On the other hand, many [illegible] and [illegible] tradesmen [illegible], and the soldiers of the garrison themselves sold products on the streets.

BIBLIOGRAPHY

1. Haring, Clarence H. *Comercio y navegación entre España y las Indias.* Mexico, 1939.

2. Veitia Linage, José de. *Norte de la contratación de las Indias Occidentales.* Buenos Aires, 1945. (Work written in the seventeenth century, which has served as [illegible] source [illegible] commerce in America [illegible].)

3. [illegible]

Part IV

RISE AND FALL OF SLAVE ECONOMY (1659-1886)

CHAPTER XIV

INDUSTRIAL CAPITALISM IN EUROPE

14.1. *The system of manufacture and the industrial revolution*

14.1.1. The economic transformation that took place in Europe beginning in the fifteenth century reached its highest expression in the process of capitalist accumulation, this being consummated in England. The driving of thousands of peasants from the land and the conversion of artisans into proletarians created the necessary conditions for the capitalist development of the nation. First to appear on the scene was *manufacture,* i.e., the plant or establishment where tens and hundreds of workers gather to handle materials with their hands or traditional working instruments. This means that the manufacturing system rather represents a concentration of ex-artisans, or of several artisan shops. Within this system a division of labor gradually takes place, i.e., the workers more and more become specialized in some productive operation, this resulting in an intensification of work without a change in technology of production actually taking place. We must bear in mind that in traditional artisan work, specialization was almost nonexistent. This division or specialization made it possible to analyze in detail each one of the phases of the production process.[1]

Meanwhile, the manufacturing system grew in importance. During the second half of the seventeenth century and the first half of the eighteenth, England carved and consolidated its great colonial empire. Its trade progressively extended throughout the whole world. Holland and Portugal failed to continue making progress as colonialist states; conquered territories began to produce raw materials and basic products (cotton, sugar, etc.) and, also, to consume, increasingly, European industrial goods. Under these circumstances, commerce constituted not only the main form of capitalist development, but the incentive to transform the system of manufacture as well. Evidently, the aim then was to produce more at a lower cost. Within the manufacturing system this objective could not be attained. Is was necessary to replace men with machines.

Ever since the early part of the eighteenth century, efforts were being accumulated to furnish industry with mechanical apparatus to replace men in a whole series of productive operations. The textile industry, at the time the most important in England, is the best example of this. But the first decisive step was taken in 1726 when coke replaced firewood and low quality coal in steel making, thus marking the beginning of the use of large capacity furnaces.

In this way, England acquired a basic metal industry capable of furthering the development of the other branches of production. Starting in 1760 the process of the application of machinery began. This is what historians call the *Industrial Revolution*. This revolution did not really change the economic and social foundation of the country though it meant a higher degree of organization for capitalism which up to then had centered on commerce and was now to depend on the progressive growth of industry. Logically, the first mechanical inventions were applied in the textile industry. Toward 1771 Hargreaves invented a spinning jenny making it possible to simultaneously produce several threads of yarn, unlike the traditional spinning wheel that had only one spindle. This apparatus was powered by hand. Immediately, Arkwright improved upon this system by utilizing hydraulic power to run the machine. Finally, in 1779 Crompton, taking advantage of the progress made by his predecessors, created the machine known as *mule jenny,* enabling one worker to run even thousands of spindles. In 1885 Cartwright went one step further when he invented the mechanical loom. This meant that not only the production of yarn was mechanized but that of cloth as well.

However, there was one problem. The principal source of power continued to be man or water, both being irregular, limited and not always available at the plant. Then, it was necessary to think of a source of energy that could be handled in accordance with the requirements of the factory. Towards 1765 James Watt invented a machine capable of producing industrial energy, based on the generation of steam. Thus, an advance was made in comparison with Newcomen's atmospheric machine which had been used in mine-pumping. Twenty years later Watt's steam engine was being successfully used in industry.

By the end of the century, the textile industry in England had already reached a stage of accelerated concentration. This was especially the case with the cotton goods industry. In order to carry out this transformation, the new class of industrialists had waged an intense struggle against the survival of artisan production. For this reason, new factories were concentrated in new zones or in small towns or near them where the resistance of the traditional craft guilds would not be found. The cotton industry almost did not exist until then. That is why the application of mechanical inventions gave it an extraordinary impetus. A contribution to this was with the invention of the cotton gin by Eli Whitney in the United States (1782). This machine separated seeds from fiber, thereby affording a great saving in slave labor on the cotton plantations of the South (U.S.A.) with the resultant higher productivity.

The "industrial revolution" spread throughout all branches of production. Moreover, as early as the beginning of the nineteenth century, metal, mostly steel, was used in the construction of machinery, resulting in much longer life. This "revolution" spread like a wave throughout the world. It appeared early in France in the nineteenth century; later it travelled to Germany and the United States as capitalist conditions ripened in each country.

The transformation resulting from the application of machinery in production was a very important one for modern history. In the first place, it made possible a continued increase in surplus-value, thus laying the foundation for capital concentration, since the application of an invention augments capital, and this increment, in turn, favors the most intensive application of machinery. From that time on, industrial capitalism would travel a straight course to ever more complex forms, to the dominance of big capital, all the way to financial capital, appearing toward the end of the nineteenth century. Secondly, the transformation of the broad masses into proletarians originated a politically active working class which struggled for better living conditions throughout the nineteenth century. Thirdly, industrial mass production demanded new markets so that traditional colonialism gave place to a system where the machinery for economic domination was more important than that of political control. Finally, industrial revolution made England a recognized world power and increased international differences in development, so that those with a larger industrial capacity became veritable masters of the world, disturbed only by their own interest contradictions. [2]

14.1.2. Precisely, difference in development, together with the fact that the most highly industrialized nations import increasing amounts of raw materials and at the same time export more finished goods, demands ever more efficient means of transportation. Sail ships and carts were, since the dawn of history, the means of transportation in use. Improvements on these did not solve the problem of driving power and of load capacity, which continued to be limited.

In England, the problem was attacked by building canals. As early as 1759 a number of zones were linked by waterways. Roads were improved through the McAdam method. But these solutions were limited, and, on the other hand, maritime transport remained without solution. This was finally solved in 1807 when the North American Robert Fulton successfully applied the steam engine to drive side paddle wheels for propelling a ship. At first, progress was not decisive: engines were too large and required a supply of fuel (coal) detrimental to the ship's pay load. Moreover, sail ships were improved upon, such as the socalled *Clippers,* affording greater speed and load capacity. For many years ocean-going ships were driven partly by sail and partly by engine and, generally, even though marine engines were continually improved upon, sail propulsion held sway up to the last quarter of the nineteenth century. Only when the *internal combustion engine* (Diesel) was perfected, sail ships disappeared almost completely.

Land transportation reached a new level when in 1826 the first railroad in the world was inaugurated in England. An engineer, Stephenson by name, commissioned to build an animal-driven railroad, applied the steam engine to drive the wheels. Though the first locomotive built by Stephenson, called *Rocket,* could not travel above twenty kilometers an hour, its traction was much greater than that of the draft animals, and was rapidly accepted. Within the short span of twenty years, railroads were built in the principal European countries and in the United States. Because of sugar transportation requirements, railroads came to Cuba as early as 1837. Railroads opened for exploitation broad areas in the interior of the continents, as was the case in the central and western United States.

During the second half of the nineteenth century, telegraphy allowed for even faster communications, first within each country and later between the continents (submarine cable).

Through these technomechanical advances, capitalist industrial economy took over the world. Another stride forward was taken in the nineteenth century through aviation, the maximum development of which has not yet been attained.

14.2. *Political revolutions*

14.2.1. The economic transformation marking the development of commercial capitalism and its evolution towards industrial capitalism, were attended by great political movements resulting in the dominance of the capitalist bourgeoisie. We have seen that in the sixteenth century the first stage of the struggle against the feudal system ended in the consolidation of absolute monarchy in England and in France, but the feudal class survived and rallied round the king, while the bourgeoisie, in which the monarchs found support when facing the great feudal lords, though obtaining certain favorable conditions for commercial and industrial development, did not possess, as a matter of fact, any power at all. In France, this class became an ally of the King, holding judicial and administrative posts and gaining *nobility,* loosing in the process a good deal of its anti-feudal character.

The accelerated process of capitalist growth in England demanded, in the seventeenth century, political changes. A series of conflicts marked the struggle between the King and the new social classes, disgruntled over the tax system which discriminated against them as compared with the feudal and landholding groups. This is the cause of the violence revealed in the Long Parliament called by Charles I that ended in an uprising against the King who, having been defeated, was executed (1642). The House of Lords was done away with and a republic proclaimed with Oliver Cromwell as Lord Protector, who not only emphasized colonial policy but, responding to commercial interests, stiffened and enforced maritime laws tending to monopolize domestic and colonial trade in an open fight with Dutch commercial power. After Cromwell's death, Charles II ascended the throne as an ally of the landowners. His brother James II encountered violent opposition. The bourgeoisie demanded a government that would guarantee its rights. Moreover, it disliked, as did the other classes, the policy of alliance with, and subjection to, France which, under Louis XIV, loomed large as England's economic, military, naval, and colonial rival. Parliament, representing the opposition, sought the help of William of Orange, son-in-law of James II, who ruled in Holland under the title of *Stathuder,* obtaining it in the form of 25,000 men landing in England. James II fled from the country (November, 1686) and in February, 1687, Parliament offered the throne to William and his wife Mary, who accepted and pledged to uphold the *bill of rights,* providing for civil liberty and the will of Parliament. With these principles, there truly began the bourgeois-democratic regime in England. There began then a firm alliance of capitalist landowners and the monarchy. This political alliance did not impede industrial and political development, but actually favored it. It was not until the nineteenth century reforms that a democratic regime came to power which was capable of guaranteeing the industrial bourgeoisie the political power enjoyed by the landowners.

14.2.2. During the eighteenth century, England's economic and military power became solid. Its colonial empire grew, producing large returns that made up a good part of the base responsible for England's final industrial victory over the other advanced nations (Spain, Portugal, Holland, and France). But England maintained and made more stringent its monopoly on trade and its political domination of the colonies. These policies collided with the commercial and maritime interests of the thirteen colonies it had founded in North America. As early as

1730, efforts had been made to keep these colonies from trading outside the empire, measures being taken to limit their production of goods which the metropolis exported.

In 1765, under the pretext of distributing the tax burden necessary to pay off the Seven Years' War expenditures, oppressive taxes on American commerce were to be arbitrarily imposed by the London government. The Americans refused to accept this and London desisted from the project, but the tax on tea importation was continued. The open resistance against these measures, begun in Boston, spread to the other colonies. A Congress was called which, after the breakdown of negotiations, proclaimed independence in 1776. With Spain supporting (from Cuba) the independence fighters and France sending an army and a naval force, military victory was obtained and the federation of independent United States was constituted.[4]

This revolution did not have a definite character, but only a bourgeois-democratic element, especially since the States (previously colonies) of the northern zone had a marked commercial and maritime character. Doubtlessly, a revolution maintaining the slavery of Africans, the essential foundation of the socio-economic structure of the States (previously colonies) of the South, from Maryland to Florida, could not be bourgeois-democratic. However, it was greatly discussed, though it was not, as some apologetic historians would have us believe, the *cause* of very important later events, such as the French revolution, the Latin-American revolutions, and the transformation of the British colonial system.

14.2.3. The French Revolution, begun in 1789, constituted the typical case of a bourgeois-democratic movement. Monarchy had not only lost prestige but had bankrupted the country after more than sixty years of war. In 1763 France lost Canada and India, part of her colonial empire. Her trade fell more and more. However, national industry grew, becoming capitalistic, as was the case with the Creusot foundry (1787), the Paris paper mill, and the coal mines, one company of which employed 4,000 workers. While the power of the traditionally dominant classes weakened, the power of the bourgeoisie increased.

Protests against the crisis broke out in 1788, in which year it is estimated there were 200,000 out of work. A plan to save the State from bankruptcy, consisting of a single-tax on property, was opposed by the nobility and the high clergy, both privileged classes. This opposition forced the King to convoke the States-General which had not been convened since 1614.

The States-General consisted of the meeting of the three "estates" or main classes of the nation: the *nobility,* the *clergy,* and the *third estate* or *Commons.* The first two were privileged, a residue of the feudal system. The third class, the Commons, made up of the bourgeoisie, not only did not enjoy any privileges but was kept from growing, as all taxes weighed upon it. This was particularly burdensome for the peasants.

The States-General met in May 1789. The Commons were in favor of joint meetings of the three groups. The privileged classes and the King maneuvered. But the Commons declared a national assembly, as some elements from the nobility and the clergy joined their ranks. A constituent assembly was proclaimed shortly afterwards. The people of Paris took to the streets in revolt and, successfully storming and destroying the Bastille, forced the King to come to the city. The nobility began to plot a bloody repression, making it necessary for the masses to organize a Revolutionary Government made up of a revolutionary municipality and militia, later transformed into the National Guard. At that point, the bourgeois revolution began. The constitution, finally adopted in 1791, limited suffrage to those who could pay a specified amount in taxes, and only property owners in the middle-sized bracket could be elected to office. This brought the protest of the poorer groups, while the nobility and the privileged emigrated to prepare counterrevolution abroad. The King secretly dealt with them to have interventionist armies attack France. However, the Constituent Assembly had become conservative, wishing to retain the monarchy and repressing the republican popular demonstrations.[5]

The attack from abroad was defeated by the revolutionary army (Battle of Valmy, September 20, 1792). A few days before —August 10— the people of Paris had established a Revolutionary Commune and the Assembly had to call a Congress elected by universal suffrage, giving the revolution a more radical turn. Monarchy was abolished and the King executed. While the danger of foreign intervention lasted, a revolutionary government was organized in which the principal role was played by Robespierre. The struggle against the enemies of the revolution became sharper since the ranks of the remaining feudal classes were now increased by groups representing the high commercial and industrial bourgeoisie, who speculated with articles of daily necessity, trying to get richer and richer. This is the period which traditional history calls the Reign of Terror. Against this stage when the revolution attained its peak, revealing itself more radical and equalitarian, a conspiracy was organized headed by Tallien, Barras, Fouché, and others, representing the enriched bourgeoisie who would not have price controls. They conspired against Robespierre, deciding to attack him on July 27, 1794 (Ninth Thermidor). He was arrested and executed together with a group of his followers the following day. From this moment, France fell in the hands of the reactionary bourgeosie, as a result of which the revolution was gradually liquidated. The constitution of 1795 set the nation back to 1791. Terror was unleashed against liberals and radicals. First through the Directoire government, later through the Consulate and, finally, with the empire of Napoleon I, the French bourgeoisie, fearing the masses, turned reactionary. [6]

14.2.4. The French Revolution had repercussions all over Europe. In neighbouring countries also, there were dissatisfied bourgeois protesting against the privileged feudal classes. But, besides, there were very grave national problems. Several nations were subjected to foreign domination and posed the question of national liberation. At the first glimmerings of the revolution, the Belgian —1789— and the Polish —1794— peoples began great battles for independence and bourgeois democracy. When in 1815 Napoleon Bonaparte was defeated, the Holy Alliance was organized with the purpose of drowning all liberal movements in Europe and, going even further, restoring Spanish rule in America. In 1829 independence was declared in Greece after fighting against Turkish domination since 1820.

By 1830, together with the revolution in France against the monarchy of the Bourbon family, new movements broke out. Belgium declared itself independent, but in Poland and Italy the liberal and national movements were defeated by the autocratic forces of the Russian tzars and of the Austrian emperor, respectively. [7]

14.2.5. Between 1830 and 1848, the political situation in France and England underwent a profound change. The industrial revolution had advanced. As a result, the working class had grown too. But living conditions were extremely miserable. While in England the workers had expressed their opposition to machines by damaging them (Luddite movement), and later forming the Great National Workers Union, founded by Robert Owen, which was subjected to brutal repression, in France there was constituted a workers movement of a pre-scientific socialist type that participated actively in the crisis leading to the Revolution of 1848. These events marked the appearance of the working class as a political force, compelling the bourgeoisie to initiate political and social reforms. The struggle against the practice of employing women and children, for a shorter work day —then of 12 to 14 hours' duration— and against unemployment, were the core of those movements.

14.2.6. In Germany, where also there was agitation in the elements of the liberal bourgeoisie and the radical petty bourgeoisie, there was an intense debate over ideas. The thinking of philosopher Hegel had many followers among the liberal university people. A group of them made up what is known as the *Hegelian left,* among whom Karl Marx and Friedrich Engels were outstanding. Marx had to emigrate, establishing contact with French utopian socialism in Paris and later, in London, with English political economy. He joined the "League of the Just", which, on the eve of the Revolution of 1848 split, the majority remaining with the "Communist League". During those years Marx and Engels had been working on a socialist theory. Towards the end of 1847 Marx succeeded in formulating the fundamentals of scientific socialism in his *Critique of Political Economy* and *Poverty of Philosophy,* thus marking his departure from Proudhon's petty-bourgeois socialism. In 1848 he drafted the *Communist Manifesto,* Marxism's central document..[8]

This Revolution explains the important role played by the French working class in the movement arising in February, 1848, against the monarchy of Louis Phillippe I. This King, who had ascended to the throne at the time of the liberal revolution of 1830, embodied the full alliance of the monarchy and the high reactionary bourgeoisie. The general economic crisis of 1845-47 had a deep repercussion in France, where the people revealed an aggressive dissatisfaction over poverty and unemployment. Elements of the bourgeoisie, and the liberal petty bourgeoisie broke with the government. Louis Phillippe abdicated in favor of his grandson, following the people's action of February 24, 1848. The Congress, with seat in Paris, proclaimed the Republic.

As had happened in 1789 and in 1830, Europe was also shaken by a revolutionary wave in 1848. In Italy there was struggle against Austrian rule and for national unity. But reaction rallied and bloodily defeated the national liberal movement, though the kingdom of Sardinia, on that island, the Piedmont, and Savoy, that is, the northwestern territory of present-day Italy, became consolidated and gained prestige from their war against Austrian domination. Other nationalities within the Austrian empire became very restless. The peoples took up the fight in Vienna, the capital, as well as in Budapest and Prague. It was necessary to grant political reforms to the Hungarian people, headed by the liberal leader Kossuth. At the same time, other peoples of Hungary —Serbian, Croatian, and Rumanian— were in a state of agitation seeking liberation. The Austrian government took advantage of this to clamp its rule over all of these nationalities. Though the government of Kossuth tried to fight the foreign intervention, the Austrian and Russian armies crushed the revolution.

The Czech revolution, centered at Prague, was rapidly quelled by foreign troops, and a dictatorial foreign government was established in Bohemia —geographic nucleus of the Czech nationality.[9]

The Revolution of 1848 was quickly suppressed in all of Europe, but it had the effect of liquidating the remnants of feudalism in the principal states. In this connection it can be stated that it closed the cycle of bourgeois-democratic revolts started by the French Revolution of 1789. After 1848 the bourgeoisie held power in the principal European countries, the most powerful and economically developed ones. At the same time that it became more and more conservative, it increasingly furthered capitalist industrial and commercial growth, to the point where, at the end of the century, financial, capitalism, and its peculiar expression —imperialism— appeared. Out of this development were to stem new conditions favoring a higher proletarian awareness.

14.3. *America*

14.3.1. America, Spanish as well as Portuguese, colonized since the sixteenth century, can be considered as a definite society as early as the seventeenth century. But we should distinguish, especially in colonial Spanish America, the existence of two zones: first, viceroyships of continental territories with heavy Indian population, the most advanced being concentrated in mountain zones with a temperate climate: Mexico (New Spain); Colombia (New Granada); Peru and Quito (Ecuador) and, second, the governments and *capitanías* (captainships) with thin and backward Indian populations, situated on low lands (sea level): Central America, the Antilles, Venezuela, Argentina (viceroyship of Rio de La Plata at the end of the eighteenth century).

Viceroyships were organized rapidly. Many settlers came to them. With the help of Indian work, mining for precious metals was developed as well as some crops and extractive industries for export (vanilla, cochineal, etc.). The production of large estates was channeled to commercial outlets on a small scale only. African slavery was developed in the low zones of those viceroyships where the Indian population was not thick. The Indians' work status was similar to that of a serf, but also doing compulsory work in the mines.

Oligarchies appeared rapidly in the viceroyships. The group of the miners was the most powerful. There were *latifundists* (large estate owners) and, among these, the Church was the wealthiest. There were commercial groups, since these countries imported heavily. Merchants had close interest links with the Spanish commercial monopoly. These merchants controlled domestic trade, which developed because of the fact that, geographically, these countries were very large, and exportable production had to be concentrated for shipping.

All this could be seen clearly in the seventeenth century. In the other colonies the process was different. It proceeded more slowly.

The practice of utilizing African slaves in the governments and *capitanías* was not stepped up until the second half of the eighteenth century. The *latifundia* (large landed estates) basically employed slaves to develop big plantations of primary products for export (sugar, coffee, cacao, indigo). There was little or no mine development. Livestock raising took on importance, as it did not require many hands and was also based on the *latifundia* system. In these colonies there was a powerful class made up of the large landowners, some of whom turned industrialists, as was the case with the sugar industry. The merchants were not so powerful, as the volume of imports was rather reduced and exports were handled, to a certain extent, directly by the landowners and industrialists. But this commercial class gained strength beginning in 1760, and became closely linked with the colonial power. The Church was wealthy, but here it did not have economic power equal to that acquired in other zones. In general, these countries started a more accelerated colonial development when, beginning in 1740, a slight capitalist rehabilitation commenced in Spain, and the industrial revolution boomed in Europe.

When Spain went into a crisis (1808) as a result of the Napoleonic wars, the majority of her colonies, and also Brazil, began their liberation process. The landholding classes, for whom Spanish commercial monopoly was an obstacle to the growth and sale of commodities in the more developed capitalist markets (England, France, the United States), these landholding classes penetrated already by liberal ideas, set up provisional governments intended to substitute the metropolitan rule that vanished as a consequence of the Napoleonic invasion of Spain and Portugal. These governments, in the form of Juntas, as the one ruling in Seville on behalf of King Ferdinand VII —a prisoner of Napoleon Bonaparte—, rapidly became independent, that is, beginning in 1810. As is generally known, the independence process appeared in three great focal points or centers: Mexico, Venezuela, and Rio de La Plata. From the struggle started in those colonies sprang the independence of almost all the Latin American nations. The struggle against Spanish rule lasted until 1825. Spain lost and the Latin American republics were set up. [10]

14.3.2. The latifundists continued ruling these republics, where the greatest class inequalities existed, where mechanized industry was nonexistent, with Indian serfs and African slaves, without good roads or adequate means of transportation. There were no basic changes in the economic or social structures. The dominant native colonial classes simply ousted the Spanish colonialist classes. There was no alteration in the forms of latifundist exploitation of land, Indians and slaves. The Church kept its lands and its power. The masses continued in serfdom or slavery. There was then formed a nucleus of the commercial bourgeois class that, precisely because of its dependency on links with international capitalism, rapidly adopted a conservative attitude, as the commercial class had done during the Spanish rule.

As a result, and because there were no important internal changes, liberated America progressively fell into a new colonialism. From then on, British and United States interests would be dominant. England was quick to grant loans to the new republics. In Argentina, it financed the building of railroads, signed commercial treaties and became very much interested in the cattle industry, with a view towards the exportation of meat. At the same time, the United States expanded its trade and, about the middle of the century, when it started its rapid march to capitalist industrialization, began to invest in mines and plantations —primary products—, and, especially, through consistent application of the Monroe Doctrine, succeed in keeping other powers from Latin America, which the United States reserved for itself as a "zone of influence". [11]

14.3.3. The transformation of Latin America's economy and society was very slow. Traditional structures stopped progress; agrarian serfdom and slavery impeded industrialization; liberal trade with highly developed European nations retarded internal production. Nevertheless, by the middle of the century, a bourgeoisie and a petty bourgeoisie were being formed, who based themselves either on the rural population or on the current of European immigration to promote the first important reforms. Towards 1850, the richest and most thickly populated nations of Latin America possessed railroads and had managed to build some internal roads, with the resultant access to new zones that were the subject of a colonization drive. Local capitalists —the merchants— had attained a certain financial capacity. Foreign investment created a proletariat that up to that time had no significance at all. There was an enrichment, by way of politics, of official persons, tending to create conditions favorable to the development of the bourgeoisie as a class opposed to, or, at least, of interests differing from, those of the old landholding class.

Then arose movements like the Mexican reform, which was carried through favored by the national struggle against the French intervention (1862) and Emperor Maximilian —imposed on Mexico by the French army. Juárez, Mexico's great leader, expounded not only political reforms, but, above all, economic ones— such as the sale of lands held by the Church. In Argentina, where land was abundant, Sarmiento, head of the reform movement, posed the necessity of colonizing the vast expanses of the pampas by settling European emigrants (in the same manner that it was then being done in the United States). In Chile, also, European immigration was promoted as a means to further capitalist transformation.

Towards 1880 Latin America was the battlefield where that reform movement and the traditional interests (landholders, merchants, the Church) which opposed progress had joined battle. The fight had not ended when already appeared in the world the imperialist forms of denomination which, in the twentieth century, would cause an arrest of capitalist development, taking over banking and the main mineral and land resources of the nations in order to exploit them to an extent suiting only the United States and England.[12]

BIBLIOGRAPHY

1. Marx, Karl. *Capital,* vol. cit.
2. Lilley, Sam. *Op. cit.*
3. Kosminsky, E. A. *Historia de la edad media.* Havana, 1962.

4. FOSTER, WILLIAM Z. *Esbozo de una historia política de las Américas.* Vol I and II, Havana, 1963.

5. MATHIEZ, ALBERT. *La revolución francesa,* 3 vol. Havana, 1962.

6. TARLÉ, E. *La clase obrera en la revolución francesa.* Buenos Aires, 1961.

7. EFIMOV, N. *Historia de los tiempos modernos.* Havana, 1962.

8. MEHRING, FRANZ. *Carlos Marx* (*Historia de su Vida*), Madrid, 1932.

9. EFIMOV, N. *Op. cit.*

10. BAGU, SERGIO. *Op. cit.*
FOSTER, WILLIAM Z. *Op. cit.*

11. GUERRA, RAMIRO. *La expansión territorial de los Estados Unidos,* Havana, 1938.

12. SÁNCHEZ, LUIS ALBERTO. *Breve historia de América.* Mexico, 1944.

CHAPTER XV

AGRARIAN EVOLUTION

15.1. *Changes during the eighteenth century*

15.1.1. Intensive cattle-raising: pastures. 15.1.2. Diversification and its little agrarian importance. Coffee plantations. 15.1.3. Enduring characteristics of agrarian operations: extensiveness; nomadism; empiricism.

15.2. *Sugar cane predominance*

15.2.1. Need of a change towards the end of the eighteenth century. Laws of 1815-20. 15.2.2. Deep penetration by sugar cane agriculture. Conversion of estates to sugar cane plantations in the central zone. 15.2.3. Effects of the sugar industry transformations and of the Ten Years' War.

15.1. *Changes during the eighteenth century*

In Chapter X we saw the changes taking place in agrarian structure up to 1659. These can be reduced to one phase only: beginning of the process of dissolution of large primitive estates as a result of slow growth of commercial agriculture. This was characteristic of the western region, the one dominated and influenced by the commercial impulses of Havana, the only seaport then regularly linking Cuba with the European economy. The central and eastern parts of the island remained stationary, with the original large cattle estates predominating. It should be remembered that in this zone large cattle farms crystalized in the form of communal estates that constituted a brake on agricultural development.

15.1.1. In the western region some of the primitives estates were dissolved and the land granted to established occupants beginning as early as the first quarter of the eighteenth century. At that time, permission for such dissolution was requested only in the case of some of the estates, the ones closer to Havana, where commercial agriculture had displaced cattle-raising, due to the proximity of the seaport.

Consequently, cattle-raising lost a considerable portion of the land it had because it did not yield an income so high as did commercial agriculture. For that reason, towards 1740, cattle fattening pastures were on the increase. These were farms of medium or large size, though incomparably smaller than the cattle *latifundia* of the sixteenth and eighteenth centuries where cattle bred on traditional farms in zones far from Havana were fattened for beef consumption. These farms had natural pasture and, as compared with the old estates, represented an *intensive* operation.

Up to this point, agrarian transformation was slow. However, towards 1740 the pace of agricultural growth began to speed up. And, as a result, cattle-raising lost land area, the number of pasture-grounds and cane-fields multiplying. There was a reduction of tobacco farms as a result of the depressing effects of the monopoly established in 1717. From 1740 on, partly because of the capitalist rehabilitation in Spain, partly because of greater participation of European commerce in Cuban exports, sugar production increased. In Spain, the capitalist upsurge promoted a slow change in economic policy. From then on, an effort would be made to better exploit American resources, in support of metropolitan industrialization. Especially, in response to the long-overdue mercantilism introduced into Spain by the Bourbons, attempts were made at progressively eliminating the monopoly held by Seville and Cadiz with respect to trade with the American colonies, so that, in the future, all regions of Spain might participate in and profit by the colonial wealth (Chapter XIX).

There was a sudden interest to know about American lands and their products, to determine whether they could produce the fibers, dyes, and other raw materials required by Spanish industry. The bureaus created after 1760 were the instruments of this new colonialist attitude.

15.1.2. As a consequence of those changes, the depth of which was favored by the English capture of Havana (1762), a stage of agricultural diversification began. This diversification was in commercial crops. From then on, expansion of trade with Spain and also, though unsteadily, with the English colonies to the north (later to constitute the United States), was a great incentive for the production of all exportable goods.

The growing of coffee, the production of white wax for export, the planting of cotton, the introduction of the mango, the attempts at the production of indigo, and many other endeavors, date back to that epoch. Of all these agricultural elements only coffee attained to a considerable development, constituting, towards the end of the century and the beginning of the 1800's, yet another factor for the dissolution of the old agrarian structure. It is true that coffee trees require high land well protected from the wind and, generally, these lands were not sought for cane and tobacco farming, but inasmuch as coffee was exported in increasing quantities up to 1830, its cultivation continued to take up land not required by other crops and cattle-raising, thus giving rise to a veritable battle in the western zone, from 1790 on, for the possession of the best located farms, causing land prices to increase. If we also consider the fact that obstacles for the easy sale of land continued in force, we shall understand to what extent that moment was important in the development of the colonial economy.[1]

The other crops that were then introduced or promoted had no repercussion on the agrarian situation. Neither was coffee itself capable of transforming the situation in the central and eastern zones where it reached a great development, occupying mountain lands that, within the slow agricultural growth process in the zone, were not sought for other purposes.

15.1.3. Land exploitation begun in the seventeenth century was marked by the absence of techniques making for a higher productivity or the conservation of soil fertility. Neither had there been much progress made in Europe before the seventeenth century, but the system of crop rotation was widely used as well as manure fertilizing. The use of slaves, the attractiveness of commercial crops, and the latifundist forms of farming (and, generally, the abundance of virgin land) favored the lack of progress in farming and cattle-raising methods. For three centuries, until 1860, the only method of stepping up production consisted of increasing the number of slaves employed in agricultural and industrial work.

So, farming and cattle-raising took on their basic characteristics in the period under consideration. Backward methods were not abandoned and extension farming was practiced exclusively. We do not know to what extent Indian farm techniques were continued in the cultivation of tobacco and minor crops (yuca, yam). It is posible that farmers from the Canary Island introduced some changes in respect to yuca, such as transplanting from seed-beds. However, all this is conjecture, pending more exhaustive investigations.

There was an abundance of land for these kinds of extensive operations. Possibly, there was an improvement in tobacco and minor crop farming methods, as land for these activities was not so easily available. This was not the case with sugar cane growing and cattle-raising. When the cattle farm suffered the consequences of soil abuse and became impoverished after fifty or more years of feeding the herd, the rancher *opened* new pastures on the same estate, or subdivided the herd, putting a part on the new section so that the cattle remaining on the old "tired" land could do better. The same thing happened with the sugar plantations. Since technology was not available to help produce higher yields, sugar planters changed to new lands to take advantage of virgin soil fertility. This explains the continuous clearing of woodlands and later will explain, partly at least, the moving of the sugar industry to lands in the eastern Havana region. This is what we might call ***nomadism*** of agrarian operations. This nomadism resulted in a change of land use in regions well situated for export crops. This change of land use was brought about mainly by the progressive ousting of tobacco farms near the Havana seaport and by the substitution of cattle-raising. The lands vacated by those operations were occupied by cane-fields and coffee plantations.[2]

However, the extraordinary growth of the sugar industry towards the end of the eighteenth century aroused the interest of sugar planters in producing more efficiently. The *Sociedad Económica de Amigos del País* (Economic Society of Friends of the Nation) became interested in science and an effort was made to imitate the sugar production methods followed in the British and French colonies. An attempt was made at studying soils to determine the best ones for sugar cane and, also, a strain of cane from Tahiti with a higher juice yield was introduced. However, none of these attempts had a decisive effect because the basic condition of the economic organization opposed progress.

The degree of empiricism and attachment to old methods was so great in agriculture that the comprehensive reform proposed by the genial agronomist Alvaro Reynoso, was not applied to sugar cane farming in Cuba.

15.2. *Sugar cane predominance*

15.2.1. The simultaneous expansion of sugar cane, coffee, and other crops towards the end of the eighteenth century urgently demanded a radical change in agrarian legislation. Farm land needed to be free of all fetters; free of the survivals of the system initiated in the sixteenth century. It was necessary to have the freedom to exchange, sell, and buy the land. Large cane growers, especially, most emphatically demanded that freedom. It is true that all those fetters did not keep them from wielding the power they had acquired. Proof of this was the violent way in which they took land away from tobacco farmers in Güines and Matanzas, to plant sugar cane, in spite of laws protecting the victims. The sugar planters wished to eliminate all those obstacles that were still in force by virtue of laws, decrees, or juridical doctrines of preceding centuries.

In short, they wanted the land transformed into an article of commerce, pure and simple, true merchandise, free of limitations. The laws and decrees impeding the free use and transfer of the land were not few in number. In the first place, the obligation of the old cattle pastures and corrals to contribute to the city's meat supply persisted. The old cattle pastures and corrals no longer existed with the same unity they had in the sixteenth century, as they had been subdivided, but pastures had to be maintained to meet the supply obligations. As a result, there were lands that could not be used for commercial crops even if this type of farming was more profitable. In order to obtain legal release from the cattle pastures obligation to supply meat to the city, an application for permission to discontinue this activity had to be made to the *cabildo* (council). Permission was not always granted.

In the second place, communal estates, predominating in the central zone of the Island, impeded agricultural utilization of the land because boundaries separating different establishments could not be set up within the property. Thus, all of the land of an estate was left for the cattle to roam about and graze freely.

Besides, regulations beginning as early as the sixteenth and stiffened in the seventeenth and eighteenth centuries, limited forest exploitation, since the state wished to have a reserve of lumber for ship-building. The sugar industry used wood as fuel in the sugar-making process, and wished to be allowed to cut trees without limitations, as had actually happened round Havana, and was to be the case in the rest of the island starting in 1820.

The fact that land had been granted, ever since the sixteenth century, by irregular grants, as in almost every case *royal confirmation* was lacking, was no little limitation in itself. The juridical doctrine establishing the King's ownership over the land was still expressed in eighteenth century legislation. This meant that the landholders did not own, but only possessed the land, being subject to political fortunes that might bring about a revision or revocation of their rights. This survival of the old law lay at the basis of all the other limitations, and impeded that the land could be the object of full, individual capitalist ownership.

The struggle against the limiting fetters lasted over forty years, from 1780 to 1820. The struggle was favored not only by the power of Cuban sugar planters, who were very influential in the Madrid court and government, but also because Spain itself was being penetrated by the more advanced forms of capitalism, requiring colonial changes. Spanish bourgeois liberalism, which grew and became strong in the crisis of 1808, coincided momentarily with the interests of the colony. On the other hand, some of the governors and high officials sent over by the Spanish government favored the interests of the sugar planters with measures that were neither consulted nor approved by the Madrid authorities. Among the functionaries most outstanding in this respect was Intendant Alejandro Ramírez, who preferred an agrarian structure based on medium-sized estates, which meant, briefly stated, that he rejected the traditional cattle latifundium in favor of sugar cane and coffee plantations, then small or medium-sized, as sugar latifundia did not come about until the end of the nineteenth century.

These circumstances led to legislation that almost completely did away with traditional laws. Royal decrees of August 30, 1815, and July 16, 1819, declared the freedom of forests and farms and established that lands obtained by old royal grants, by settlement thereon, or held during a period of over forty years, were the free property of the holders thereof. In this way the land was freed of juridical fetters, thus being transformed into an object of commerce and of individual capitalist-type ownership. While this legislation preserved some communal rights (collection of palm tree fronds and wild fruits), from then on nothing would for long stand in the way of the landowner's rights, to the point that in certain zones, as in Sancti Spíritus, there were law suits and conflicts between the people who were deprived of those communal rights and the land owners.

The problem was not only attacked with regard to these basic aspects, but also the legal procedure for the right to dissolve the traditional landed estates was begun, with the result that the first norms thereto were established by the Tribunal of Puerto Príncipe.

15.2.2. We have repeatedly explained that in western Cuba the process of commercial agricultural growth produced a subdivision, or dissolution of original latifundia, but in the central zone (Chapter X), the most backward forms of operation remained as *communal estates* and other forms of latifundia. The advisory vote of the Tribunal of Puerto Príncipe on the dissolution of communal estates tended to facilitate, in that zone of the country, the transformation that had been brought about by the growth of commercial crop agriculture in the western part of the island.

However, as long as the great sugar industry remained confined to the western region and did not invade the central zone, that legislation practically was not applied. It was not until 1830-40 in Las Villas, Camagüey, and Oriente provinces that the process of dissolution of the traditional estates was begun. It was started in the zones near the new seaports (Sagua la Grande, Caibarién-Remedios, Nuevitas) because sugar industry concentration was taking place there. However, inasmuch as sugar industry growth came to a stop towards 1860, a substantial number of the old estates remained, especially in Camagüey and Oriente. Such men as "El Lugareño" (Gaspar Betancourt Cisneros) for years criticized the "barbaric" system of exploiting the cattle or communal estates. Their efforts were not very successful due to the slow sugar development in that region. The building of the railroad running from Nuevitas to Puerto Príncipe did not come in time to favor the appearance of a new agrarian structure.

15.2.3. Towards 1840 the sugar industry reached a stage of profound technological changes largely copied from the European beet sugar industry. At that time, the industry was concentrated in a great producinz zone —Güines— of very fertile land, as will be seen in chapter XVIII. These technological changes took place mainly in the western region, causing the industry to move east, i.e., the growth of the industry tended to occupy the plains of Matanzas, especially the Colon zone.

The technological transformations referred to (three-roll horizontal grinding mills, steam engines, and vacuum pans) resulted in greater production capacity and, consequently, the sugar mills thus equipped required more cane-fields than did the old ones. Since the Havana region was "saturated" with commercial agricultural farming, the industry sought those lands —needed in greater abundance and virgin rich— in the plains of Matanzas and, farther east, though to a small extent, in the western part of Las Villas.

The important thing is that the new mills required more land, and, on the other hand, produced as much as three or four of the old ones. This meant that each factory's plantations tended to grow while the old mills tended to disappear, as they were subtituted by new, more efficient machinery; that is, that within the agrarian structure, the foundation was being laid for the formation of the sugar latifundium that was to dominate the Cuban economy beginning in 1880-1902. It should be kept in mind that the introduction of the railroad in 1837-39 contributed greatly to the expansion of cane-fields, as it facilitated the hauling of cane to the mills. All this means that within the structure created by the growth of sugar industry since the end of the eighteenth century, arose the forces which were to destroy that very structure to build the capitalist latifundium on its remains. This took place from 1840 on in the western zones of the country, and in part of Las Villas Province, where there were sugar mills with 200 *caballerías* (6,667 acres), before 1860; in Camagüey and Oriente provinces —where traditional estates could not be done away with— the sugar capitalist latifundium appeared and spread after 1880 until 1926.

Why this process stopped is due to deep causes which we shall go into in Chapter XVII. One thing is certain: in 1860 the colonial slave structure practically had gone into a crisis and growth had stopped. This crisis proceeded to the Ten Years' War which laid waste part of Las Villas, Camagüey, and Oriente. Camagüey, especially, suffered *the effects of agrarian destruction.* This means that the war, besides liquidating to a considerable extent the landholding class, destroyed all the material vestiges of the old forms of farming. Thus, at the War's end, in 1878, a great part of the country's lands were not being utilized, and were free and available for the most modern sugar mills, in need of large plantations, to become established there. And that is exactly what happened, especially after the abolition of slavery (1886), when United States investments began. It can be stated, then, that Camagüey and Oriente went, without discontinuity, from the original latifundium to the capitalist latifundium that dominated our basic resources until 1959.

BIBLIOGRAPHY

1. Pérez de la Riva, F. *El Café,* Havana, 1944.
2. Le Riverend, Julio. La economía cubana durante las guerras de la revolución y del imperio francés (1790-1808); *Revista de historia de América,* No. 16, Mexico, 1943.
3. Guerra, Ramiro. *Azúcar y población de las Antillas,* 1st ed., Havana, 1927. Ortiz, Fernando. *Op. cit.*

CHAPTER XVI

TOBACCO ECONOMY

16.1. *Spread of tobacco farms throughout the territory*

16.1.1. In Chapter X we examined the form in which the penetration of agriculture into the fertile interior took place. We already know that towards the end of the sixteenth century and the beginning of the seventeenth a great part of the country, especially the best located lands (on the coast) were occupied by cattle latifundia. By the middle of the seventeenth century, this process of "latifundization" was practically consummated in the western region, which, as we have said elsewhere, attained development before the other regions of the country. Therefore, beginning approximately in 1640, the economic occupation of the interior of the country was carried out fundamentally through the agricultural spreading process that had already begun at the end of the sixteenth century. Tobacco farms were very important in this spreading process to the interior. The driving force for their movement to the interior was provided by the opposition of cattle latifundists who, by dint of decisions of the Council of Havana, deprived tobacco farmers of their lands near the city. Tobacco farmers had to "emigrate" to the interior.

This "emigration" was a very important thing since it represented a much more vigorous process of colonization than the penetration of cattle-raising. It was an intensification of the process, because farming, as is generally known, increases and concentrates the population. The emigration process meant, above all else, a factor of dissolution or fracture of the primitive latifundium.

We should not lose sight of the fact that tobacco began to be a product of increasing exportation since the early 1600's. This meant that a small plot planted with tobacco produced revenue that possibly was much higher than yielded by cattle-raising. That was the reason the latifundists wished to: 1) oust the tobacco growers, to go into that activity themselves and, 2) have the tobacco growers farm their land as tenants, thereby obtaining a substantial income.

These facts are not disconnected. Rather, on the contrary, they form a united whole since the latifundists attacked the tobacco growers to either oust them or force them to pay rent or tax as was done until the middle of the nineteenth century.

After being the victims of repeated attacks, the tobacco growers emigrated to the interior of the country, following the course of the rivers.

Tobacco farmers of that epoch did their planting on lands naturally suitable for that activity (*vegas*), that is, lands which were level, fertile, and moist: alluvial soil. Later, in the nineteenth century, the name *vega* would be applied to any tobacco farm even if it were not situated by a river. Early farmers preferred these lands because of an abundance of water, means of communication (the rivers) and great fertility.

16.1.2. There were two drives by the latifundists: one before 1620, the other towards 1650. This explains the fact that before the latter date there were settlements of tobacco farmers in rather remote zones, such as Guane (Pinar del Río province), and Güines. Towards the end of the century there were *vegas* even along the course of the Sagua la Grande River, and in the northern part of the province of Oriente (Mayarí and Tánamo). The zones nearer Havana were not all evacuated by the tobacco growers, but some of them were occupied by cane-fields and sugar mills which also produced a high income, this being the reason why many of the cattle latifundia were subdivided into sugar cane plantations.

On the other hand, the zone of farms known as *estancias,* i.e., truck farms supplying the urban population —increasing in area as Havana became a larger city— also had to start moving farther out, as many of those areas were turned into urban zones.

Thus, by reason of the latifundist agricultural structure, there was a kind of emigration wave in agriculture throughout the seventeenth and first half of the eighteenth centuries. This produced in the oldest zones a change in the use of the land. Truck farms near the city were transformed into urban zones, such as happened towards 1730 in what are today Zanja and Monte streets; tobacco farms became sugar cane fields —along the Almendares River—; and cattle lands near the city were transformed into sugar cane plantations.

As can be seen, there was in the period between 1659 and 1780 a real struggle to control the most fertile and best located —closest to the city— farm lands which were, since the end of the sixteenth century, held by cattle latifundists —the primitive colonial oligarchy. This brought about an intercrossing of forms of land exploitation later affecting primitive cattle latifundia which thus began to dissolve, to subdivide. [1]

16.2. *Tobacco growers*

16.2.1. What, and who were the tobacco growers? It should be explained that most of these were immigrants from the Canary Islands which, during the sixteenth, seventeenth, and eighteenth centuries, had the privilege of trading with the Spanish-American colonies and particularly with those in the Antilles, by-passing the port of Sevilla, the center of Spanish trade monopoly. These "isleños" (islanders) were farmers in their own country and continued as such in Cuba where the oligarchy had already taken over practically all the land by the end of the 1500's. Once in Cuba, they went into the interior in search of fertile soil. They settled on state lands, as was the case in Santiago de las Vegas, or on latifundia, in which case they had to pay rent. The "isleños" were good farmers, hard-working, sober, steadfast, and set in their ways. These virtues and traits were inherited by the Cuban peasantry.

These immigrants learned rapidly to cultivate tobacco. It seems that the local Indian farming traditions predominated in the growing of this crop.

Unlike the practice in the thirteen English colonies of North America (i.e., in Virginia) where tobacco was cultivated on large plantations employing many slaves, tobacco in Cuba was grown in small farms and almost without slaves. The reason for these differences may be due to the fact that the Virginia tobacco trade was organized from the beginning on a very definite and massive capitalist basis, while in Cuba production at first was for domestic consumption, growing very slowly as foreign trade increased. In present-day United States, those who grow tobacco are true capitalist landowners, while in Cuba, where the latifundists preferred cattle-raising and sugar production, tobacco growers were small farmers. Consequently, they were not able to employ a large number of slaves.

On the other hand, the tobacco growers very soon fell under the domination of the merchants and the large landholders. The reason for this is as follows: the tobacco farmers were dependent on the merchants, especially those in Havana, to export their crops; in the case of the large landowners, the farmers had to pay rent to them. Sometimes, the landlord was the Church. The merchants bought the crop for export; thus, they manipulated prices according to their own interests. They financed the growers' crops and, consequently, these farmers' dependence on certain merchants dates back to the period under review, ending only with the triumph of the Revolution. [2]

16.2.2. These farmers were marked by a combative spirit. Their fight against the latifundists began at the end of the sixteenth century. For this reason, when towards 1680 the treasury became interested in monopolizing the whole tobacco crop and the first purchases by the government were made, the growers expressed their dissatisfaction and, in some cases, they quit planting tobacco. In reality, the tobacco purchase monopoly by the King's treasury paid lower prices than the merchants had been paying.

Later, in 1717, when monopoly was formally decreed, the tobacco farmers rebelled against the authorities, took the city of Havana and forced the high colonial officials to flee to Spain. In 1721 and 1723 there were two new movements by the tobacco growers, the latter being crushed by a bloody repression.

16.3. *Tobacco industry and commerce*

16.3.1. Though the exportation of Cuban tobacco during the 1600's was mostly in the form of leaf, there was since that time a simple tobacco industry that followed the orientations of European market consumption. Tobacco was consumed in two different products: cut for pipe smoking, popular in northern Europe and with the poorer populations of France and Spain; rappee or snuff, the use of which predominated in France, Italy, Spain, and especially, among the aristocratic class. By reason of her trade links, Cuba specialized in the production of rappee or snuff. Rappee or snuff was manufactured in tobacco mills equipped with millstones. These were in operation as early as the first half of the seventeenth century. But their number increased as commerce grew in volume. In Cuba, possibly in addition to the forms of consumption popular in Europe, "pure" cigars were made for home smoking. Perhaps those were the fore-runners of today's *vegueros* (country cigars).

Early in the 1700's, the sudden development of trade with Europe, especially with France, and the increase of consumption in Spain, produced a general economic upswing lasting through 1720, approximately. During this period, close to twenty tobacco mills (besides some one hundred sugar mills) were built, all of them near the cities of Havana and Matanzas. These mills possibly utilized hydraulic power, as they were located particularly along the Almendares River. But the monopoly decreed in 1717 progressively stifled this industry to the point that towards 1760 only three mills remained, two of them owned by the Royal Treasury, and the other by the Marqués de Jústiz, in Matanzas. The object of this prohibition was to strengthen the monopolistic position of the royal factories in Spain promoted by the mercantilist economic orientation of the Spanish monarchy.

16.3.2. The tobacco monopoly was organized in 1717, providing for a superintendency of tobacco in charge not only of purchasing the leaf, but also of assigning quotas to the various zones, according to the consumption as fixed by the royal decree itself. There were, also, factors, i.e., agents, of the monopoly in all cities to handle the monopoly's transactions. The rebellion of the tobacco growers that same year brought about some modifications, though not really substantial ones. At any rate, towards 1730 the Royal Treasury discarded that policy, granting the right to purchase Cuban tobacco to privileged merchants or lessees. These were grandees of the Spanish court, such as the Marquis of Casa Enrile or Don José Tallapiedra. After 1740 the right was granted to the Royal Trading Company of Havana. When this company lost its privilege in 1760, the State superintendence was reorganized, resulting in a new monopoly of purchase similar to that of 1717.

In this second stage, purchasing offices, or delegations were organized throughout the country. The growers, in turn, had been creating a defense institution which would now function fully. This consisted of representatives of the growers of each zone who would deal with the authorities of the superintendence and of the purchasing offices, regarding problems of prices, regulation and size of the crops, and, especially, the problem of the land, because the large estate owners continued harassing the farmers to make them leave their land or pay rent or tax.

It can be stated that the purchasing offices contributed greatly during this stage in fixing tobacco farming norms in the various zones of the country. The differentiation between the product of the western, central, and eastern zones was then fixed.

However, the effect of the monopoly was contrary to the development of production. On the other hand, it brought about a certain concentration of farming, since the conditions imposed on the farmers were unfavorable to them; and so towards 1770 already there were tobacco growers or landowners of certain importance or capital. The poorer farmers could not endure the policy of exploitation and delay in payment that made them fall prey to ruthless money lenders. The delay in payment was caused by the fact that crop purchase money came from Mexico and often took several months to arrive.

16.3.3. Towards the end of the century there was open talk about the need to protect the growers so production would not be completely ruined. At that time the first changes in consumer orientation took place, since the use of rappee or snuff was declining, being substituted by cigarettes which were then made by workers in their own homes. This production was then for a very limited market. The use of cigars was beginning to increase also. This brought about the end of the tobacco mills, the remnants of which finally disappeared by 1820, approximately. This was the beginning of modern tobacco industry with which we shall deal in a later chapter.

BIBLIOGRAPHY

1. RIVERO MUÑIZ, JOSÉ. *Op. cit.,* Chapter VII.
2. ORTIZ, FERNANDO. *Op. cit.*

CHAPTER XVII

EXPANSION OF SLAVERY

17.1. *Evolution*

17.1.1. Slow pace during the seventeenth century. From monopoly "trade" to free "trade": Thesis of Arango y Parreño. 17.1.2. Struggle against the "trade"; England's position; beginning of Cuban opposition. 17.1.3. The situation after 1844. 17.1.4. The situation at the end of the Ten Years' War. Abolition: significance of the event (1880-86).

17.2. *System of slave work*

17.2.1. "Degrees" of slavery. Intensification of work in the sugar mills. 17.2.2. Urban slaves. Unequal distribution of slaves over the territory.

17.3. *The free worker*

17.3.1. The situation towards 1830. Appearance of the tobacco industry. 17.3.2. Beginnings of labor organization.

17.1. *Evolution*

17.1.1. The system of slave production begun in the sixteenth century, was marked by a slow pace of growth during the 1600's. It could even be stated that after 1620 the rate of slave introduction into the islands decreased or became stationary, though no statistics are available to back up this statement.

Cuban historians and publicists seem to favor the thesis that colonial economic development was delayed by a lack of laborers. This idea is implicit in the attitude of sugar mill owners since the end of the 1700's. It would be an error to readily accept this opinion, since, as a colonial country, the decisive driving factor for development was its capacity to export or, rather, its possibilities to export. If the metropolis and other European markets did not increase their purchases of Cuban products, it was obvious that production would remain stationary or at a low level and, consequently, a new addition in labor force was not necessary. Cuban history of the eighteenth century proves that whenever the possibility of exporting was greater and there was need for increasing production, slaves immediately appeared, brought by the same commercial capitalists who wished to acquire more Cuban products. This explains, for example, the fact that Europeans and North American planters delivered slaves on credit to be paid for in Cuban commodities from 1702 on. This means that between trade, production, and slave growth there was a very close, reciprocal relationship.

The fact that the English and North Americans in 1762-63 brought many slaves to Havana indicates that they purchased more Cuban products and delivered, as a needed production "article", hundreds and thousands of Africans. And the English occupation and domination in those years was coupled with an expansion of European trade in general, and Spanish trade in particular, thus stimulating the production of more sugar, and demanding, for this reason, an increasing "importation" of slaves.

The slave commerce or "trade", begun in the sixteenth century, was carried on by companies or individuals who had obtained the corresponding privilege or monopoly. But early in the 1700's when Cuba became closely linked with the European economy in full capitalist growth, this system varied in its manifestations. Then slave trade monopoly was granted: first, to the French Company of Guinea, and secondly, when the treaties of Utrecht were signed (1713), to the English *South Seas Company*. French and English traders purchased Cuban commodities in exchange for slaves. But, inasmuch as they possessed their own colonial sugar industry, they did not buy sugar. Instead, they acquired tobacco, hides, and wood. This meant that sugar production did not increase extraordinarily and, for this reason great numbers of slaves were not needed, since these were always destined mostly to work in the sugar industry. The English company complained that Cuba did not purchase many slaves. This is understandable, since it operated in Cuba after 1720, when exports of tobacco as well as sugar declined. [1]

At the end of the English monopoly on slave trade, the privilege was granted to Spanish grandees (Marquis de Casa Enrile, and Don José Tallapiedra) and to the *Real Compañía de Comercio de La Habana* (Royal Trading Company of Havana), founded in 1740. These maintained the characteristic slow pace of that stage. In fact, the latter took advantage of its privilege to deal with English traders of Jamaica who were the true suppliers of slaves. However, the situation began to change towards 1760 and, with commerce on the upswing there was an intensification of slave importation. After 1765 some English firms, like Baker and Dawson, were granted the right to sell slaves in Cuba.

This situation went on until 1788. Trade with the United States, which after independence from the English empire tried to secure new sources of supply of molasses and sugar, had expanded production. Spain also had developed its colonial trade. Large numbers of slaves were needed to take care of rising production and to build new sugar mills. The sugar mill owners, speaking through their spokesman, Arango y Parreño, stated the case for freedom of slave trade rather than monopoly trade by merchants or companies. Arango y Parreño claimed that the free system, established in the French and the English possessions in the West Indies, was the cause of the "splendor" of those colonies. He did not stop to think that the system had been successful there by reason of the great interest of the colonial powers to obtain sugar. It was then necessary to establish that system in Cuba because the demand for sugar had grown. In 1789 the Madrid government granted the petition of the Cuban sugar oligarchy. So the mill owners were able to obtain a "supply" of slaves to build a great number of new mills from 1790 to 1802.[2]

From then on, every year thousands of slaves were brought in. Towards 1820, by virtue of the treaty of 1817 with England, the Madrid government abolished the slave traffic, thus creating the era of African slave contraband lasting, though decreasingly, until 1860. Why was the slave trade prohibited? We shall look into this matter immediately.

17.1.2. At the end of the 1700's there began in England a great movement against African slave traffic. This change was related to the general conditions of the capitalist industrial development in England. On the one hand, the sugar production of the West Indian colonies (Barbados, Antigua, and Jamaica) had been turned into a monopoly of the landowners who maintained profiteering conditions in empire markets to the detriment of rising sugar consumption which, besides, could not be satisfied by the West Indies due to limited land area. Then began the importation of sugar from India which, being produced by native workers and farmers, served as a means of opposing West Indian sugar monopolists. The new colonialist interests were opposed to African slavery because they realized that the system of wage-labor —of extremely low wages— was more advantageous to them.

On the other hand, the demand of certain raw materials by English industry, in a process of growth by reason of the industrial revolution, made it necessary to effect a change in connection with African commerce. Instead of delivering merchandise in exchange for slaves, it was traded for other products necessary to the metropolis. This new form of trade with equatorial Africa was progressively pushed forward, and early in the 1800's there was begun, in the zones dominated by England, the growing of primary products and the production of raw materials which she needed for her industrial development.

The economic movement stimulated propaganda against the slave trade and against slavery. Favored by bourgeois liberalism, the current against both spread over western Europe. In 1807 the "trade" was abolished in the United States. Previously, the French Revolution had dealt a death blow to both the slave trade and slavery in the West Indian colonies under France. At the fall of Napoleon Bonaparte (1815), in the congresses of the European powers that were then held (Vienna, Verona, etc.), England was able to secure agreements against the slave trade, which was declared illegal and considered as piracy The political influence exerted from then on by British interests in Spain achieved the signing of a treaty to abolish the slave traffic in Spanish colonies (1817), going into effect in 1820.

Cuban mill owners did not accept that measure passively. In 1811 they fought tooth and nail against the abolition of slavery by the Cortes (Spanish parliament). The abolition proposal had been made by a Mexican delegate. However, the mill owners accepted the outlawing of the "trade" because the contraband of Africans was immediately organized. Merchants and United States adventurers, Englishmen and

Spaniards, in spite of the treaty entered into with England, joined with Cuban traders, Madrid functionaries, governors and colonial officials, and sugar mill owners to participate in that illegal traffic netting the highest of profits.

However, by 1830 there were expressions of a certain opposition to the slave contraband in Cuba. The most progressive elements of the sugar mill owners' class began to have their doubts about the slave system and the traffic. They were especially concerned over the increase in the slave population which was on its way to outnumbering the white people, as it did by 1840. The spectre of a general slave uprising horrified the ruling classes, though, of course, it was useful to Spanish colonial interests, who played it up in order to keep reformist and liberal Cubans within bounds. By 1823 Varela had worked out a plan for the abolition of slavery, and towards 1828, Arango y Parreño was wondering if it would not be better to produce sugar in Cuba the same way it was produced in British India, that is, without slaves. José A. Saco attacked the slave traffic denouncing its illegal existence, thereby earning the enmity of the Spanish Captain General Tacón.[3]

17.1.3. In 1836 England was successful in obtaining a new treaty with Spain in which measures against smuggling were stiffened. English consuls were established in Havana for the purpose of observing the fulfillment of that international agreement. These delegates denounced the "cargoes" as they came in and played up the matter among the Cubans most subject to fearing the uprising of the slaves.

Circumstances grew worse in 1843. Spanish authorities uncovered a conspiracy which, historically, is hard to prove. It supposedly included whites, free Negroes, and slaves. It was called *Conspiración de la Escalera,* being one of the most horrendous collective crimes ever commited by colonialists. Doubtlessly, there were at that time a number of slave revolts. That, together with propaganda by the authorities, terrorized the sugar mill owners and the colonial middle class.

That situation produced a change of opinion among many of the sugar mill owners, for whom it was necessary to take steps to stop the steady growth of the slave population. Miguel Aldama expressed that the only way out of that situation was brutal repression, but at the same time recognizing that the slaves, naturally, aspired to freedom and liberation by force from the yoke under which they suffered. For the first time a document was drawn up requesting measures against the slave traffic. Of course, that request was opposed by quite a few of the sugar mill owners, government authorities, and other participants in the slave contraband.

Besides, another development had taken place, producing disillusionment among the sugar mill owners. Restrictions (surveillance of the African coast and of ships on the high seas) imposed by England to fight slave smuggling and the resultant higher fees demanded by conniving authorities and ship owners, had inflated slave prices. Also, the intensification of sugar production work and the necessity of employing more slaves in the mills, due to the application of more efficient machinery, demanded a greater importation which meant a much larger "investment" than in the other cost elements in sugar production, thus creating a very serious crisis in the slave industry.

Fear and increased slave prices, as well as their rising weight in *cost* formation, brought about a change of attitude regarding the traffic. However, since free manpower could not be obtained or a system secured to conserve the slave population stretching their useful lives—an impossible attainment because what the slave owners wanted was high and fast output—intermediate formulas were sought which were based on the forceful importation of hands.

Irrespective of some attemps at employing free workers in the sugar industry and in other productive activities, which were complete failures, sugar mill owners worked hard to find substitutes for the African slaves. Pure and simple traditional slavery was not possible. For this reason, the workers secured then were enrolled under pretences of freedom covering actual semi-slavery.

First, thousands of Indians from Yucatan were brought in. The so-called Caste War in Yucatan, brought about by the protest of the native, especially rural, population, resulted in frightful repression by the landowners and authorities of that Mexican States. As a "humanitarian" formula, the pure slaughter of the Indians was replaced by the practice of selling them to Cuban landowners. Supposedly, they were to work a number of years — as many as were necessary to recover transportation cost, after which time they would be free.[4]

In the same manner, Chinese coolies were secured. These were purchased at the Portuguese colony of Macao. The number of workers brought into Cuba by this method before 1870 ran into the thousands. This was the epoch in which colonialist powers cut China into pieces and divided her among themselves. Also in the case of Chinese workers brought to Cuba there were supposed "contracts" providing for a limited number of years. These unfortunate workers were designated as "settlers".[5]

However, it was difficult for them to work the specified number of years, especially because of the fact that any serious offense, and particularly running away from the plantation —even for a few hours— was punished by disregarding all the time served prior to the infraction.

Also employed then were emancipated Negroes, that is, those whose clandestine introduction into the island had been reported, resulting in their being declared free men, though subject to work during a certain period of time for the emancipation administration board.

Lastly, the shortage of new slaves brought about the employment of rented ones. Many slaveholders without land or industry in which to employ them, rented their slaves for a monthly fee.

The use of Yucatan Indians and Chinese coolies, as well as the practice of slave renting, meant that the system of slave work was in decline, but during all those years the sugar mill owners and planters would not recognize that the time had come to free the slaves. Historically, the reason and the basis of their own existence was slavery, and so were unable to face abolition, which meant the disappearançe of their own class. This is what took place, as we shall see further on.[6]

17.1.4. The situation of slavery grew worse as a result of the Ten Years' War. In the first place, many slaves joined the Cuban insurgents, thus becoming free men, *de facto* at first and *de jure* later (1878). Moreover, the destruction caused by the war in the central and eastern zones freed many slaves without the formality of any declaration. Their exiled or dead master could not claim them. Though slavery was continued with varying degrees of solidity in the western region, unaffected by the fighting, the internal process of decomposition worsened due to the death of childless slaves. Moreover, it was declared, towards 1872, that all children born of slave parents would be free. This finally *closed* all possibilities of replacing slaves with other slaves. A resource was had to the employment of free workers and rented slaves, to the extent that, in 1878, there were in the sugar mills groups of workers representing all possible work systems.

The demand for the abolition of slavery did not take long to be made. In 1880 began the process of "guardianship" (*patronato*), providing for several years of paid labor by the slave so as to compensate his master. In 1886 slavery was declared completely abolished. Abolition was possible because in practice it no longer was very important. While towards 1850 it is estimated there were some 400,000 slaves in Cuba, in 1877 the number was 200,000, of whom only 100,000 remained unfreed in 1883.

Abolition brought important consequences: 1st, the transformation of the working population into a social class with unity characteristics: the proletariat, and 2nd, it favored the transformation — already begun in 1840 — of the sugar industry into a capitalist industry. In this respect, it can be said that it made possible the formation of the sugar cane planters' group.

17.2. *System of slave work*

17.2.1. The system of slave work was the base of colonial economy in Cuba. This economy reached its peak between 1790 and 1860, as we have seen in this chapter. Its specific characteristics and its own evolution should be explained by historians without resorting to psychological or racial arguments or causes. We must make an effort to situate the evolution of this work system within the conditions distinguishing it at any given stage.

This evolution has not been understood by traditional historiographers. It has been said that slavery was in Cuba, and generally in the other Spanish colonies, a mild system, at least as compared with the system in the other European possessions. This is attributed to the Spaniards' nature — prone to breeding with Indians and Africans or to employing slaves in home services. With the maintenance of this thesis, the fact that the institution was one aspect only is lost sight of. Alexander von Humboldt expounded that thesis in his work on Cuba, thus stimulating the continuation of this historical error.

In the first place, if we only consider the system of domestic slavery, it is easy to see why slavery would seem "mild", as long as we do not forget the punishments those slaves were subjected to. Possibly, Humboldt and other observers did not see at close range the lives of the other slaves. The closer the slave was to primary activities (for export), the worse his condition. For this reason, in the nineteenth century, domestic slaves were threatened with being sent to work on coffee plantations, and those at the coffee plantations with being sent to work in sugar mills. In the next place, the abusive and exploiting character of slavery became more pronounced as commercial crops were started and expanded and their intensification was sought. From 1790 on, the growth of the sugar industry progressively transformed slavery into a repressive system demanding the last drop of vital energy from the slave. Arango y Parreño in his *Discourse on Agriculture in Havana* complained about the number of religious holidays granted the slaves working in the sugar industry, to the detriment of production. He advocated a more stringent demand on the slaves so as to obtain higher output. That trend continued throughout the period, resulting in higher production and a shorter life for the slaves. The situation worsened from 1810 on, when fear of the slave population growth arose.

Finally, it should be realized that two basic elements existed: slave cost and slave output. As the cost of slaves rose, efforts were made to extract more work from them. Moreover, the growth of industry and the relative limitations of technology produced an increasing desire in the slaveholders to obtain an intensification of production at the expense of the slaves' lives. For that reason, the important thing then was to rapidly obtain large profits from slave work; that is, the useful life of the slave was shortened by increased exploitation. While in the middle of the 1700's only 3% of the slaves had to be replaced annually; one century later 5% or 8% had to be replaced, according to contemporary accounts. That is why many people then complained of the fast rate at which slaves became worn out. However, for the owners of the sugar industry that "wear and tear" had its compensations because with stepped-up production the slave produced in a few years much more than he did one century before. Thus, his cost was more than recovered. The repressive system in the period of the "intensification" of slave work produced the worst manifestations of that system's character. Slaves lived in miserable barracks, almost like prisoners. Occasionally, they were granted a holiday so that, stimulated by their misfortune, they might dance and sing. They could not have a normal family life; had no opportunity to earn extra money that might enable them to dream of buying their freedom; and as for education, they received none. Their lot was reduced to exhausting work, whippings and the stocks.[7]

17.2.2. The urban slave lived in his master's house. Occasionally, he was able to obtain a minimum of learning with respect to reading and writing or some trade. He wore rather smart, clean clothes. Depending on personal factors, he could attain to his master's confidence, which he could turn to his own benefit or to the detriment of the other slaves. The situation of the family coach driver is very typical because the slave aristocracy gave him training under special instructors, transforming him into a kind of confidant.

In cases where the slaveholder did not have many slaves — only one or two — the slave might be put to work for another master and thus have the opportunity of earning some money for himself.

However, in Havana and other larger cities on the island there were homes where domestic slaves were given the punishment prescribed by their masters: whippings, the stocks, etc. If their behaviour did not improve, they were sent to do harder work in other activities or were sold. In this latter case, buying masters would be informed of the slaves' faults so that they might be adequately repressed.

However, we should consider certain characteristics that seem to have manifested themselves in Cuba more definitely than in other colonies. Of course, in all colonies slave population was more abundant in rural zones, that is, on commercial crop *plantations*. This was logical because slaves were the foundation of the country's exporting economy. This was the case in Cuba, though it occurred with more intensity in the western region (Havana and Matanzas) where the large sugar centers were located. In Las Villas, Camagüey, and Oriente the rural slave population was less numerous. Ramiro Guerra has made a statistical analysis of this in his work on the Ten Years' War.[8]

But what distinguished slave distribution in Cuba in comparison with other colonies, is, without a doubt, its relative abundance and concentration in the cities. The creation of a very wealthy oligarchy and a middle class with high incomes in Havana and other cities favored a high utilization of domestic slaves who lived in their masters' homes. In other European colonies, the formation of an absentee oligarchy — residing in the metropolis — caused the opposite result.

17.3. *The free worker*

17.3.1. The great impulse produced by the growth of trade towards the end of the 1700's was also reflected in an increase of free — or wage-workers. This type of worker existed since the sixteenth century in the cities, holding jobs in the various trades or crafts, in occupations depending on commerce or under intermediate or disguised forms, such as the administration of farms. It can be readily understood that they did not have great importance in the social and economic picture of those days (16th, 17th and 18th centuries up to 1790).

But the expansion of production after 1790 favored the appearance of new elements of this type. Of course, in the tobacco industry, now oriented towards the manufacture of cigarettes and "puros" cigars, non-slave workers had to be employed. Cigarettes were made by free piece-workers in their own homes for an entrepreneur furnishing the raw materials and distributing the finished products. "Puros" were made by convicts and by children of the orphanage, that is, nonslaves, but, on the other hand, inmates; the reason for this being that the manufacturers wished to secure those workers who, in the slave system, were not permitted to take employment for wages so as to avoid jobs regarded as fit for slaves. However, growth was so rapid and the demand for workers so great, that attractively high wage offers transformed into wage-workers tobacco growers who could no longer hold on to their land.

In the sugar industry there were offers of some jobs employing free workers. Of course, those workers were part of the group representing the owner, but nevertheless, they worked for wages, which characterized them socially and economically; chiefs of production, ox-drivers, health officers, foremen, etc., were salaried workers in great demand in the sugar mills during those days, in the same way that later, in the middle of the 1800's, mechanics and engineers were needed.

Finally, trade development created a sector of free workers in the personnel of importing firms and in the internal distribution of goods. This became more pronounced towards the middle of the 1800's with the establishment of the railroad companies and with urban commerce development. Unlike the situation in other branches of production, in this case the bulk of wage-workers came from Spain. They were immigrants forming the nucleus of the famous *voluntarios* (volunteer Spanish Militia), common Spanish people who were aroused by their employers, wealthy Spaniards, against the Cubans.

Towards 1830, this process of formation of a working class was crystalizing in the tobacco industry. On the one hand, large cigar shops or factories, sprang up. Sometimes, dozens of salaried cigar makers were grouped in those shops. In a sense, factory owners then resorted to mechanisms attempting to transform this system into something similar to slavery, because in a basically slave society the free worker tends not to remain as such, but to seek less dependent occupations or where there are no slaves with whom he must live. The mechanism holding the tobacco worker was the *contract of apprenticeship* which is known since the sixteenth century. The apprentice was bound to serve a number of years and the owner had the right to punish him severely (the same as if he were a slave). In 1863 the newspaper *La Aurora* denounced the case of a cigar manufacturer who would punish his adolescent apprentices to the extent of using the whip and the stocks.[9]

In the cigarette industry, though home production continued, regular work shops began to appear. However, that form of production did not become established until after 1853 when mechanized factories were built.

The formation process of the tobacco proletariat is revealed by statistical data. Towards 1835 there were some 2,000 cigar makers; in 1850, 15,000. It was an important nucleus within the economy and society of Havana. It was also in the process of formation in the other important cities and in towns near the capital, such as San Antonio de los Baños. At times of crisis, towards 1860, there were 5,000 of them unemployed.

17.3.2. The degree of concentration of these workers and their extremely low standard of living produced in them the first manifestations of a common class interest, giving rise to the earliest work organizations. These were aid and benefit societies grouping the cigar makers, and later extending to other professional groups, such as the typesetters and store clerks. The tobacco workers published the first newspaper of the labor movement, *La Aurora*.

Many of those associations strictly maintained their mutual benefit character, even preserving ethnic or other type differences customary within the colonial slave system. However, out of those associations would arise the trade unions that developed after 1880, when slavery was on its way out and all working men in Cuba were becoming a part of one single wage-earning class.[10]

BIBLIOGRAPHY

1. Saco, José Antonio. *Historia de la esclavitud,* 6 vols. Havana, 1937-1940.
2. Arango y Parreño, Francisco. *Obras,* 2 vols. Havana, 1952.
3. Guerra, Ramiro. *Manual de Historia de Cuba,* Havana, 1962.
4. Le Riverend, Julio. *Historia de la nación cubana,* vols. III and IV.
5. Jiménez Pastrana, Juan. *Los chinos en las luchas por la liberación cubana,* (1847-1930). Havana, 1963.
6. Cepero Bonilla, Raúl. *Azúcar y Abolición,* 2nd Edition, Havana, 1960.

CHAPTER XVIII

INDUSTRIAL EVOLUTION

18.1. *The sugar industry*

18.1.1. Sugar industry during the first half of the eighteenth century. 18.1.2. Expansion towards the end of the 1700's. Its causes. Growth process in the western part. Penetration in central and eastern zones. 18.1.3. Techno-mechanical transformation (1840-60). Effects of the crisis and of the Ten Years' War. 18.1.4. Appearance of the *"central"* sugar mill: "division of labor".

18.2. *The tobacco industry*

18.2.1. End of the monopoly. Cigar and cigarette factories. 18.2.2. Different "brands". Processes of concentration.

18.3. *Mining*

18.3.1. Efforts in the eighteenth century. 18.3.2. Resumption of copper mining in the nineteenth century. Expansion of mining: diversity of operations.

18.4. *Railroads*

18.4.1. Spreading process and financial organization. 18.4.2. Concentration of railroad companies.

18.5. *Other industries.*

18.1. *The sugar industry*

18.1.1. The sugar industry, founded towards the end of the sixteenth century, developed slowly until 1659. From that date on it is possible that some new mills were built, especially in the Havana area, around the Bay of Matanzas, in Remedios, and in Trinidad, that is, near the seaports, since, as we have already seen, that industry sought transportation facilities for its heavy and bulky products. As a rule, sugar trade conditions did not favor the expansion of production in Cuba. Spain produced sugar and, in addition, imported from Brazil which, by reason of the union of the royal crowns of Portugal and Spain, from 1580 to 1640, had secured a market for herself in the metropolis. Towards the end of the 1600's, when the people of Havana requested, through Viana Hinojosa, the Governor, greater market opportunities for Cuban sugar in Spain, the King replied that it was not a matter of opinion but of State interest to continue importing Brazilian sugar.

The situation began to change after 1700. The crown of Spain went to a French prince, Philip V, and war raged in all Europe until 1713, against the powers supporting the Archduke of Austria, who also aspired to the Spanish throne. French and English mercantilist capitalism had entered the stage of industrial promotion. The most advanced powers themselves discarded piracy as a means of struggle against the Spanish Empire. This new policy was definitely established in the Peace of Ryswick (1697). From then on, the policy of every state would be to assert its economic superiority, imposing terms and obtaining concessions from weaker and more backward nations, as in the case of the Treaty of Methuen (1703) between England and Portugal.

The war produced an economic rise that had been developing since the end of the 1600's. There was a coincidence, in England and France, of conditions causing an inflationary process that spread to all zones and countries with which they traded. During this period Cuba established close links with French commerce and improved her trade with Spain. As a result, there was a stage of sudden production growth. This was so in respect of tobacco, as can be seen from the fact that from 1710 to 1720 the number of mills for the production of rappee more than doubled. Sugar production was also favorably affected.

In the early 1700's, that is, from 1701 to 1720, one hundred new sugar mills were built in the environs of Havana, and the first ones appeared in the vicinity of the City of Santa Clara. Trade with the French and, later, with the British brought a definite increase in the production of sugar.

Beginning in 1720, there was a recession of the causes of that growth as a result of depression in France and England (bankruptcy of Law, in Paris, and failure of the *South Seas Company,* in London). By 1740, some 60 sugar mills of the one hundred newly built had disappeared, and very few of the tobacco mills had managed to remain in operation.

However, with regard to the sugar industry's development, it did not stop completely. The *Real Compañía de La Habana,* founded in 1740, in spite of not being profitable, did not effect a retrenchment. Towards 1750, the metropolis had initiated a policy representing the ascending capitalist interests, and favored the purchasing of Cuban sugar.

18.1.2. The capture of Havana by the English (1762) brought about a contact of the North American colonies with Cuba. Those colonies needed molasses and sugar, due to the fact that the sugar mill owners of the British West Indies demanded, within the Empire, stringent monopolist profiteering terms. The War of Independence of the United States (1770-81), supported by France, and by Spain from bases in Cuba, favored an expansion of those trade relations. North American merchants bought sugar and sold flour and wooden containers for sugar. They also purchased precious metals, taking advantage of the price differential existing between the two countries in respect of these products.

Meanwhile, Spain had moved towards a liberalization of the old trade monopoly. From 1765 on, and especially in 1778 (free trade regulations), as we shall see in chapter XIX, she increased her commerce with Cuba. The expenditure of large sums of money for military purposes in Cuba from 1776 to 1785 strengthened the accumulation process begun before 1740, facilitating sugar growth.

In conjunction with all those events, worked the effects of the revolutionary fighting and the imperial wars of France (1791-1815), because the United States, in its neutral position, became the transporters of Cuban sugar production. Finally, the Haitian people's rebellion produced the ruin of that country's sugar industry, at that time the main producer and supplier of the product.

There was a rapid concatenation of events, the outcome of which was an increase in sugar production in Cuba. As the result of a strong trade stimulus, many sugar mills were built then, mainly in the western zone of the country. That bonanza or "fat cows" period lasted until 1804, approximately. However, as in 1720-40, the depression did not completely eliminate the progress made by the sugar industry. Cuba's road to capital colonialism was paved with those periodic sugar crises, after which the industry gained new vigor, though always at the expense of the rest of the Cuban economy, weaker and more vulnerable.

Along the northwest coast of the island, from Matanzas to Mariel, the sugar mills became very numerous. They were concentrated round Havana and moved steadily into the interior. That inland penetration posed a transportation and communications problem for the solution of which plans for building a canal running from Güines were made, but, later, in 1837, a railroad was constructed instead. When sugar mill owners learned of the richness of the soil in the valley of Güines, they moved rapidly to occupy it, constituting there the first great production center. The largest and most complete sugar mills were built there with the help of hundreds of slaves.

Little by little, the sugar industry expanded to the east, taking over the flat lands in the province of Havana, penetrating into the Matanzas plains along the area of Bolondrón and Unión de Reyes and, by the decade of 1830-40, going as far as the great Colón plains where the other large sugar center was built, the biggest in the nation until after the Ten Years' War. That sugar area joined with the one that had been established round the Bay of Matanzas, thus becoming one. In this new stage, the sugar mills were equipped with more modern machinery, being, as a rule, more powerful than the ones built in the remaining zones. Those were the mills where steam engines, three-roll grinding mills, and vacuum pans were mainly used.

That invasion by the sugar industry moving from west to east stopped almost completely in the Colón plains. It advanced beyond Colón only along the north, towards the zone of Sagua la Grande, and along the south, in the direction of Cienfuegos, coming to a stop at both places when the crisis of 1857-66 and the Ten Years' War (1868) broke out.

The central and eastern zones to a large extent remained outside that process. However, new mills sprang up, mainly in Sancti Spíritus, Nuevitas, and Puerto Príncipe, where the possibility of exporting sugar directly had opened. The fact that at the time large cattle estates in the zone began to be dissolved was a reflection of sugar penetration. However, in this case the impulse was not decisive. Nor were the mills established there of the more modern type. On the contrary, small mills with traditional equipment predominated in that zone.

In Oriente province the sugar industry underwent almost no alteration between 1820 and 1868. Here, the sugar industry was in the most backward state in the whole country. To a large extent it was made up of *cachimbos* (small, inefficient mills), with few cane-fields or slaves and remaining in the same original zones where the industry had started in the sixteenth century, that is, Bayamo and Santiago de Cuba.[1]

18.1.3. This dispersion, representing, in essence, an increase of sugar mills, was carried out beginning in the decade 1830-40 under the influence of great technological transformations.

Irrespective of the fact that the sugar mill owners sought to increase their profits, the application of certain chemistry principles and of more efficient equipment was due to advances made by the industry in Europe and in the United States, and, consequently, to changes in the capitalist sugar trade.

In effect, the beet sugar industry had spread over Europe and, being a new industry, had proceeded from more solid technical-scientific and mechanical bases. That industry was born favored by and to have the benefit of all the positive factors of the industrial revolution. It was helped by the great strides made in chemistry and by the equipment and devices technology could produce since the end of the eighteenth century. Though not representing an immediate danger to the Cuban sugar industry, its growth since 1810, mainly in France and Germany, was very rapid. There were Cubans who in the decade 1820-30 became alarmed over the effects its development would soon have — so they thought — on the national economic situation.

Besides, the example of that capitalist industry spurred the Cuban mill owners to apply better technology and equipment. In point of fact, some of the techniques in use since the decade 1820-30, as the application of boneblack to decolor cane juice, and filters to clarify it, were adopted from the beet sugar industry.

Those advances were favored by the beginning of the slave system crisis. On the one hand, the price of slaves rose, which meant that their wholesale application was no longer possible because there is a limit to what a simple addition of hands can do to intensify and increase production. Moreover, slaves made up a very high element of cost while the international sugar price progressively went down in a century-old trend reaching a crisis in 1882-84. As early as 1830 there were Cubans who began to have their doubts about the economic advisability of slavery. And since the end of the 1700's Cuban sugar mill owners discussed technological improvements to produce as much and as cheaply as in the French and British West Indies. They were not ignorant of the effect of those improvements. That is the reason why, since the period 1835-40, they planned to replace traditional equipment, the so-called "Jamaican train", with more efficient machinery.

Since that date, the use of steam engines to drive the mills spread rapidly, together with the installation of horizontal rolls which were more efficient and suitable. These mechanical improvements resulted in a substantial increase in cane juice yield, a benefit contributing to strengthen the position of sugar mill owners. Moreover, there was a reduction in the cost of production as a result of the elimination of oxen to move traditional vertical mills.

The next step was the application of vacuum apparatus to concentrate juice. Two types were in use: Rillieux and Derosne. After tests, it was proved that they obtained more sugar from the juice, as they eliminated molasses inversion, a frequent phenomenon in open vessels of the "Jamaican train". Derosne, himself, made two trips to Cuba between 1840-42 to supervise the installation of the equipment.

From then on, modern mills with this type of equipment multiplied. According to contemporary statistical data, we see that mills equipped with modern machinery: 1st, produced more sugar and 2nd, as a result, required more cane due to larger capacity. Some of the early Rillieux and Derosne mills had to process juice from neighboring mills that could not fully extract the sucrose content in cane because they were equipped with traditional machinery. The result, then, was a substantial increase in the sugar mill owners' profits.

The sugar manufacturers had visions of great profits. All the mill owners with sufficient financial resources wished to modernize their plants. In this transformation they saw a way to: 1st, reduce costs and 2nd, bring down the number of slaves employed to run the machinery. However, inasmuch as cane-fields would have to be expanded to satisfy the greater capacity of the mill, more slaves would have to be used on the plantations, thus losing a good part of the advantages obtained; that is, slavery continued to appear as an obstacle to the industry's growth.

This movement came to a stop towards 1860. There were several reasons for this. We shall only cite the main ones. In the first place, there was the impossibility of applying new improvements because the slave system prevented the African from becoming a qualified worker to run the new machinery. Also, increased numbers of slaves on the plantations and difficulties in substantially improving agricultural techniques kept costs at uneconomically high levels, thereby reducing the possibility of achieving an accumulation that would permit the continuation of industrial transformation. The lack of sufficient loan and credit facilities kept many sugar mill owners from modernizing their old plants.

The crisis of 1857, and the depression of 1866, caused an accelerated liquidation process of the slave industry with the consequent financial ruin of many small mill owners who had to mortgage their property. On top of this came the consequences of the Ten Years' War (1868-1878) that destroyed a large part of the sugar industry in Las Villas, Camagüey, and Oriente.

What is the significance of the stagnation in technological transformation of the sugar industry? It meant, in sum, that the highest degree had been reached in the relationship between capitalist technology and machinery, and the system of slave-labor. The abolition of slavery remained as the basic problem.

18.1.4. The increase in production capacity and in yield of modern mills had a deep effect on the industry's structure. A mill equipped with the most efficient technology and machinery could produce more than two or three of the old ones, and with greater profits for the owner. This means that, due to an inevitable capitalist production law, new factories eliminate old ones. Many of the owners of antiquated mills did not have the financial means to replace them with new modern plants. They went into a crisis and were eliminated by the more efficient competitors. There was thus begun the process of *sugar industry concentration.* This process reached its highest peak after 1880 and would lead to the formation of sugar latifundia and to the benefit of foreign capitalists.

When the need arose to expand the cane-fields to supply the greater grinding capacity of the new mills, the problems of slave sugar cane agriculture sharpened: it required more slaves, better means of transportation, technological transformation: in sum, the structural crisis of slave economy worsened.

The mill owners sought to resolve the problem through the so-called "division of labor". Stimulated by a group of enterprising mill owners and by technical experts like the Count of Pozos Dulces and others, the thesis was advanced that in Cuba sugar production should be done as in Europe, by the industrialist, who would buy the raw material —sugar cane— from specialized growers, that is, sugar production and cane production should not be in only one hand as it had been in the past.

In this way, they claimed, the number of free planters would spread all over the country. This would be one more step toward the abolition of slavery to help make it a slow process devoid of fears by the mill owners. The truth of the matter was they sought immediately to create a farmer class to face the grave problems of cane agriculture.

The idea was tried out in 1863-64 at the "Tinguaro" mill (Colón), owned by Fernando Diego. But, actually, the situation was as follows: those planters did not own the land; they had to employ the mill owner's slaves; the system of hauling cane —with oxen— was expensive. Those things did not constitute an incentive to the planters. Moreover, they were paid two pesos for one hundred arrobas of harvested cane landed at the mill, which made the system much worse. In point of fact, those "growers" or farmers were actually salaried foremen and administrators. The project ended in failure.

Contemporary writers explained that the system could not be successful as long as industrial equipment did not increase the sugar yield, that is, five to six arrobas of sugar per 100 arrobas of cane. Their argument was not false, since —based on that yield— neither the mill owner nor the planter could meet the inefficiency and the high cost of sugar growing. However, the conditions imposed on the growers were no stimulus for them. Actually, the system of cane planters was established after the abolition of slavery at the time the modern sugar mills were built, after 1886. In this new stage the price paid for cane by the mills was not a good one either. Since the end of the century and during the Republic the planters had to fight hard to obtain a reasonable price for their cane.

With the failure of the "division of labor" the last effort made by the mill owners to solve the problem of slavery failed. However, Alvaro Reynoso, a genial Cuban agronomist of that time, in 1862 proposed a system of farming based on scientific principles which, essentially, called for irrigation. This would raise the cane yield in juice and sucrose. However, in order to install this system, the planters would have to transform their plantations and invest heavily. As always, they preferred to continue with a backward agriculture utilizing low-paid workers and peasants. [2]

18.2. *The tobacco industry*

18.2.1. In a previous chapter we saw the characteristics of primitive tobacco economy. In this one we shall take up that process and continue with its analysis. The establishment of the tobacco trade monopoly in 1717 brought about the elimination of rappee mills which had multiplied between 1701 and 1720. Towards 1740 only three mills remained out of a total of over thirty in 1720. The policy of restricting colonial development in favor of the Spanish tobacco industry (mostly in Seville) had been successful. Moreover, tobacco growing became depressed to the point that in the first decade of the 1800's Spain bought this product from Virginia (United States) to complete its supply.

Towards the end of the 1700's, important changes in consumption began to take place. Tobacco, which had been mostly used in the form of rappee or smoked in pipes, became widely used as cigars. This form of smoking originated with the Indians and had been popular in Cuba since the sixteenth century. It was no accident that "puros" cigars spread to Europe when Cuban trade and economic relations expanded greatly towards the end of the 1700's. The use of cigarettes also became widespread, possibly as the manufacture of thinner paper was improved. Before cigarette paper was available, they were wrapped in corn husk. Of course, all these new uses represented the "democratization" of consumption and meant a progressive decline in the use of rappee.

Cuban industry sprang up about that time. In order to have a steady supply of workers, convicts and orphanage children were used. Nevertheless, cigar workers and home cigarette makers arose. The production of those domestic workers and artisans was purchased by merchants and distributors, true entrepreneurs, who handled and sold the finished product.

The abolition of the tobacco trade monopoly by a royal order of June 23, 1817, favored the expansion of production of the cigar makers who could from then on sell and export their product freely.

18.2.2. The exportation of cigars began to take on importance in the early 1800's. Foreign merchants attracted by the fame of Cuban tobacco, purchased the product. The industry then made big strides as the result of the concentration of workers in shops, producing for only one merchant, whose "brand" had become well known. Thus arose the great capitalist tobacco industry, examples of which can be found from 1830 on. Progressively, larger shops were formed with as many as sixty or even one hundred workers. The owners of the "brand" became the industrial entrepreneur. They were then known as *marquistas* (brand owners).

The process of concentration was rapid. Towards 1850 there were a small number of *marquistas* and many shops without brand producing for the brand owners, whose shops could not produce enough to meet foreign demand, especially from the United States. Unlike the sugar industry process, concentration was not obtained through the application of more efficient machinery and equipment, but rather by the employment of increasing numbers of workers. In Havana alone there were some 15,000 cigar workers, constituting a very important nucleus of wage-workers. However, they were subjected to *contracts of apprenticeship* and other bonds making their situation a reflection of the slave system prevailing in that era.

Throughout the 1800's the industry continued in that concentration process. Moreover, reforms were initiated then that were to reach our day, such as cedar containers —holding 25, 50, and 100 cigars— decorated with ornamental lines and lithographs, constituting the distinctive mark of that Cuban product, later imitated by the tobacco industry in other parts of the world.

However, the protectionist policy begun by the United States towards 1857-60 brought about a deep crisis in the industry. This, coupled with the effects of the political situation in Cuba at the time, caused the emigration of cigar workers and factory owners to the extreme south of the United States, establishing a vigorous tobacco industry there. From then on, sometimes there were thousands of unemployed cigar workers in Havana, and the situation of the "brandless" cigar shops worsened. For this reason the first organized workers movement sprang from the cigar sector, beginning in the decade of 1860-70.

The cigarette industry had a faster evolution. Home cigarette makers continued to predominate. However, towards 1830 work shops sprang up. As a matter of fact, unlike cigar-making, in which operations are complex and for a long time mechanical devices could not replace the workers' dexterity, the production of cigarettes could not be expanded if done by hand. When in 1853 the first mechanized factory, "La Honradez", was put into operation, the industry rapidly became concentrated into a few large units employing very few people.[3]

18.3. *Mining*

18.3.1. Copper mining did not stop completely. However, exportation practically ceased since 1610. Later on, some foundry operations were carried on in order to make industrial equipment (boilers, vessels, and pans), for the sugar industry. Neglect of this activity continued during the 1600's. At the beginning of the eighteenth century an attempt at starting it anew was made, with the administration of the Cobre or Santiago del Prado mines granted to private entrepreneurs. The plan failed for various reasons, it being worthy of mentioning the fact that the King's slaves previously employed at the mines had multiplied and become free in fact, and so firmly refused to go back into slavery, so that in the last quarter of the century the King recognized them as free men.

18.3.2. European industrial development was to pave the way for new explorations of the mines. Capitalist industry, based as it was on machinery made from metals, consumed large quantities of copper, requiring an increasing supply of that mineral. This explains the fact that, towards 1830, an English company, named La Consolidada, obtained a concession to work the mines of Cobre. There also was another English company, and a Spanish-Cuban enterprise devoted to copper mining. No effort was made to concentrate the mineral; it was shipped abroad in an unrefined state. During thirty years Cuba was the principal supplier of copper to British industries until mines in other countries —which had become more readily accessible due to improved ocean transportation— were worked, such as those in Chile, Mexico, and other underdeveloped nations. Mining activities in Cuba thus came to a stop again. Along about those years the capitalist interest of the United States revealed itself when it sent several of its mining experts to explore the mineral wealth of our country. Spanish-Cuban companies were organized and worked other less important mines, including mineral tar, sands, and marble.

After the Ten Years' War, United States monopoly companies began to work iron deposits in Oriente Province. [4]

18.4. *Railroads*

18.4.1. The history of railroads illustrates very clearly the process undergone by the Cuban economy between 1830 and 1860. Railroads were built due to the demands of the sugar industry which, as it penetrated farther into the interior, required more efficient and cheaper means of transportation. Sugar at that time was put in boxes containing 16 arrobas, a heavy and bulky load, difficult and expensive to haul over the roads of those days. With the idea of solving this problem a project was considered to build a canal running from Güines to the north coast. Sugar from this zone was to be transported along this waterway. The project was not carried out. However, when news of the first successful railroad in England (1826) reached Cuba, the local mill owners became keenly interested. The Development Board, formerly the Royal Consulate of Agriculture and Commerce, and the Economic Society, rapidly advanced the negotiations to build a railroad. In August 1833 permission was requested to bargain for a loan of 3,000,000 pesos from the English firm Robertson and Co. Authorization for the loan was granted by royal order of October 12, 1834.

With these resources and the help of A. Kruger, an engineer from the United States, the first railroad was built. It was inaugurated on April 19, 1837. This railroad ran from Havana to the town of Bejucal, 27 kilometers away. In December 1838, another section, running from Bejucal to Güines, was opened. Even before the work was finished on the first road, many new projects were being planned providing for other sections to link the province of Matanzas with Havana. Sugar mill owners did not take long to realize that railroads not only solved the problem of sugar transportation, but also were a good source of income. For this reason, pressure was applied by these interests for the sale of the Havana-Güines railroad to a private company made up of sugar mill owners. A price of over three million pesos was agreed upon and the sale consummated on January 11, 1842. [5]

Inasmuch as, besides Güines, the great sugar zone was the plains of Matanzas, the movement of railroad building developed mainly in those two directions. There was keen competition between the different capitalist groups in obtaining concessions, and, later, the rival companies competed with one another in so reduced a portion of the country. The section Güines-Unión de Reyes was built, and from there to Matanzas Bay (1845). Later on, a railroad running directly from Güines to Matanzas was completed (1861). But, so as to make matters still more disorderly, another railroad from Havana to the Bay of Matanzas was built (1861). The worst thing about this was that for a good part of the way this railroad ran parallel to the Güines-Matanzas one.

The speculative boom in business ending with the crisis of 1857 was marked by large investments in railroads. The first railroads were built in Oriente (El Cobre, Santiago - El Cristo) and in Las Villas (Cienfuegos - Villa Clara, in 1860 and Sagua la Grande - Encrucijada, in 1863; Casilda - Paso Real, in 1860). Most of these railroads remained unconnected with each other, serving limited zones only and, generally, linking the interior with the main seaports. Ever since 1854 the convenience of joining these isolated railroads to form a *central railroad* had been proposed. But this project was not fully realized, from one end of the island to the other, until the present century.

18.4.2. It can be stated that, from 1865 on, the railroad building movement came to a stop, to be restarted with the United States economic and political penetration in 1899.

Before 1880 some of the companies were purchased by other companies or were merged with them. But this concentration process was rather slow. Financial concentration took place in another way, that is, by the close connection between sugar, mercantile, banking, and railroad businesses.

The fact that the ownership of large sugar mills, banks and railroads sometimes was held by companies where one powerful stockholder or a small number of stockholders predominated was highly indicative of the degree of ripening of capitalist conditions arisen within the slave system. Those conditions —indicative of the possibility of a more complete capitalist development— were eliminated by the socio-economic events taking place between 1857 and 1878, and particularly, later on, by imperialist investments.

18.5. *Other industries*

18.5.1. It is worthy of notice that there were other industries in the nineteenth century. For the first time the fishing industry was organized as a capitalist activity, though, due to circumstances, it was rather a screen covering up large-scale smuggling of merchandise, and slaves (mainly Indians from Yucatan).

Foundry was the most interesting of these other industries. Along about the middle of the century a large foundry works was built at Bemba (Jovellanos) employing 80 slaves and supplying the sugar mills with spare parts. As Matanzas was the great sugar center, other foundries were set up in that zone towards the end of the 1800's.

Other industries were begun after 1860. However, they were less important than the ones mentioned in the preceding paragraphs. Needless to say there were minor industries, such as tile and lime kilns, and others related to building and construction, in every city or important town.

BIBLIOGRAPHY

1. LE RIVEREND, JULIO. *Historia de la nación cubana,* vols. cit.
2. CEPERO BONILLA, RAUL. *Op. cit.*
3. RIVERO MUÑIZ, JOSÉ. "Origen y primeros tiempos de la industria tabacalera cubana." *Tabaco.* Havana, December, 1945.
4. CALVACHE, ANTONIO. *Historia y desarrollo de la minería en Cuba,* Havana, 1944.
5. ORTIZ, FERNANDO. "Las perspectivas económicas sociales del primer ferrocarril de Cuba," *Revista Bimestre Cubana,* November-December, 1937.

Chapter XIX

COMMERCE AND ITS MODIFICATIONS

19.1. *Commercial policy*

19.1.1. Cuban trade in the eighteenth century. Beginning of relations with the United States. Changes in trade policies until 1822. 19.1.2. Maintenance of exclusivist trade policies. Multiple customs tariffs.

19.2. *Characteristics*

19.2.1. Structure of commerce towards 1850. Commercial organization. 19.2.2. Banks and wholesale establishments. United States credit.

19.3. *Domestic trade*

19.3.1. Its primitivism. The merchant-banker in rural zones. 19.3.2. Small-scale urban commerce. The general merchandise store.

19.1. *Commercial policy*

19.1.1. The commercial organization and policy prevailing in Cuba during three centuries, did not undergo any substantial change. The monopoly system reigned supreme, the benefits therefrom going to Seville, in Spain, and to Havana, in the colony. The system of fleets of merchants ships continued, though progressively declining. This decline was reflected not only in the reduced number of them —years would pass without a fleet sailing— but also in the lower tonnage of cargo. The red tape established by the Commodity Exchange authorities of Seville became worse and worse. Everything favored the Seville commercial interests maintaining their unearned profit-making and their association with foreign merchants (English, French, and Dutch). The custom duties known as *almojarifazgo* were a heavy burden. Besides, many other taxes were added every time the State Treasury required additional funds.

Moreover, as a result of the fact that during the 1700's there were other colonies producing sugar, as Brazil, and the English and French possessions in the West Indies began to also produce sugar, the possibilities of Cuba expanding her trade were sharply reduced. It is safe to conclude that contraband, both rather openly as well as covertly, was the only way to increase colonial trade. Foreign traders and shipowners would remain for months around the Cuban coast bartering with the planters. Sometimes, under pretext of taking on provisions or repairing damages, foreign ships would put into port and sell their cargo of merchandise. Cuba also maintained trade relations with other Spanish colonies through Veracruz and Campeche, as well as Cartagena de Indias.

The change in commercial policy had towards the end of the seventeenth century produced an effect on the situation. Indeed, from then on, the trading powers placed a greater trust on treaties imposed by war, than on traffic carried on by pirates, corsairs and buccaneers. Moreover, the war of succession to the Spanish throne brought Cuba into close contact with the European economy, especially with French commerce. The natural result of increased trade possibilities was the expansion of the sugar industry.

The dynasty change in Spain stimulated capitalist development. Philip V and his advisers —who favored a policy of mercantilism— initiated reforms, stimulating industry and trade. In 1720, the first modifications to the fleet system were made. The practice of chartering single ships, "out of fleet", to carry merchandise from Spanish ports (Seville and Cadiz) to Spain's colonies in America was accepted and favored. This reform was a very timid one, but it would be followed by other measures, thus liberalizing the trading system. As a matter of fact, though a series of wars took place, the threat of attack to merchant ships had disappeared. This was in sharp contrast with the situation when pirates, corsairs, and buccaneers had roamed the seas (seventeenth century).

Traditional commercial policy was still reflected in the founding of the Royal Trading Company of Havana (*Real Compañía de Comercio de La Habana*) in 1740. It was made up of Spanish and Cuban merchants and was granted the monopoly of trade in Cuba, resulting in constant complaints due to abusive practices. Also complaining were Spanish stockholders, because the management by Havana-born company officials, headed by Martín de Aróstegui, founder of the company, left much to be desired. But if, from a political standpoint, the founding of this company presupposed the maintainance of the monopoly principle, from the point of view of the development of Cuba it meant that a commercial class had been formed that, in alliance with the Crown's interests (the King had subscribed to one hundred shares of stock) and the Spanish merchants, claimed a greater participation in the profits of colonial trade. However, the company did not develop its own strength, but combined with traders and shipowners of Jamaica, who supplied it with slaves and European industrial goods.

The company's privilege ended after the English capture of Havana (1762-63). That event caused the Spanish government to adopt new measures leading to a liberalization of commerce. Indeed, the capitalist impulse in Spain was already demanding the reform of traditional trade monopoly. That was the reason the Royal Order of October 16, 1765 eliminated a number of taxes and charges weighing on trade in the Caribbean possessions and, also —which is of primary importance— authorized these colonies to trade with several Spanish seaports, thus doing away with the trade monopoly of Seville and Cadiz. Though this new policy was called *free trade,* it was only an extension of the monopoly to all Spain, as commerce with foreign countries was still prohibited. Such an extension of trade meant that all economic regions of Spain would be benefited by the exploitation of those colonies. Though limited, the measure favored an increase in colonial trade.

In truth, the most important change was brought about by the regulations on free trade of October 12, 1778. In the first place, they opened new colonial ports to direct commerce with Spain (in Cuba, besides Havana, those of Santiago de Cuba, Trinidad and Batabanó were qualified). Ships at sea were now allowed to change destination, including that of the cargo, which had been strictly prohibited before. Foreign trade was allowed upon the payment of exhorbitant taxes. These regulations, though not completely satisfactory to Cuban exporters, propitiated an increase in colonial trade.

That increase in trade, moreover, was favored by the United States' War of Independence. By reason of the aid Spain extended to the American colonies in their fight for liberation from England, U.S. ships freely put into the port of Havana, loading sugar and other commodities, and unloading flour, industrial products, and slaves. That phenomenon was decisive for colonial trade, leaving an imprint that lasted until 1959.

Trade with the United States meant the opening of an increasing market for Cuban sugar and molasses, thus linking the sugar mill owners' class to foreign interests. For that reason, at the time of the French revolutionary and of the imperial wars (1790-1815), the watchword of Cuban sugar people was to struggle for direct commerce with the "neutral" nations, that is, with the United States. From 1782, the entrance of U.S. ships into Cuban ports had been prohibited, and after 1790 this decision to allow entry was reversed back and forth, according to the gravity or easing of naval operations. Often, during those years, United States traders were the only regular buyers of Cuban products, which they exported to Europe, thus realizing a very profitable business. At the same time, they supplied flour, an indispensable staple for the Cuban population. During this long period of twenty-five years, the high colonial officials authorized this commerce without consulting Madrid. This was in the interest of the large estate owners' class, which constituted the dominating economic group. Thus, by favoring the export of sugar, the colonial government secured that group's allegiance. [1]

19.1.2. On February 10, 1818, freedom of trade was decreed. But the customs tariffs established in that connection were ferociously protective of Spanish commerce and ships, discriminating against foreign competition. For this reason, when the constitutional regime was re-established, Havana sugar mill owners were successful in obtaining a reduction of Spanish trade protection with the adoption of tariffs (in 1822) ranging from 20% to 36% *ad valorem*. By comparison with prior rates the new ones seemed moderate! Moreover, the 1822 tariff established import duties on a differential basis, that is, setting different "per cents" depending on whether the merchandise and the ship were Spanish or foreign. Accordingly, there were four columns or duty types: one for Spanish merchandise carried in a Spanish vessel; another for foreign merchandise in a Spanish ship; another for Spanish merchandise in a foreign vessel, and another for foreign merchandise in a foreign ship. Naturally, the last category was the most heavily taxed.

The tariff system applied to Cuba under the so-called free trade policy was none other than the Spanish trade monopoly wearing a new face. This system lasted through the nineteenth century with occasional changes to increase protection against foreign products. [2]

The Spanish trading class maintained its privileges and thus continued profiteering, under the protection of the tariff, on both Spanish and foreign goods.

19.2. *Characteristics*

19.2.1. Naturally, the changes in the trade policy went hand in hand with an increased volume in commerce, thereby revealing, more and more, the dependency of the commercial structure, as befits a colonial nation within the capitalist system. It is difficult to know the details of mercantile flow distribution before 1790. However, we do have enought data to determine its basic characteristics. This matter is important because in dependent colonial economies, commerce volume and distribution are very significant elements to determine the degree of dependency. Moreover, they are economies in which the basic incentive is the possibility of exporting. Therefore their growth can be measured, to a great extent by their export production and since it is an abnormal growth, its pace and amount are an index of their progressive structural deformation.

In the first half of the nineteenth century, the characteristic fact of the structure of Cuban commerce was a marked tendency to increase trade with the most advanced nations and to decrease commerce with Spain. This explains the powerful protectionist tendency of Spanish interests, especially in connection with United States commerce. Cuban export interests, (sugar, coffee and tobacco) fought to obtain the United States market. But the Spanish government would not easily give up Cuban imports. However, the alliance of those interests with the colonial government was maintained during the period between 1790 and 1860.

Towards 1860 export commerce was distributed in the following manner: United States, 62% ; Great Britain, 22% ; and Spain, 3%. The rest was divided among many nations with which no regular trade was held. With regards to the first two, the balance of trade was favorable to Cuba; with Spain, it was unfavorable. We must come to one conclusion: the predominance of the buying position of the United States was consolidated, since that country's sugar refining industry was substantially supplied by Cuban raw sugar. With this predominance, there was a deep and progressive penetration by United States capital. This explains why Spanish colonialist interests redoubled their protectionist policy — raising import duties on foreign goods, as in 1853.

Import commerce was not equally distributed. Spain supplied 30%, while the United States and Great Britain each exported 20%. Those figures reflect the protectionist policy of Spain. However, it should be kept in mind that included in the figure for Spain are foreign goods re-exported to Cuba from Spanish ports.

Export commodities though few in number were rather varied: refined sugar, raw sugar, coffee, wax, leaf tobacco and tobacco products, cane brandy, residual molasses, and copper ore were the main items. Export of manufactured goods (refined sugar and cigars) was higher than it would be later on. Imported articles on the other hand were many, running the whole gamut of manufactured goods required for the survival of the population and the maintenance of industry.

19.2.2. Increased trade and close relations produced more complex and specialized forms of commercial organization. The traditional sugar mill owner going to market with his sugar disappeared rapidly. Not only did the banks spring up but also wholesale establishments combining commercial and banking operations. There was, since the decade of 1840, a savings and loan bank, created with the participation of the sugar mill owners, to facilitate funds to them. In 1844, wholesale establishments were opened in the town of Regla, and the *Banco del Comercio* was founded. Other such institutions followed, with the participation of the sugar mill owners. Other wholesale establishments were opened in Matanzas and Santiago de Cuba.

Previously, the tobacco merchant had arisen. This merchant was a specialized one by reason of the peculiarities of the product. However, the large wholesale dealers in leaf tobacco for export date back to that period.

To a great extent, both types of merchants operated on the basis of financing by United States business firms. Since the decade 1820-30 there were businessmen at the great seaports in the United States specially devoted to dealing in Cuban sugar. The firms Moses Taylor, and Atkins were famous. Many sugar mill owners did not sell their sugar production through the local wholesalers, whose dealing capacity was limited, but through the United States wholesale dealers who, in order to secure the purchase of the product and augment their profits, extended credit to the Cuban sugar producers. This credit took the form of merchandise, slaves, or tools and machinery. Thus, there was established throughout that period a tight bond of interests, linking United States importers to the Cuban export group.[3]

It can be stated that until 1886, and even later, the trade system continued operating on those bases. However, we should point out that financial dependency worsened as a result of the crisis of 1857-66. In effect, during those years, in spite of certain business upturns, the financial institutions created by the Cubans were liquidated, thus leaving the Banco Español (Bank of Spain) and the United States businessmen without competition, the absolute masters of the Cuban market.

19.3. *Domestic trade*

19.3.1. Internal trade expanded. In the first place, because coastwise shipping became stable through the use of regular steamships. Other reasons were the building and extending of railroads, and a certain very small improvement of the roads. All of the large cities and seaports were points of entry for the imports of each respective zone, though Havana was becoming the supply center for the whole country.

19.3.2. Nevertheless, domestic trade maintained its primitivism. In the first place, distribution was carried out through a great number of small stores, both urban and rural, basically dependent on the importers. Of course, limitations for the establishment of this type of business place disappeared as the cities grew in size, with the resultant proliferation of such stores. There was a certain specialization in this type of small retailer, serving as an instrument of credit to the population. However, in the rural zones and in areas near the cities, the general merchandise (not specialized) store was outstanding, continuing into the twentieth century.

Needless to say that the system was based on unbridled profit-making, as would be verified later on. The whole credit pyramid weighed heavily on the consumer.

In rural zones, the merchant turned financier. In thickly populated rural areas with important crops, the merchant of that zone, almost without competition, doubled as financier or money lender. This double role enabled him to set his own terms and reap tremendous profits.

BIBLIOGRAPHY

1. Le Riverend, Julio. *Op. cit.*, chap. XV.
2. Guerra, Ramiro. *Manual*, cit. chap. XVII.
3. Ely, R. T. *Comerciantes cubanos del siglo XIX*. Havana, 1963.

CHAPTER XX

FINANCIAL ORGANIZATION

20.1. *Monetary system*

20.1.1. Antecedentes. "Natural" economy. Appearance of the *macuquina.* Monetary dislocations of the late eighteenth century. Influence of U.S. trade. 20.1.2. Multiple currency. Problems caused by the Sevillian pesetas. 20.1.3. The inflationary crisis of 1868-78.

20.2. *Credit, banking and crisis*

20.2.1. Influence of commercial credit. 20.2.2. The early banks. 20.2.3. Speculation: the stock companies. 20.2.4. Crises of 1847 and 1857-66. 20.2.5. Conditions up to 1895.

20.3. *Fiscal system*

20.3.1. Antecedents. Policy of indirect taxation. Introduction of the sales tax. 20.3.2. Incidence and proliferation of customs duties on foreign trade. 20.3.3. Fiscal Administration. Provincial management. The Villa Nueva Reform. 20.3.4. The peso of the fiscal system: the information office and its results.

20.1. *Monetary system*

20.1.1. Beginning as far back as the conquest, Cuban currency not only was minted outside of the country, but suffered all sorts of vagaries caused by external conditions and needs. The Spanish monetary system, based on the legal circulation of gold and silver pieces, was characterized by frequent alterations in the precious metal content of the coins. Coins were constantly minted and re-minted for purposes of devaluation, as the inflation caused by the influx into Spain of metals from American mines might dictate.

Cuba provided herself with coins produced in Mexico, whose value was stable and proportional to extraction, carried out constantly, of silver from mines there. This money, however, did not stay in Cuba. Its high value, compared with the Spanish silver piece, which suffered a devaluation of almost 100 percent between 1537 and 1686, made it highly attractive to foreign and Spanish traders in the colony. Therefore, only the gold pieces remained. These were very scarce and, moreover, were sought after primarily for hoarding, as they were not a convenient medium of exchange for ordinary business transactions. The result of all this was that throughout the colonial period, which lasted up to the mid-nineteenth century, a constant shortage of tender prevailed. Only during a portion of the eighteenth century (1730-1780) did there exist an adequate coin, the silver piece known as the *macuquina,* which we shall discuss further on.

This scarcity lent itself to the emergence of a barter or "natural" economy, that is, one based on direct exchange of goods rather than currency. Up until 1691, the residents of Santa Clara were obliged to pay for their meat with agricultural produce, although the ranchers resisted this type of payment. This was also true in Remedios and frequently even in Havana. In the capital, ranchers in their turn pressed to pay their taxes in produce also.

Cuba began to receive a more adequate monetary supply around 1720. Remittances of funds (called *allocations*) from Mexico to pay soldiers and finance military installations began to increase because of tobacco purchases and the establishment of a great naval base and of the Havana shipyards. The 1737 monetary reform of Philip V established the value of a heavy peso as five pieces of two "royal units" each (these pieces were the *pesetas*) but did not alter the American exchange rate which was four pieces of two "royal units" per peso. Naturally, then, it was advantageous to give four Spanish *pesetas* for a heavy peso of silver, since on arrival at Spain, the trader received five *pesetas* for his peso. Consequently, silver pesos were constantly drained away from Cuba, to the detriment of her inhabitants.

Because of their lesser value, the Spanish pesetas were, of course, not popular with the settlers who tried to get rid of them as rapidly as possible. The situation improved when the Mexican treasury began to send silver *macuquinas* to Havana. These were perforated silver coins, which, despite the reduced weight caused by cutting pieces from them, circulated at face value. For this reason, Spanish and foreign traders did not export these coins and they remained in domestic circulation. In fact, in foreign trade they were considered as devaluated currency, thus favoring the export of domestic products.

The coins were first perforated in Mexico, and subsequently met with further tampering in Cuba, where the silversmiths were short of raw materials and used pieces cut from these coins in their handiwork. In the course of the eighteenth century, the *macuquina* became accepted Cuban currency. However, the State Treasurer and the traders would not accept it at face value, but only at its real value, its actual weight in silver. State policy was directed towards taking this money out of circulation, since the inhabitants used it freely in their transactions, and in 1771 an order was issued to call it in, to be exchanged for the State peso. This exchange meant that the coin lost up to 50 percent or more of its face value. The process of withdrawing it from circulation went on for years, since the people needed money for everyday transactions and the new currency did not arrive until 1787. As the *macuquina* became scarce in various parts of Cuba, it was necessary to improvise. For this purpose, paper counters, bits of tin, and even French playing cards with denominations printed on them, circulated as tender.

The poor residents protested a great deal because this "money" lent itself to extensive speculation and to flagrant abuse of consumers. It is also important to realize that between 1770 and 1790 economic activity was on the increase, so that the disappearance of the *macuquinas* and the shortage of new currency caused significant dislocations. The sugar exporting oligarchy was particularly discontented, as one can gather from Arango y Parreño's *Discourses,* since the lack of a devaluated currency now discouraged exportation.

20.1.2. Later, towards the end of the eighteenth century, increased trade with the United States caused further dislocations, since foreign traders exported the new silver money to exchange it for gold. This was because the monetary system of the United States set a premium on silver, whereas in Cuba gold was at a premium. However, gold was of little use to Cubans in their everyday exchanges, and so there was again a great scarcity of money. When the "remittances" ceased to come in from Mexico, about 1811, silver again recovered its value and the value of gold went down. This time it was not U. S. traders who went off with the silver, but the Spanish themselves and Latin Americans in flight from national insurrections, leaving debased gold behind them in Cuba. In this period Cuba was also overrun by the so-called Sevillian pesetas (5 to a peso), which in Cuba were exchanged at 4 per peso, so that speculators brought them into the country and exchanged them for heavy pesos, which they later exchanged in Spain at a comfortable profit of 20 percent. As a consequence, Cuban currency came to consist almost entirely of Sevillian silver. Since this constituted a debased currency, the same speculative phenomena as had risen toward the end of the eighteenth century recurred and were aggravated by the circulation of counters of cardboard, wood and tin, owing to the scarcity of small change. In 1841 the Sevillian pesetas were called in at their true value, 5 to a peso.

From then on the monetary situation tended to stabilize, even though Havana and other cities were sites of multiple circulation because of the great expansion of trade, and particularly because of the remittances of gold brought by travelers from California where the gold rush had attracted millions of fortune seekers.

In 1868 the formal peso divided into 100 *centavos* was officialized, but immediately thereafter foreign money, such as the French louis also became acceptable.[1]

20.1.3. For a time things went smoothly, disturbances not breaking out again until the decade 1868-78. When troubles did begin, they were caused by the increasing issuance of colonial paper money, whose volume was augmented as costs increased. Naturally this paper money went on depreciating, so that in 1874 an ounce of gold was worth 163 paper pesos. Consequent speculation and harm to consumer interests was enormous. The very colonial authorities were obliged to make a show of repressing this evil, even persecuting some speculators closely connected with officialdom. This situation was not ironed out until the 1830's. Nonetheless, since bank issues were in actuality State loans, the people of Cuba were snowed under by a load of debts which helped further to impoverish them.

20.2. *Credit, banking and crisis*

20.2.1. Up until 1840 credit practices were confined exclusively to the use of commercial credit. A considerable number of rich planters speculated with their sugar; others combined importing with sugar trading and very many of them depended on the great merchants to finance their sugar crops. When, towards the end of the eighteenth century, United States traders appeared on the scene, they became the supplier of a substantial part of this credit, taking this function over from the French and English, through sales of slaves and machinery.

Of course, subsequently the Cuban economy underwent an impressive process of development, with great spurts of activity which made possible the creation of massive sugar capitals capable in some degree of financing themselves.

But the predominance of the commercial credit, of an usurious nature, remained as a characteristic of the colonial economy. Arango y Parreño complained of its unbearable pressure upon the large estate owners, and even later, by the middle of the nineteenth century, there was evidence of the extremely high interest rate on loans (14% to 24%).

Documents of that era reveal the importance of the firms dealing in Cuban sugar. Many of them were established only in Cuba and others were in the United States. Some of them had offices or agencies in both countries. The large business transactions carried out during the period 1830-50 not only transformed many of these firms into veritable banks but also demanded a more flexible and powerful financial organization at the service of the sugar mill owners.

20.2.2. Overlooking the attempts made for the establishment of a bank prior to 1830 and the effective constitution of the Bank of San Fernando, no true reference can be made regarding any banking before the foundation of the Savings and Loans Bank of Havana, founded by a group of capitalists headed by Carlos del Castillo (1842).

Although this bank's operations were not very liberal, as compared with the traditional forms of credit and neither did they encompass a substantially large proportion of the sugar business deals, its success and strength, which allowed it to survive the 1857 crisis, indicate that it adjusted itself to current needs.

Its historical significance rests upon the fact that it showed a way to be followed at a time fraught with great changes in technology and productive equipment, and on the other hand, it presupposed the formation of a powerful though small nucleus of Cuban capitalists, allied to United States merchants.

The great investments required by new sugar mills equipped with horizontal mill trains, vacuum vats, steam engines, and railroads could not be obtained through traditional methods and resources. A vigorous financial impulse came into being, as shown by a combination of railroad and sugar interests and the establishment of stock companies devoted to banking. Towards 1850 this development became deeply significant: in addition to the creation of wholesale establishments which were in fact veritable banks, the foundations were laid for what was to become the Bank of Spain in Havana.

20.2.3. The ever-increasing bond with the international capitalist economy following the 1840's, the high level of activity attained due to the export of sugar and the construction of railroads were instrumental in bringing about, following the 1850's, an era of increasing speculation. It was the era of sugar industry expansion in Matanzas, especially in Colón and Cárdenas and in the zones of Sagua la Grande and Cienfuegos. Beginning in 1855, the process became a veritable landslide. The capitalist trend towards the proliferation of stock companies overshadowed the picture of the national economy. Companies such as the Territorial Credit organized sugar, railroad, banking, and commercial enterprises, under the guidance of a group of Cuban capitalists headed by Miguel Aldama. All sorts of companies were created to carry on all kinds of projects: sugar plantations, railroads, insurance, manufacturing industries, newspapers, etc. Concurrently with the land and railroad speculations taking place in the United States and England, conditions for a powerful financial development in Cuba were beginning to ripen. These conditions arose from the colonialist slave organization, as an expression of the transition towards a fully capitalist economy.

20.2.4. This was a new phenomenon in the history of Cuba — as was the 1857-66 crisis. The crisis, originating in England in 1845-47, was not felt deeply in Cuba, even though, in contrast with the 1837 depression, its effect was reflected in a sudden, significant drop in prices and the volume of sugar exports.

On the other hand, the speculative, inflationary process of 1855-56 led to the crisis of 1857, closely following the great panic in the United States. Numerous stock companies went into bankruptcy and others were unable to gather the capital needed for their operation. The demand for reinbursement of funds from stock companies and banks brought about a sudden recession with the consequent bankruptcy. The Bank of Spain was saved by a contribution made by Spanish merchants and sugar mill owners, including other banks such as the Territorial Credit and the Savings and Loans Bank.

Inasmuch as the crisis made a great impact upon business, it took several years to overcome it. This was made more difficult by the fact that sugar prices and exports moved irregularly, due to the depressed state of the United States and British economy, lasting through 1866.

20.2.5. The Ten Years' War (1868-78) served as a cover-up for the financial situation which had emerged in a very bad condition from the 1857-66 crisis. So far, the great Cuban capitals, which had created the financial development, had been liquidated, and only the Bank of Spain remained, operated very restrictively, reflecting the interests of the Spanish merchants. To a certain extent, the old system of usurious credit was revived and, on the other hand, foreign credit became invested with a decisive importance.

The decade of the 1880's witnessed a great change in sugar prices, remaining at a permanently low level as a result of the appearance of the refinery monopoly in the United States and England, as well as by the fact that the sugar policy followed by the most developed countries gave Cuba the almost exclusive role of raw sugar purveyor. At that moment, not only did the United States commercial capital become predominant, but direct investments were made as well. A new stage had begun.

20.3. *Fiscal system*

20.3.1. If the monetary system was disordered, the fiscal system fared no better. No basic philosophy underlay its practices, so that taxes and levies were imposed according to the needs of the Spanish government and confusion reigned. It should be clarified here that the majority of these imposts were indirect, that is, levied not on capital or profits, but rather on sales, so that all of them were borne essentially by the unfortunate consumer. It should also be noted that until the eighteenth century, State funds were collected predominantly through customs duties, known as *almojarifazgo*. Customs duties were easy to collect, since both importation and exportation were conspicuous and continuous economic activities. It is true that duty evasions abounded in the customs offices and that extensive contraband cut down on revenues, but, in the long run, this was still the most effective source of government income. Duties were levied both at point of entry and point of departure, that is, on imports and exports, the former exceeding the latter greatly. Payments were calculated on percentage of the declared value of the merchandise. Generally, such tariffs were very high, thus causing merchants to raise prices proportionally, to the detriment of the consumer.

20.3.2. All through the seventeenth and eighteenth centuries, additional taxes were constantly being created parallel to the customs duties. These were extremely numerous, although they were partly consolidated in 1765 when "free trade" with Spanish ports was first initiated. Local taxes were also set up to meet city expenses and those of the colonial governors. Some of these were the aqueduct tax, whose funds were used for constructing the Royal aqueduct to bring water from the Almendares River to Havana; the galliot tax, allocated for maintaining a coast guard vessel, and a tax for financing the construction of the walls around Havana. There was one other regular tax, the tithe or a tenth part of all agricultural products. Although this tax was originally paid entirely to the church, as the monarchy became stronger, it arrogated almost the total proceeds from this tax to itself.

Another characteristic of this fiscal system was the farming out of tax collections. All important taxes were farmed out to tax collectors who advanced the money to the State. The State, of course, did its best to obtain the maximum from these collectors, who, in their turn, did not scruple to enrich themselves through the abuse of their fiscal privileges. Speculation in taxes was rife, and the colonists defended themselves by falsifying their records and thinking up all manner of ways to circumvent the law.

The first changes in this system were made in the eighteenth century. The Bourbon monarchy with its policy of centralization of authority decided to eliminate the intermediary tax collectors and set up a system of direct State administration. The government also tended towards the simplification of the tax system. At the same time, however, increases in State expenditures provoked new and increased levies. Therefore, in 1758, began the enforcement of the sales tax, which had previously been established but not made effective in Cuba. The ordinance of March 23, 1764, fixed a tax of 4% on all sales made in the country. Protests were widespread, adding even greater force to the resistance against a direct tax of 3% on income from real estate which had recently gone into effect. In 1765 the real estate tax was abolished but the sales tax raised to 6%. Later on, the sale of farm property was subject to a double sales tax (12%) and a minor tax was also levied on the buyer of such property (6% of 6% of sales price).

This last tax rounded out the fundamentals of the treasury system. From then on (the late eighteenth century), changes made were secondary and predominantly quantitative. As a matter of fact, taxes collected in Cuba during the sixteenth, seventeenth and eighteenth centuries had been quite inadequate to meet administrative costs. They had been supplemented by the remittances from Mexico made annually to cover largely military expenditures. From 1790 on, the growth of trade and of production favored more ample tax collections. Beginning in mid-nineteenth century, Cuba became a great source of income for the Spanish colonialist regime.

20.3.3. Improvement in the system of tax collections was greatly aided by the establishment of the central office for administration of finance created by royal order on October 31, 1764. These central administrative offices originated in Spain and spread to America through the influence of French mercantilism, that is, the existence of a centralized fiscal policy, tending to reinforce the economic interests of the State with elimination of local or regional peculiarities. This office was created to superintend all matters of tax collections, State monetary rights and State property. It was characterized by a consistent effort to improve tax collections in order to guarantee the public treasury those revenues necessary for the carrying on of public financial transactions. Generally speaking, the financial office was in the hands of an official who, by virtue of his very position, wielded power, and who, at times, was a very competent and loyal servant of State economic interests.

Among the most eminent fiscal administrators were Alejandro Ramírez, Arango y Parreño, and Claudio Martínez de Pinillos, Count Villanueva. The last is remembered for his great reforms. However, these reforms did not go to the root of this system, but rather affected only administrative procedures and manners of collecting taxes in such a way that State income increased considerably. It is true also that about the time of Villanueva's incumbency, 1830-40, the Cuban economy flourished vigorously, thus increasing State proceeds automatically.

20.3.4. The treasury system, through which Spain extracted great sums from Cuba, increasingly constituted a heavy drain on the Cuban people, tending towards impoverishment of the local population. Protective customs barriers for Spanish trade and industry increased throughout the nineteenth century, and a proliferation of stamp taxes, monopolies on the sale of game cocks and playing cards, sales taxes and a multitude of other levies, ended up by bleeding white the propertied classes and the people. General discontent led to the inclusion of the fiscal problem on the agenda of the Council of Information meeting, held in Madrid in 1865. The Cuban delegates proposed that many of the taxes then in effect be abrogated and that a property tax be established, but the Spanish government refused to modify the system and also imposed a direct tax which constituted an additional burden for the landowners. This event contributed to the Revolution of 1868, since the wealthy farmers of the central and eastern parts of the country felt the deleterious effects of the official economic policy more than did the great landowners of the western part of the Island. In general, the treasury system weighed more heavily on the native sectors of the population and those dependent on exportation than it did on the Spanish traders, whose connections with the colonial power gave them an advantage.[3]

From that time on, there were no changes in the fiscal policy. And when the economic structure was further impaired by the effects of the Ten Years' War (1868-78) and the abolition of slavery, the tax burden became increasingly intolerable.

The impoverished Cuban people were paying heavier taxes than peoples in countries where capitalism was advancing rapidly, and with all their misery were supporting thousands of government functionaries and foreign personnel as well as financing State activities which were of no benefit to the country.

BIBLIOGRAPHY

1. Villanova, Manuel. *Economía y civismo,* Havana, 1945.

2. Le Riverend, Julio. *Op. cit.,* Chap. XVII.

3. *Information on reforms in Puerto Rico and Cuba,* Vol. I, p. 228 on. New York, 1867.

Part V

THE CUBAN ECONOMY DURING THE IMPERIALIST ERA (1886-1958)

CHAPTER XXI

IMPERIALISM

21.1. *Finance capital*

21.1.1. Industrial capitalism and transportation. 21.1.2. The special development of certain branches of industry. 21.1.3. The process of capitalist concentration. 21.1.4. Finance capital and its characteristics.. Imperialism. 21.1.5. Imperialist manifestations in capitalist countries.

21.2. *Colonialism*

21.2.1. The struggle for the division of the less developed territories. 21.2.2. Pre-imperialist manifestations. 21.2.3. Appearance of imperialist wars. 21.2.4. The world wars.

21.3. *Socialism*

21.1. *Finance capital*

21.1.1. Industrial capitalism, which came to full development in Europe during the eighteenth century, developed a series of new characteristics during the nineteenth century. The effects of the industrial revolution began to take definite form, with their sequelae of increasingly acute contradictions among the more highly developed nations and between these and the less developed countries. All this was accompanied by the expansion and development of processes for the application of scientific and machine techniques to industrial production. With the spread of these mechanisms and techniques, industry became increasingly complex, demanding more and more extensive financial investments on the part of the capitalist. As a result, those entrepreneurs who succeeded in acquiring modern industrial plants found themselves more powerful than those who were saddled with outdated installations. In the long run, manufacturers who were unable to supply themselves with modern equipment had to go out of business. This industrial growth, which was also concomitantly one of concentration of economic resources, was greatly abetted by the use of better means of transportation.

Industrial capital needed more efficient means of transportation in order to sell its ever increasing products and in order to open up new markets for them. More rapid vehicles and those with greater freight capacity were necessary. The United States attempted to solve this problem by the building of canals towards the end of the eighteenth century, but this solution was serviceable only within the capitalist country itself. They did not solve the problem of how to send goods overseas or across vast continents. These needs were met by the advent of the steamship and the railroad.

Railroads came into being first in England, the most highly developed country and therefore that in greatest need of improvements in transportation and communication. The first railroad began to operate there in 1825. Its utility in the expansion of capitalist industry was soon appreciated. Moreover, the railroad companies themselves were capitalist enterprises with their needs for massive investments and employment of thousands of workers. The English port cities, devoted to the export of finished products and the import of raw materials, soon established close ties with the cities of the interior, the great centers of production. Before 1850 the railroad had spread to all of the more advanced cities of Europe, and even, as in the case of Cuba, to some colonial countries where the importance of some export product required good transportation between the interior and ports of embarkation. In some countries, such as the United States, the growth of industrial and finance capital was in large part dependent on the establishment of railroad companies and the building of railroads over vast areas previously little exploited, but lending themselves to exploitation now that rapid transport was available.

Steamship travel did not develop so impetuously. Although the steam engine was applied to ocean navigation before 1820, through the ingenuity of the U.S. inventor, Robert Fulton, maritime transport problems were not solved for many years. The reason for this was that the steam engine originally was massive and inefficient, taking up a great deal of space in the ship and requiring enormous quantities of fuel. This, of course, diminished the capacity available for cargo, outbalancing the fact that by 1850, the steamship was obviously more rapid than sailing vessels. Moreover, the sailing vessel industry, faced now with competition, modernized its methods and developed new types of sailing ships of greater speed and capacity, such as the clippers. The contest went on for several years until at the end of the century the internal combustion (Diesel) motor was invented, which, fueled with petroleum, did not take up much space itself and, moreover, permitted the construction of very large ships. The sailing vessel thus lost out and was relegated to a secondary role in world transport. [1]

The combination of railroad and maritime transport permitted the more advanced countries increasingly to inundate far-away and more primitive countries with their industrial products, and, at the same time, favored the acquisition of basic commodities and raw materials produced in colonial or backward countries. For this reason the more highly developed countries built up great merchant marine fleets and navies.

21.1.2. Along with these advances rose great technological changes. Industrial chemistry came into being and made great progress, and new methods for the manufacture of steel to make it increasingly more resistant and adaptable for a multitude of pressing industrial uses were evolved. The Bessemer and Martin processes for the smelting of iron and refining of steel not only made for increased steel production, thus augmenting the power of the steel magnates, but also permitted improvements in quality needed to satisfy the growing demands of the shipbuilding, railroad and heavy machinery industries. The eventual discovery of electrical energy gave growing industrial capitalism a cheap and adaptable source of power, alleviating the danger of exhausting natural fuels; and one, moreover, which could be easily taken to any part of the country. By 1850 the manufacture of machines and tools constituted a fundamental aspect of industrial development in the more advanced countries. Progress in this industry in turn was reflected in the prominent role played by the steel industry.

21.1.3. All of these changes caused a steady increase in capitalist enterprise. Between the middle and the end of the nineteenth century, capitalist enterprise, based on these techniques, had become infinitely more complex than at the beginning of the century. This enterprise then tended to eliminate all industry not having access to the use of the new machinery and techniques or unable to obtain the financial resources necessary to install them. The elimination of handicraft production also proceeded apace, this type of manufacture being replaced by the much cheaper mass production of the great mechanized factories.

In order to achieve this growth and concentration of industry, the banks had to participate more and more in the formation of capitalist enterprises. The banks themselves also underwent a process of concentration. In all of the more advanced countries their numbers decreased and those which survived became increasingly wealthier and more powerful. The banks used the great sums of money they had accumulated as a result of industrial growth in order to create gigantic enterprises, so complex that they could not possibly be financed by a single capitalist. The banks then benefited more and more from the profits of these enterprises which they had created or helped to create, thus increasing the volume and power of banking capital. This relation between industrial capital and banking capital coalesced into finance capital. So by the end of the nineteenth century, the economic power of the bourgeoisie was in the process of concentration into smaller and smaller groups of entrepreneurs and bankers, who became more and more powerful as time went on. This concentration marks an important development in the history of capitalism.

21.1.4. The finance capital which grew out of this process presents unique characteristics. It is a pooled capital of variously associated capitalists so as to control large sectors of the economy. Examples of this type of organization are trusts, capitalist syndicates and cartels, their common feature being the grouping together of capitalists who, through mutual agreements, control an entire branch of the economy of one or more countries.

This means that the development of finance capital entails the constitution of monopoly conditions in production and distribution. These conditions prevail not only in the country where the monopoly is located, but also in countries under its control. That is, monopoly conditions spread to moderately developed countries and to more backward ones, colonies or economic colonies. And as each group extends its influence, it becomes stronger in its competitive position. It is only detained by two factors. One of these —and a partial one— is the resistance and competition of similar groups which arise in the capitalist world. The other is the increasingly victorious struggle of the peoples to rid themselves of the monopoly system.

Monopoly capital, by virtue of its concentration, obtains greater and greater profits as a result of the exploitation of thousands and thousands of workers and of vast colonial territories. Under these conditions a mechanism arises which permits the monopolies to extend their power even further: the export of capital. The theorists of finance capital state that this exportation occurs when a country's development leads to an excess of capital which must be invested outside of the country. This attemps to furnish a justification for imperialism, which is the control of nations and territories by foreign capital. However, it is not true that there is excess capital, as Lenin points out in his classic work *Imperialism, the Highest Stage of Capitalism.* What happens is that the big capitalists seek higher profits through the exploitation of the masses of the underdeveloped countries, diverting the exported capital from the needs of the capitalist country itself. Indeed, even the most advanced capitalist countries still have room for investment in agriculture, not to speak of the great masses living in substandard conditions whose improvement would require the investment of great amounts of capital. But instead of taking on these problems, finance capital goes in search of ever increasing profits.

21.1.5. The United States, England, and Germany are the capitalist countries in which finance capital has developed most rapidly and most comprehensively since the last quarter of the nineteenth century. Lenin has used the statistics and theoretical formulations of each of these countries as indices of the inner working of imperialist development and as indications of its characteristics. The process, of course, is not limited to these countries. In other advanced countries, however, it developed later or more slowly and therefore did not reach the degree of consummation achieved in the countries mentioned. In France, for example, finance capital did appear, took over the economy and exploited colonial territories, but it never rose to such power as in Germany or England. In Russia there were manifestations of finance capitalism, but side by side with them backward feudal conditions prevailed, as in the case of agriculture.

Moreover, the process extended through only a small group of countries because one of monopoly imperialism's characteristics is that it holds back the development of those areas it penetrates. Therefore, a full-blown capitalist development could hardly have been possible in other countries, since the control of their production and markets by the minority of highly developed countries prevented this. And today this phenomenon has gone even further. Powerful United States imperialism exploits not only the backward countries but also other less powerful imperialist countries, such as England herself, France, West Germany and Japan.

21.2. *Colonialism*

21.2.1. The industrial revolution and the independence of America brought about the need for a new type of international organization based on world exploitation and its division among the more advanced countries. The conditions of capitalist development required forms of control different from those which predominated until the eighteenth century. And the transformation undergone by industry demanded increasing importation of raw materials and basic commodities, on the one hand, and ever greater exportation of industrial products, on the other. This was made possible by better transportation. Consequently, the most highly industrially developed countries began a fevered search for outside sources of raw materials and markets for their industrial products.

All through the nineteenth century colonialist activity, responding to the ambitions of growing capitalism, was intense. British capitalism not only revamped methods of exploitation in the colonies it had held since the eighteenth century, as with India and Canada, but also got a firm hold on Australia and equatorial Africa, where the character of its trade changed: instead of acquiring slaves to resell, it obtained industrial raw materials and began the production of basic commodities on plantations.

French capitalism launched new adventures in the hope of making up for the loss, in the 1700's, of its colonial empire. Starting in 1830, it went into Tunisia and Algeria, vied with Great Britain for the control of Egypt, took over Madagascar, and forcefully subjected Indo-China (Viet Nam) and New Caledonia.

Towards the decade of 1880-90, the great powers, such as Great Britain, France, and Germany, with the participation of the Netherlands and Belgium, divided Africa among themselves.

21.2.2. Even though the colonial powers had conflicting interests, they banded together to subject China and Japan to their will. Against China they organized the shameful intervention which went under the name of the Opium War (1840-42). The resistance of the traditionally nationalistic Chinese brought about an alliance between France and England, later joined by Tzarist Russia —an incipient colonial power— to partition China. These powers, later accompanied by Germany, secured commercial ports and naval stations in China by force. In the meantime, France was penetrating Indo-China.

In 1854, Japan was forced by U.S. Commodore Perry, under threat of bombardment, to open up her country to foreign trade with the highly developed nations.

America was not out of the picture in this violent colonialism. However, her process was somewhat different, disguised as it was as colonization and exploitation of the great plains and the West of the United States. Latin America, on the other hand, saw the colonization and exploitation of the Argentine pampas and British financial penetration into many countries in South America. Millions of European immigrants settled in these territories on the free land and became advance agents of capitalist penetration.

Local wars occurred, as that of Texas, where the United States snatched a great part of Mexico's territory away from her. There was also a growing rivalry between the United States and England for control of the Gulf of Mexico and South America.[2]

21.2.3. The coming into being of finance capital intensified the the struggle for world control among the imperialist powers, notwithstanding the fact that nineteenth century colonialism, prior to the imperialist era, had left practically no scrap of world territory unclaimed by the predominant capitalist groups.

The only way, then, to resolve the contradictions of interest among the more powerful countries was war in which one country tried to aggregate to itself the economic resources of another. These wars were at times economic: tariff wars, the imposition of commercial treaties on weaker countries, the granting of economic aid or advantage to other nations with a view to blocking penetration of competing capital therein, etc. But all of these "peaceful" methods eventually led to ruinous wars.

Japan waged the first imperialist war in 1894, against China, bringing on the intervention of the other powers, especially Russia, to prevent Japan from taking over all of China's wealth for herself. The Spanish-American war of 1898, in which the United States' pretext for participation was the liberation of Cuba, was another early imperialist war and one which opened the gates for United States expansion in America and Asia. Another was the Boer War, through which British imperialist interests took over South Africa.

21.2.4. Greater conflagrations were in store, however, since Germany, who had reached the peak of capitalist development in the late nineteenth century, had no colonies. She had participated in the plunder of China and penetrated economically in some areas but aside from negligible holdings in Africa and the Pacific, she held no colonial territory. She therefore launched an offensive in North Africa and, in general, against British interests the world over. European history after 1900 is marked with crisis arising among these various interests, who fought among themselves not only over colonial possessions, but also over the control of the less developed areas of Europe, such as the Balkans. In the end, the First World War broke out, lasting from 1914 to 1918 and resulting in the crushing of Germany and the annihilation of the Austro-Hungarian Empire. This war's toll of millions of dead, wounded and handicapped for work, of thousands of cities and towns destroyed, hundreds of ships sunk, constitutes one of the most horrible episodes in human history. As a result of this war, the United States, who had taken part against Germany in its final phase, became the chief creditor of the European countries, since she had come to their aid by selling them arms and food. Also she effectively became the creditor of defeated Germany, since the "Peace" of Versailles obliged that country to pay thousands of millions of dollars as war damages to the allies (France, Belgium, and England).

Living conditions at this point produced profound people's protest movements, and the first socialist state appeared in the USSR (1917-18). Contradictions sharpened, since the general crisis of capitalism, becoming acute with the great world depression of 1929-32, brought a resurgence of Germany's aspirations. There, the discontent and misery of the people provided a springboard for action on the part of the most reactionary capitalists, who financed the Nazi movement headed by Hitler. In Italy, shortly after the First World War, the reactionary bourgeosie, threatened by the vigorous popular movement which had sprung up, brought Mussolini's fascism to power. Japan, in the meantime, was attempting to extend her influence in Asia and entered into an alliance with Germany and Italy against the bloc constituted by the United States, France and England. Thus the Second World War originated. But this time a new factor entered into play: the Soviet Union had become consolidated as a socialist state.

The entrance of the USSR into the war when the Nazi government invaded her territory was a decisive element in the triumph of the democratic forces throughout the world. The German invaders suffered a crushing defeat in the Soviet Union.

The end of the war was succeeded by changes in the balance of world social forces. The socialist camp, previously limited to the USSR, spread out to include Czechoslovakia, Poland, Rumania, East Germany, Hungary, and China. The immediate effect of these changes was that capitalism lost a substantial part of its forces. Another result of the war was to give the United States hegemony of the capitalist world, which certainly did not eliminate the contradictions within imperialism but did impart to them a new form.

21.3. *Socialism*

The growth of the socialist camp was a vital blow to the capitalist system. In the period before the Second World War, the Soviet regime had proved that a socialist economy not only could survive, but that it was the most effective way to overcome the problems of economic underdevelopment and improve the living conditions of the masses. The five-year plans rapidly put the USSR in a position to reach production levels very similar to those of the most highly developed capitalist countries. Moreover, the rate of growth in the USSR far surpassed the rate of growth in capitalist economies where a marked tendency toward stagnation was observable.

The incorporation of China and the European peoples democracies into the socialist camp set limits on imperialist control. The capitalist powers began to find the colonial peoples more and more resolute in opposing their ambitious attempts. The aid and example of world socialism stimulated these peoples to wage continous battles for liberation, especially in Asia and Africa. In America, the Cuban revolution showed the epic force of the peoples when guided by socialist ideals.

Between the Paris Commune of 1871, the first attempt to set up a Socialist and truly democratic state, and today, the world situation has changed substantially. The days are past when a small group of capitalists could bring the world under their control and divide it among themselves despite the loss of innumerable lives and the existence of infinite misery. [3]

BIBLIOGRAPHY

1. BIRNIE, ARTHUR. *Historia económica de Europa* (1760-1933), 2nd ed. Mexico. Havana. 1963.
2. JVOSTOV, V. M. AND ZUBOK, L. I. *Historia contemporánea,* Havana, 1963.
3. REVUNENKOV, V. G. *Historia de los tiempos actuales* (1917-1957) ; Havana, 1963.

CHAPTER XXII

THE BASIS OF IMPERIALIST DOMINATION

22.1. *Events until 1903*

22.1.1. The new stage of Cuba's history is framed within a process of great transformations within the capitalist system dealt with in the preceding chapter. All industrially advanced countries present a similar development, as England, France and Germany. The same is true of the United States.

What had happened in the United States? In the first place, its territory had been aggressively extended; originally, it consisted only of a narrow strip of land along the Atlantic coast, which had been colonized by the English. The United States extended towards the interior of what today constitutes its territory, that is, towards the west; it obtained Louisiana and Florida through negotiations and finally gained Texas, by means of an abusive war of depredation. It also extended towards the south, going as far as the Gulf of Mexico.

Each of these steps emphasized even more the aggressive and expansive plans of the ruling class and of United States political leaders. The last stage of all this process was the War of Secession (1861-65), whose real motive was beyond that of liberating the slaves of the southern United States, that is, the establishment of the hegemony of the northern states. Definitely that war ended in the triumph of the northern part of the country (the industrialized one) with the states having a larger capitalist development than the southern ones (agricultural, feudal latifundist, using African slave labor). The war ended with the triumph of the North, but this was not simply the victory of a political group over another group within the nation; in reality, the northern forces occupied the South as a conquered country. During some years the South played the role of a conquered zone that was becoming transformed into an appendix attached to the industrial North.

When this war ended, the great industrial development accelerated. The United States rapidly marched towards an economic organization which in a few short years, reached the height of its old metropolis, Great Britain, which had had the largest capitalist development during a century and a half. As a result of this organized development, the phenomenon of industrial concentration took place: an economic concentration that was perfectly illustrated by the presence of great railroad companies derived from the union of independent companies, the trust of sugar refineries, the great steel mills and the large banks. Financial capital came into being. Also, within that period (1880-1890), the first imperialist type of investments in Cuba began.

The economic evolution of Cuba led to ever closer commercial relations between Cuba and the United States during the end of the nineteenth century. It can be stated that Cuba was the first great market of the growing United States capitalism.

When the United States was still a country where large English investments were made during the nineteenth century, already the Baltimore, New York, and Boston businessmen had sugar credit investments in Cuba. This credit was fundamentally given for the purpose of supplying slaves on credit, the supply of sugar industrial machinery and advanced payments (actual financing) on the sugar that the United States businessmen bought in Cuba to supply the eastern market of the United States, as well as the import of the United States products into Cuba. These trade relations favored the establishment in Cuba of

United States citizens who bought and operated some mills, as well as large commercial houses. But such relations changed radically when the sugar refining industry of eastern United States concentrated itself from a financial point of view aiming at the exclusive purchase of its raw material, unrefined sugar, from Cuba, since the year 1880.

22.1.2. It was then that the direct United States investments in the sugar industry of Cuba began. Along with these sugar investments, there were others, such as in the mining industry. The interests of the United States refining industries and the interests of the United States investors in Cuba joined in such a way that the latter become allied to and an appendix of the former. Likewise, these interests allied themselves with the manufacturers of export articles to Cuba. Towards 1895, the United States had invested approximately $50,000,000 in Cuba.

During the War of 1895, the Cuban cause became popular among the people of the eastern United States, who immediately sympathized with it and with the exploits of the liberators. But this popular sympathy would soon be vitiated by the economic interests who profited from their businesses and investments in Cuba. Havemeyer, who was the visible head of the great United States sugar trust, even said at a certain moment, that the stockholders of his enterprise would be sufficient to draw Cuba under United States domination, clearly indicating that if the United States would agree, the economic interest groups would act by themselves. The campaign in favor of the rebel Cuban people transformed itself into a campaign in favor of the United States groups interested in subjecting Cuba. All the ultra-reactionary United States jingoism displayed itself through the press, in the Senate and all the executive bodies of the United States government with the object of vitiating the popular sentiments, [2] leading the public opinion towards expansionist objectives.

22.1.3. The repressive policy of Weyler was, without doubt, the first pretext to introduce interventionist plans, arguing that the United States could not permit the crimes that the Spanish colonial government was committing in the small, rebellious island. Two incidents, which took place at the beginning of 1898 definitely triggered off the jingoist campaign. The first was the publication of a letter that Dupuy de Lome, Spain's Ambassador to Washington, wrote to the Spanish politician Canalejas, during his visit to Havana. This letter, although written with all the rancor of the defeated Spanish aristocracy, made a just appraisal of Mr. McKinley when he called him a politicaster.[3] In connection with this letter, a press campaign was begun which pretended to raise the United States war spirit. The other incident was the explosion of the United States cruiser *Maine* which had been sent to Havana on a "courtesy" visit at the same time that in the United States ports there were some ships of the Spanish Navy on a similar visit. The *Maine* exploded mysteriously on February 15, 1898, an incident used by the U.S. propaganda to blame Spain, although from the moment it occurred, there were United States authorities who testified against that possibility. Better still, this great disaster must be attributed to the interventionist interests that took advantage of it to unleash a war.

Towards the end of March 1898, President McKinley presented an ultimatum to Spain. Even though there were official manifestations that seemed to have a pacifist desire, the aggressive Theodore Roosevelt, Under-Secretary of the Navy, had already taken the necessary measures to prepare for war. It is logical that the warmongers would not accept any explanation on the part of Spain, and McKinley, in one of the characteristic maneuvres that United States governments perform at the moment in which they must decide on international problems, sent a message to Congress, putting the matter presented by Spain into their hands. The Congress, already sufficiently committed to the warlike campaign, declared by the Joint Resolution of April 20, that Cuba was and had the right to be independent; but in another paragraph, where it should have recognized the validity of the Cuban revolutionary forces, the Teller Amendment was introduced, which announced and justified the United States military intervention with the sole objective of "pacifying" the island.

It is not our intention to relate the incidents of the war here. In Felipe Martínez Arango's work the principal aspects can be studied. Among them it is necessary to emphasize the decisive role played by the Cuban liberators in the military triumph that the United States generals attributed to themselves.

The surrender of the Spanish forces at Santiago de Cuba put an end to the hostilities that officially ended with the Treaty of Paris, signed on December 11, 1898.

22.1.4. United States military interventionist policy was aimed at the creation of political mechanisms that would favor economic penetration. The first thing was to disarm the people in the cities as well as the liberation army.

Throughout the government of General Brook, established in 1899, there was a clear manifestation of a Cuban sentiment contrary to the annexationist solution. This sentiment was specially expressed each time the constitution of a civil foreign interventionist government became the matter of discussion, since this type of government meant permanency of the occupation by the United States. Even though the appointment of Leonard Wood as military governor represents, towards the end of 1899, the triumph of the aggressive annexationists. These forces, afraid of the possible competition of the Cuban products, were also very powerful and kept Congress and the government in a state of uncertainty.

On December 5, 1899, in a message to Congress, President McKinley took the first steps towards the policy of subjecting Cuba, based on the formal maintenance of an "independent" Republic. By this means, without annexation, the interests who were in favor of this solution were satisfied. For McKinley, Cuba had to be necessarily linked to the United States by special relations, be they organic or conventional. The future should decide whether the destiny of Cuba would irrevocably be united to the United States. The reference to the "conventional links" in the message clearly indicated that a formula was already being prepared which was later confirmed by the imposition of the Platt Amendment. Leonard Wood had been selected to enforce the policy without hesitation. When the year 1900 had just begun he set himself to "conquer" the spirit of the Cubans. His first attempt was not successful, since the assembly of outstanding personalities that he had planned had to be held by sectors. His meeting with the Generals of Cuba's Independence proved their great resistance to and suspicion of the United States policy. General Bartolomé Masó's position in relation to this matter was firm and outstanding. The rest of the year 1900 was used to hold the first elections for municipal posts, in order to organize the three parties: the *Nacional,* in Havana; the *Republicano* in Las Villas and the *Unión Democrática* also in Havana. Even though there were no marked differences in the program of the first two, the *Nacional* party represented the group that had taken sides with the attitude adopted by Major General Máximo Gómez, in favor of disarming the liberators in exchange for $75.00 for each rifle and the *Republicano* party of Las Villas represented, to a certain point, a more radical group which inclined itself to the Assembly of Cerro, contrary to disarmament in the way proposed by the United States government. In those elections there were many regional-type groupings. The *Unión Democrática* party represented the conservative side, as it assembled many of the autonomist elements allied to a certain number of old partisans of independence.

The elections were held under a law that restricted the vote to Cubans who could read and write or those that had at least $250,000 in properties or had served in the liberation army.

The policy of the government of Washington followed a preconceived plan that included the visit to Havana of the Secretary of War, Elihu Root, with the customary commission of senators formed by Platt, apparent father of the Amendment; Aldrich, who had participated and would also participate in the senatorial discussion on the economic relations with Cuba; Teller, who proposed an amendment to the Joint Resolution promoting the annexationist thesis; and Phelps. This commission held a series of interviews with the principal leaders of the Cuban radical group; even though they limited themselves to stating that they would have to inform the government of Washington, they were able to detect the profound division of opinion that existed within the Cuban political panorama. On the other hand, Wood was recalled to Washington and his trip, though the objective was not officially expressed, caused much public comment, above all, due to the fact that some ideas of the government of Washington leaked out, that is, that they were studying to "solve" the problem of the military occupation.

All speculation became clear when, by decree of July 25, 1900, Wood called a meeting for a constituent assembly.

What verified the suspicion of the Cuban radicals was a paragraph of the decree which pointed out the following as the objective of the Constituent Assembly: "draw and adopt a constitution for the people of Cuba, and as part of it, provide, in accordance with the government of the United States, the matters in connection with the relations that were to exist between the government of the United States and Cuba". This paragraph makes explicitly clear McKinley's message of December 5, 1899. A wave of protest immediately spread. A meeting of all the parties was called and they agreed to protest to McKinley; the *Nacional* party, although present, did not stand by the agreement which, suspiciously, was never sent to McKinley.

The elections were held on September 15, 1900, choosing the proprietor-members and their corresponding substitutes, and on Monday, November 5, the work of the Constituent Assembly began. Very soon, within its body, there was a general feeling that the relations with the United States was not a matter to be discussed, due to the fact that it had nothing particularly to do with the Constitution. It is not necessary to outline the incidents of this assembly in connection with the drawing up of the constitutional text. Immediate resistance on the part of the liberal group, was expressed by Manuel Sanguily, Juan Gualberto Gómez and Salvador Cisneros Betancourt who voted for all the liberal solutions in each of the debates. The Constitution was signed on February 21, 1901.

Immediately the relations with the United States became a matter of discussion in the report committee, stating its opposition to consider the principles of such relations a constitutional appendix, indicating that the government of the Republic to be constituted in the future should sign a treaty with the government of the United States to formalize these "special" links. To curb the Cuban patriotic resistance, the Congress of the United States decided to approve as part of a law an appendix that the Cubans did not accept.

Although the legislative period was just ending, the procedure to introduce this text as an amendment to the law of the United States Army's budget was adopted, an amendment which consisted of what in the United States corrupt parliamentary practice is called a "rider" and in the no less corrupt Cuban parliamentary practice was called a "percha". Such an amendment, drafted by Elihu Root and proposed by Senator Platt was approved on March 2, 1901. The Washington government informed the Cuban radicals that, in fulfillment of what the Congress had decided, the occupation was not to be recognized as ended as long as the Platt Amendment was not accepted as a constitutional appendix, since it was thus established by the law approved by the Congress. In one of his multiple "sweetening" declarations, Root affirmed that the amendment had only a relative value, since all it contained was actions that the United States could perfom without a specific law; but that the United States government needed the Platt Amendment in order to guarantee itself, before the other nations, the "right" to subject Cuba. This traditional policy of the United States of disguising its acts of violence under supposed consecrated rights in international negotiations is well known by all.

The report committee of the constituent convention remained firm, especially because of Juan Gualberto Gómez' attitude. But the reaction of the government in Washington was final, demanding that the Cubans should not modify a single word of the Amendment and should purely and simply accept it, without discussion.

A few radicals of the constituent convention thought of yielding before the overwhelming force, and finally, on June 12, 1901, the Platt Amendment was passed by a very small majority.

The Platt Amendment later became a permanent treaty between Cuba and the United States on May 2, 1903. Prior to this, on February 23, 1903, the treaty leasing the military and naval bases was signed. This was one of the objectives pursued by the government in Washington in its policy to subject Cuba, and whose remnant is the naval base at Caimanera. The best analysis of the process and the meaning of the Platt Amendment was expressed by General Wood in the following way: "Of course, Cuba has been left with little or no independence by the Platt Amendment... and the only thing to do now is to look for annexation. This, nevertheless, would require some time and during the period in which Cuba maintains its own government it is very desirable that it have one that will conduct its progress and development. It cannot enter into certain treaties without our consent, nor secure loans above certain limits, and it must maintain the sanitary conditions which have been indicated. All of this makes it evident that Cuba is absolutely in our hands and I believe that no European government would consider it otherwise: a real dependent of the United States and, as such we should consider it. With the control that we have over Cuba, a control which, without doubt, will soon turn her into our possession, soon we will practically control the sugar market of the world. I believe that it is a very desirable acquisition for the United States. The island will be gradually 'Americanized', and in due course we will have one of the most rich and desirable possessions existing in the world..."

Speaking in the same vein, General Wilson, ex-governor of our province of Matanzas until 1902, in a speech published in the magazine "Cuba and America" said: "ten years will not elapse without having the Republic of Cuba feel the fear that will cause the end of the provisional arrangement (commercial) and ask for its admission into the Union; I cannot keep myself from stating that it is my belief that this period will justify that it is worthy of such fortune". Wilson was a "sweet" annexationist because he considered that Cuba would be worthy of being annexed.

The treaty of reciprocity was introduced during the process of the United States military occupation in a very peculiar way. First, the military government of occupation approved tax reductions on United

States imports to Cuba in 1898, 1899 and 1900, reductions that were not compensated by an equal percentage on Cuban exports to the United States.

The policy of economic control in Cuba was made to depend on the definite establishment of the instruments for imperialist domination of Cuba. The United States government first adopted a line of action based on the political status of Cuba, and later decided on the basic line of economic submission. If the political decision meant annexation, there would not be any need for specific economic measures to perpetuate the Cuban submission. If the political decision was to disguise the annexation by means of the Platt Amendment, there would evidently be a need for an economic penetration mechanism.

The annexationists were opposed by the United States beet and tobacco growers' interests, whose privileged position in the domestic market made possible by the tariff of 1890 and 1897 ran the danger of being strongly hurt by Cuba's evidently extraordinary sugar and tobacco production capacity. However, solution through annexation had the enthusiastic approval of financial interests (individual investors, banks, trusts, exporters) moved by the great possibility for profits that could be gained by the development of the Cuban economy at the service of financial United States capital. It is clear that the political thesis of domination was surrounded by arguments which were not precisely economic. There were those who maintained that Cuba should be annexed due to the fact that it lacked a civilized people capable of living in liberty; others considered that the "security" of the United States, very interested in dominating all the "American Mediterranean", so demanded. There was some "Superman", who had the idea that Cuba could be a colony utilized to receive the Negro inhabitants of the United States and to produce raw materials at a very low cost, based on miserable salaries. Others went so far as to state that the United States' "mission" in Cuba was God's will.

The problem of reciprocity, though raised since the year 1898, had a colonial background; the rationale made by Spanish government officials in 1897, offered the opportunity to designate an ambassador of Spain to Washington (March 17, 1898) along with the representatives of the autonomous government of Cuba, to initiate the negotiations in order to sign a treaty of reciprocity. Nevertheless, this project was never again brought up until Cuba's opposition to the Platt Amendment became manifest. Undoubtedly, the government of Washington as well as the military authorities in Cuba, specially Leonard Wood, were in favor of dominating the Cuban economy by means of a mechanism based on "reciprocity"; but both sides considered that the political question was a prerequiste to "guarantee" the investors and the United States businessmen a situation that would permit them to operate their businesses in Cuba at will. For this reason, the proposed treaty of reciprocity was presented as a concession by the United States to Cuba as compensation for the acceptance of the Platt Amendment. The double fraud was evident, since the Platt Amendment as well as the "reciprocity" tended to benefit United States capital and its allies, the Cuban mill owners, but not the people of Cuba. It is not strange that in the year 1901 the United States army of occupation would reach the maximum of its excesses by using Cuban funds to finance the propaganda made in the United States in favor of the reciprocity; a propaganda principally displayed by the Association of Exporters of the United States. This means that the United States authorities were the ones who promoted the matter in connivance with the Cuban mill owners.

It is not a mere coincidence that, at the moment in which the report committee of the Constituent Assembly was debating the problems raised by the Platt Amendment, (March, April and May of 1901), a movement was begun by some Cuban organizations such as the Mill Owners' Circle and the Economic Society of Friends of the Nation in favor of the Platt Amendment and, of course, of the reciprocity. On this occasion, the circle of mill owners, in a statement made December 30, 1899 to the military governor, asked for "free trade" with the United States (that is, annexation) and if this were not possible at that moment, to set up duties on the basis of reciprocity, established by the McKinley law of 1890.

In this atmosphere of propaganda favoring reciprocity the commission of the Constituent Assembly, formed by Méndez Capote, who presided it, Portuondo, Tamayo, and González Llorente, visited Washington. During interviews with Elihu Root they stated, on two occasions, the need for a solution that, logically, consisted of establishing tariff reciprocity. The Cuban request brought forth the usual declarations of good will as well as Washington's insistence that the Platt Amendment be approved as a previous step.

The Platt Amendment having been accepted, the problem of reciprocity mentioned by Estrada Palma in his program letter of September 7, 1901 continued being a matter of discussion.

On October 9, 1901, a public demonstration took place in Havana in favor of the reciprocity treaty and immediately a special commission was sent to Washington, composed of the representatives of the mill owners whose purpose was to encourage the negotiations.

Theodore Roosevelt having substituted President McKinley, who had been assassinated, sent a message to Congress at the end of that year requesting the study and solution of the question of reciprocity with Cuba, arguing the usual "moral duties" and the need to strengthen the Cuban economy.

When it was submitted to Congress, the matter found a very strong resistance on the part of the beet growers' interests, and the bill was shelved in the Senate. Roosevelt then decided to negotiate the treaty of reciprocity with the government-elect of Cuba, submitting on July 4, 1902 a draft treaty to the Ambassador of Cuba in Washington, Gonzalo de Quesada. On October 18 the government of Cuba presented its counter-proposals and days later, in November, the government of Washington appointed General Tasker H. Bliss to negotiate in Havana, while the government of Cuba appointed two of its cabinet secretaries. Two meetings were enough for the Cuban negotiators to accept the conditions presented by the foreign government.[8]

Consequently, the treaty was signed on December 11, 1902, subject to ratification by the U.S. Congress and the Cuban Senate. The former did not approve it until December 17, 1903, going into effect on December 27.

The mechanism of "reciprocity" established in this treaty consisted of the following:

First: The products that had entered duty free into the United States would continue enjoying the benefits of this freedom.

Second: A series of Cuban articles established on a special list would enjoy, when imported by the United States, a preferential tariff 20% lower than the tariff applied to similar products coming from other American or European countries.

Third: The U.S. products specified in the list, would enjoy, when imported by Cuba, preferential tariff ranging between 25% and 40%.

Fourth: The tariff could be increased but always having a preferential margin, and

Fifth: The preferences agreed on in this treaty could not be extended to any other country since it constituted a special treatment, different from those traditionally known as the *most favoured nation clause*.

22.1.5. We have made reference to United States investments in Cuba prior to 1898. Let us take a look at how things developed until 1902 under the military government of occupation. There had been not only one army of occupation in Cuba but several after the surrender of the Spanish army in Santiago de Cuba, and one, especially, showed the Cubans what kind of new dominating power ruled the country. Charles M. Pepper offers a very important testimony on the army of promoters, profiteers, colonizers, drunks, and cheaters of all kinds who landed like a predatory rear guard when Leonard Wood took charge of the government of the eastern region of Cuba. These are the ones mentioned by Sanguily in an outstanding paragraph of his speech against the treaty of reciprocity.[9]

The scandal re-echoed in certain United States sectors who did not favor the annexation, considering it harmful to their interests. For this reason, in March 1899, a "rider" was added to the budget of the army (the same was to occur in 1901 with the Platt Amendment). Such is the origin of the Foraker Amendment, which prohibited the concessions for exploitation of natural resources or the economic activities of enterprises or individual United States entrepreneurs. Naturally, this "unselfish" provision, as Leland H. Jenks ironically termed it, was opposed by Mark Hanna, an old enemy of Foraker in the political struggle for leadership in Ohio, and skillful handler of the political stage where, due to his wealth, he was a political sponsor in several elections including McKinley's, whom he supported, thus ensuring his victory.[10]

Of course, that "unselfishness" did not go beyond the letter of the Foraker Amendment, since, in fact, the United States promoters and entrepreneurs were given a free rein in the conquered Island. Suffice is to mention what occurred with the mining concessions, which was clearly stated in the military order of February 8, 1900, excluding them from the established prohibition in the Foraker Amendment. No less interesting is what happened with the concession of the central railroad. When Van Horne, an international railroad tycoon, began to plan a unified system of Cuba's railway lines, he found himself faced by the Foraker prohibition, and after a personal interview with McKinley came to Cuba and easily solved this difficulty. It was argued that the provision prohibited the concessions but did not prohibit the *provisonal* authorizations and above all did not prohibit a private owner selling a strip of land to any railroad company. Of course, the provisional authorization, since it was a railroad investment, was a concession in fact, that the future Republican government of Cuba would have to recognize and ratify by all means. Otherwise, it would have to indemnify the railroad company for the road, the stations, and the equipment.

In no way this looting of Cuba's resources and exploitation of her manpower can be considered as exceptional. The dastardly intrigue of Panama took place under the same United States government. General Wilson said in his aforementioned speech, that if the Latin American countries agreed to the establishment of a commercial union with the United States, they would sell their raw materials and "would buy the major part of the products from our factories". This was the imperialist dream disguised under benevolent words while Teddy Roosevelt wielded the "Big Stick".

Suffice it to say that the United States military occupation was an accelerating stage of the imperialist investments.

BIBLIOGRAPHY

1. NEARING, SCOTT. *El imperio americano,* Havana, 1961.
2. JENKS, LELAND H. *Nuestra Colonia de Cuba,* Madrid, 1929.
3. BOLETÍN DEL ARCHIVO NACIONAL. Havana, LXI, January-December, 1962.
4. MARTÍNEZ ARANGO, FELIPE. *Cronología de la guerra hispano-cubana-norteamericana,* Havana, 1958.
5. MARTÍNEZ ORTIZ, RAFAEL. *Los primeros años de la independencia,* 2 vols. Havana, 1927.
6. ROIG DE LEUCHSENRING, EMILIO. *Historia de la Enmienda Platt,* 2 vols. Havana, 1935.
7. SPEECH BY GENERAL WILSON "Cuba and America", Havana, 1902.
8. MARTÍNEZ ORTIZ, RAFAEL. *Op. cit.*
9. PEPPER, CHARLES M. *Tomorrow in Cuba,* New York, 1899.
   SANGUILY, MANUEL. "El tratado de reciprocidad", *La lucha anti-imperialista en Cuba,* vol. 1, Havana, 1960.
10. FLYN, JOHN T. "Hanna. El hombre que hacía presidentes", *Bohemia* magazine, Havana, October 23, 1949.

CHAPTER XXIII

IMPERIALIST PENETRATION AND ITS EFFECTS

23.1. *Principal Events until 1925*

23.1.1. Without a doubt, at that time and more so later, the principal group of United States investments in Cuba were made mainly in the sugar industry. We have outlined the ways in which the United States capital was invested in Cuba during the second half of the nineteenth century. We pointed out as well that when the United States refining industry transformed itself into a trust during the 1880's, under the aggressive initiative of Mr. Havemeyer, the nature of United States investments in Cuba changed. In the future, these would be direct investments of financial capital with a definite policy that would completely respond to the interests of the United States industry. Edwin Atkins is considered the pioneer in this type of investment. In 1883, he foreclosed the Soledad mill in the zone of Cienfuegos. This movement begun by Atkins became widespread as a result of the McKinley tariff of 1890. In fact, the McKinley tariff tended to violently eradicate from the United States market the best-quality sugar imported from Cuba, to which higher tariffs were applied, while favoring a reduction of the duties on raw sugar that constituted the raw material needed for the refining industry. The United States capitalists realized that it was a prosperous business to produce raw sugar in Cuba. On the other hand, this action left Cuba totally subjected to the United States industrial needs; consequently, many of the Cuban producers that could not supply raw sugar as needed by the refining trust, went into a crisis and were eliminated in the concentration process of the sugar industry.

Other financial groups followed in Atkins' footsteps.

Atkins himself, allied to Havemeyer in 1892, acquired lands where he installed the Trinidad sugar mill (Central Escambray) built from ten inactive mills between 1868 and 1890 and later bought more lands which contributed to the disappearance of a small number of mills that were left in the zone. The Rionda family, who in 1893 went into business under the name of Tuinicú Sugar Company, acquired in 1899 the Francisco Sugar mill (now called Amancio Rodríguez) and in 1910 the Washington sugar mill (today's George Washington).

In 1899 the group named Hawley appeared on the scene, organizing the Cuban-American Sugar Company, owner of Mercedes and Tinguaro sugar mills (now 6 de Agosto and Sergio González, respectively) in Matanzas. In 1901 they also obtained a refinery in Cárdenas, the only one in Cuba at the time.

Of course, they took the precaution of engaging General Mario García Menocal as their agent in the country, who recommended the purchase of 1900 *caballerías* (63,333 acres) in the north of the province of Oriente, where Chaparra sugar mill (today's Jesús Menéndez) was built. This company grew with the addition of new holdings, constituting in 1910 a true "holding company" with 11,000,000 shares of stock issued. It should be emphasized that Hawley was a member of Congress during the period of the Spanish-Cuban-United States War, representing the State of Texas.

Moreover, the United Fruit Company which had been growing since the decade of the 1880's with plantation businesses in Central America and the trade of bananas in the United States market, had previous links with the Cuban banana zone of northern Oriente, where the Messieurs Dumois were outstanding businessmen and planters.

Logically, it invested in the zone, known to be fertile for this type of crop, and for this reason in 1901 acquired near Nipe, at a ridiculously low price, 2,200 *caballerías* (73,333 acres) for a mill called Preston (today's Guatemala sugar mill). As a result of this penetration, there were 29 sugar mills owned by U.S. citizens in 1905 whose production amounted to 21% of Cuba's total sugar crop. The voracity of the great companies and its Cuban allies, (landowners, and politicians) was unlimited to such an extent that veterans of the War of Independence who were established on State lands (Zavala and Cebolla in Oriente) were driven off.

On the one hand, this grabbing of the best lands, especially in Camagüey and Oriente, created a difficult agrarian situation by reducing the possibility of a diversified agricultural development and greatly limiting the purchase of lands by the Cubans. That is, the only bourgeois land owners who could and did exist, and as a matter of fact, were linked to the sugar mills in a progressive dependency, were those of the cane growers. The rural population had to become proletarians. Towards 1915, a witness who could not be suspected of being radical used to say that the small farms were decreasing, that every day there were fewer farms and fewer *haciendas* due to the action of the powerful companies. On the other hand, to obtain cheap labor, the great sugar interests imported laborers from Jamaica and Haiti, as well as from other countries, such as India, and even Russia and Norway. The Agrarian League organized in 1905 was the spokesman for the Cuban sugar producers who proposed this reactionary solution to the demographic problem produced by the great death toll of the War of Independence (1895-1898). [1] In 1912, the "Promotion of Immigration Society" advocating the same policy and formed by landowners, shipowners, and other interests, was founded.

Furthermore, the rising emphasis on the production of sugar, a trend that increased during World War I, transformed Cuba into a country whose essential imports were foodstuffs.

Agricultural and cattle-raising lands were exclusively devoted to cane, while United States' and other countries' products flooded the nation.

23.1.2. In the agricultural sector there were other direct United States investments governed by the motto "we must 'Americanize' Cuba". This means that a real U.S. colonization campaign had started. The aforementioned landowners were located in almost every province, especially on the Isle of Pines. At that time a magazine called "Cuba Review" was published, in charge of promoting this movement. The preference for the Isle of Pines explains itself since at all times during the years of the United States occupation and the beginning of the controlled Republic, the United States government reserved the definition of the status of that island for a later occasion. This was due to the fact that the United States naval and military circles on the island considered it important from a strategic point of view and wanted to reserve it in order to establish one or several naval bases there.

In 1905 there were around 13,000 United States farmers who owned land amounting to $50,000,000. They had spread throughout the whole country, although the majority owned lands on the Isle of Pines.

The farmers of the Isle of Pines distinguished themselves by the stir they made against the authorities of the controlled Republic. They organized a movement in order not to recognize the authorities, not to pay taxes, and to demand from the United States government that the Isle of Pines be annexed to the United States. It was a movement that coincided with all other annexationist-type plans. The government in Washington definitely lost interest in establishing naval bases on the Isle of Pines; nevertheless, the recognition that the island formed an integral part of the territory of Cuba was not made until the treaty of 1924.

The investments in the tobacco trade were of great significance, since they contributed to set an example as to how the tobacco trust penetrated into Cuba, as had happened in the sugar industry. The first step consisted in the sale of the interests of F. García and Bros. to the commercial enterprise known as the Havana Commercial Company (in 1900). In 1902, the American Tobacco Company, a United States trust, and also a branch of Havana Commercial Company, acquired a number of trade marks and industries as well.

The tobacco trust operated on the basis that the Cuban and Spanish-Cuban owners who sold this product could not establish new manufacturing plants or link themselves to the tobacco business; through this procedure the possible competition from factory owners who were skilled and well-known in this specific trade would be eliminated.

In 1903, the larger part of the important brands were in the hands of the trust that during the early years of the Republic controlled 85% to 90% of the total cigar exports.

The mining investments were the first to take place in the established chronological order, since already in 1883, the *Juraguá Iron Company*, a branch of the *Bethlehem Iron Works* of Pennsylvania, was constituted. In 1889, it purchased the great Daiquirí ore deposits. *The Sigua Iron Company* was founded in 1894. And in 1889 they established the *Spanish-American Iron Company* that was later acquired by the *Bethlehem Iron Works* in 1916.

With these investments and with the mining concessions that were obtained by the United States interests during the military occupation and in the early years of the controlled Republic, practically all the principal supplying sources of iron that the steel industry of eastern United States needed were owned by imperialist capital. The United States enterprises controlled no less than 80% of the minerals exported during the early years of the Republic. The larger part was in the hands of the above-mentioned Bethlehem Company which, in addition, acquired the so called *Ponupo Manganese Company*.

United States capital was also interested in the transportation business, where they used the financial means and decisive influence of Van Horne. Van Horne understood that the great business of the moment consisted in integrating all the independent railroad lines that had existed in the Spanish colonial period and set upon the task of promoting this idea, reaching his goal in a brief period. Consequently, in 1899, the *Cuban Central Railway Limited* was founded. Later, in 1908, the *Cuban Eastern Railroad* was established. In keeping with the role which it had played during the sugar development period, the railway business was fundamentally expanded to handle sugar transportation, rather than towards general Cuban production. This implies a close link between the two groups of investors, as many of the companies devoted to both sectors were financially related.

23.1.3. The United States banks did not immediately come to Cuba. In any case, they did so slowly. Logically, private banking was never an instrument of economic promotion, but rather the rear guard in the development of a zone or a region. In 1901, the *North American Trust Company* began to operate under the innocent name of the National Bank of Cuba. There was nothing national about it, and it was the financial institution which had the closest relations with the various governments until the crisis of 1920-21. Its president, Mr. Merchant, was a man of great influence in the life of the country during those years. This bank obtained from the occupation government the handling of all the state accounts, and in addition, played the role of attorney and paying agent, a privilege it maintained for several years. Its financial privileges permitted the spread of its branch offices throughout the whole country, as well as the payment of fat dividends.

In 1906, the *Bank of Nova Scotia* was established. However, the large banking movement did not rapidly develop until 1915, a period when an extraordinary sugar expansion took place. As we shall see later on, between that year and the crisis of 1920-21, the United States and British banks managed to control almost all of the sugar industry.

Right after the constitution of the controlled Republic, United States banks penetrated into Cuba by means of loans. The first important operation was the $35,000,000 loan to pay the army of liberation. The loan was made by Speyer and Company of New York. What we must emphasize concerning this operation (the birth of a system used by United States imperialists time and time again in order to give the reward demanded by the submitted governments for their shameful traffic with the national interests), is the fact that the above-mentioned Bank had complete official support, from President Roosevelt down to the least important government official. The secret lay upon the personal friendship of the President of the United States with Mr. Speyer, as well as on the fact that Elihu Root was the banker's lawyer. Furthermore, in order to insure the negotiations, Speyer and Company named Horacio S. Rubens as its lawyer in Cuba. Rubens had close ties with Tomás Estrada Palma on account of previous services rendered to the representatives of the Cuban revolution in New York.[3] The fact that Speyer operated in other Latin American countries during those years shows him to be the first imperialist banker; on the other hand, he had connections with German imperialism, whose purpose was to penetrate into the continent also and ally itself with United States capital.[4]

A new $16,500,000 loan was agreed on by the government of President Gómez, with the same Speyer Banking House in 1909. Even when Gómez had announced that he would seek a domestic credit, he preferred to obtain the funds from the "international" market. Speyer and Company, of New York, were "fortunate" enough to secure the corresponding contract. This good fortune was due to, among other reasons, the fact that its representative in Havana was no one else but the well known "friend of Cuba" Mr. Steinhart, whose numerous financial activities were well protected by his official post in the United States consular corps.

When this point was reached and the great investments were made, (whose principal examples we shall later indicate), the strangulation of the independent economic development of Cuba became emphasized. Not only was an absolutely predominant industry that would play the principal role in the national income and trade created, but also the economy was deformed into an economy that graphically could be compared to a midget with a giant's head. It also introduced an obstacle to the diversified development of Cuba which reduced its role to that of a supplier of raw materials to a sole market. Consequently, all Cuban economy came to be absolutely dependent of any change, minimum as it were, occurring in the economic structure, the market and the consumption by the United States population. It was therefore an economy subjected to such a degree that would totally impede compensation for the faults within its own structure and, consequently, along the years would not do anything but emphasize the maladjustment, with a worsening of its political and social effects.

23.1.4. The final reason for the acceleration of the direct investment process in Cuba is the fact that the United States market grew extraordinarily. Nevertheless, towards 1912, Cuban production exceeded United States consumption and was forced to look for customers in the world market. The crisis that the situation was supposed to impose on Cuba was prevented by World War I which turned sugar investments into a frenzy. The First World War, foreseen three years before, began in 1914, originating great disturbances in the European sugar industry and making transportation from relatively far off places, such as Java, difficult. Of course, the United States investments would not be used exclusively in the sugar sector. In order of importance, there were also large investments in the mining industry, railways, the manufacturing industry and in Government bonds until 1919, even though, by then, the sugar investment surpassed the rest by a wide margin.

Not only could we speak about the acceleration of the investments but also of the appearance of what we shall correctly call an economic super-corporation, a phenomenon that is nothing but the reflection of the process of capitalist concentration through the "holding companies", also occurring in the United States economy. This super-corporation had the financial support of very important groups from the United States industry and especially from the banking circle. On the other hand, they collected a large proportion of the private national savings which were attracted by their promises of fat profits that, in the long run, would be lost by the middle or small savings account holders.

We must also mention among the most significant investments of those days the one made by the well known Edwin Atkins in 1915, who added to the enterprises he managed, *Punta Alegre Sugar Company* which controlled the Florida and Punta Alegre sugar mills in Camagüey, (now Argentina and Máximo Gómez, respectively).

Perhaps the most characteristic phenomenon of this acceleration was the creation of the *Cuban Cane Company* in 1916 by the famous Rionda family, known for their large investments during the first republican stage. The *Cuban Cane* launched itself into the sugar business on this occasion with a $50,000,000 capital and bought 6 mills, all at once (Conchita, Asunción, Mercedes, San Ignacio, Jagueyal and Lugareño). Its violent policy of control was characterized by the fabulous price paid for the mills, well over their real value. But the promoters, very closely tied to the United States policy, and well informed of the future of the business, acted thus because they considered the investment would turn out to be a success. The venture, which they largely controlled due to their relations with the United States policy, certainly was no failure. In the same year, 1916, they had a profit of $10,000,000 and in the following year the amount rose to $38,000,000. This means that in two years invested capital was almost fully recovered. Naturally, when the situation changed in 1918, their profits decreased. It must be observed that the decrease in profits was due to the fact that some Cuban and United States directors of the *Cuban Cane Company* established the *Cuban Trading Company,* an enterprise which was in charge of the sale of sugar produced by the mills belonging to *Cuban Cane.* It is evident that the profits of this Company were being transferred to the new enterprise; but it is also evident that this transfer was not due to a mere coincidence, but to an internal scheme of the corporation with the intention of defrauding the investors of *Cuban Cane.* This way, in expectation of the end of the war and the consequent normalization of trade, *Cuban Cane* was left heavily indebted in mortgage loans and current liabilities, while the trading company was reaping large profits from the sale of sugar. This also represented a way to evade the agreement that *Cuban Cane* had made with the Cuban mill owners, from whom they had bought the mills, keeping them in the organization on the basis of paying them participation in the profits as well as large salaries.[4]

At that time the Hershey Corporation also came on the scene. It bought large strips of land and old sugar mills to the north of the province of Havana where later it built the Hershey sugar mill (today's Camilo Cienfuegos). Finally, we must mention the *West Indies Finance Corporation,* which in the year 1920 acquired Palma Sugar mill (today

Dos Ríos), built by Menocal with the "savings" which, due to his good personal "management", he had "managed" to save during his term of government.

Logically, neither the anti-imperialist sentiment, nor the concern over the progressive foreign domination had totally disappeared in Cuba. The old issue of prohibiting the sale of land to foreigners, raised by Sanguily in 1902, was debated again in the years 1916-17 and 1918. Representative Wilfredo Fernández, who had a regrettable participation in the dictatorship of Machado, introduced a bill similar to Sanguily's, while other notorious men of the time, such as Antonio Sánchez de Bustamante, became firm defenders of the sale of lands to foreigners, and furthermore, they attempted to prove that the sale of mills to United States corporations was not harmful to the national interest. Logically, within a political structure of submission to the foreign interest, nothing was done in relation to this matter.

We must emphasize that it was not only the large United States corporations that took advantage of the circumstances, but also that Cuban and Spanish-Cuban sugar millionaires came forth, among whom was the famous "Pote" (José López Rodríguez), skillful speculator who had managed to control the National Bank of Cuba and who extended his businesses in sugar and other activities by taking advantage of the money deposited in the above-mentioned bank. All of this ended in the well known crisis of the year 1921.

23.1.5. We must not disregard the fact that after the impact of the crisis of 1920-21, investments continued, and the sale of sugar mills to U.S. enterprises and foreign industrial control increased; the latter being fundamentally represented by the banks, whose position as creditors before the crisis permitted their foreclosing Cuban property. The sugar investment movement was so strong that it lasted through 1926. A totally new sugar mill, the Santa Marta, built by ex-President Menocal, began to operate during that year.

It might be well to review the bank penetration process.

As we have previously said, banks in general, and especially United States banks, never pioneered the development of any zone but rather followed in the wake of that development. This was the case in Cuba. United States banks also accelerated their penetration beginning 1915, when the National City Bank of New York appeared for the first time, purchasing the Bank of Sr. Carlos Zaldo. Logically, this bank, along with the Bank of Canada and the Bank of Nova Scotia, an English bank previously established in Cuba, directed its activities to the sugar business, profiting from the crisis of 1920-21.

The boom in sugar business, owing to the World War, resulted in the creation of numerous banks, generally small, owned by Cubans and Spanish-Cubans. But new United States firms continued to appear such as the *American Foreign Banking Corporation,* the *Merçantile Bank of America,* and the *Guaranty Trust Company,* the last two of New York, which entered into an association, to form the *Banco Mercantil Americano de La Habana.*

The banks which had Cuban and Spanish-Cuban capital could not be considered as being independent from the foreign banking system. Practically all those small banks were agents of large foreign financial institutions, such as in the case of the H. Upmann firm, closely connected with the James Speyer Company, which had made the first loans to Cuba. This was the more necessary for the Cuban and Spanish-Cuban institutions because their limited capital and their deposits would not have permitted them to compete with the large foreign banks which had a more daring credit policy which could be considered very liberal, if we take into consideration the boom in commerce and sugar prices. This policy was too liberal during the boom. Therefore, when in 1920 the price of sugar went down within a period of six months from 20 cents to 3 cents a pound, in New York, most entrepreneurs were unable to meet the loans which had been made based on higher prices, and so lost their businesses to the foreign banks. Next chapter will deal with the fate of the Cuban banks.

BIBLIOGRAPHY

1. This Agrarian League Requires a Thorough Study. Comisión Consultiva Agraria, *Memoria de sus trabajos,* Havana, 1960.
2. Jenks. *Op. cit.*
3. Katz, Friedrich. *Op. cit.*
4. Primelles, León. *Crónica cubana,* 1917-1922. Havana, 1958.

CHAPTER XXIV

SUBJECTED ECONOMY

24.1. *Stages*

24.1.1. The whole process described in Chapters XXII and XXIII led to a state of permanent crisis, that is, of breakdown of the economic structure that could not be resolved because foreign domination sharpened and worsened in its retarding effects.

The evolution of that subjected economy had two stages: one extended from 1898 to 1925 and it could be said that it began in the decade of the 1890's without essentially altering its characteristics; the other one ran from 1926 through 1958.

1898-1925. This is the stage of the growth of the subjected economy, hence that of the progressive increase of the influence of United States interests, that is, a growth leading to an increasing subjection. This process was based on the increase in exports, and, consequently, on increased sugar production. Hence, it was also the growth of economic deformation called *single-production.* At the end of this stage, Cuba was already an irretrievable prey of the exclusive cultivation of cane and sugar production as well as of Yankee monopolist capital. Increased investments of foreign capital were necessary to bring about this abnormal growth. This capital adopted methods of exploitation which were most adequate to accomplish its purpose, leading to the appearance of large sugar mills capable of manufacturing hundreds of thousands of bags of sugar in a short harvest period of from 90 to 120 days. Simultaneously with the large mills the great cane latifundia came into being, that is, the obsolete, low capacity sugar mills disappeared and the concentration of land held by the companies increased. While in 1899 there were 207 mills, in 1926-27 the number was only 177. Though exact data are not available, it can be stated that the land area held by that group of mills increased throughout the years, including those of the crisis and even after 1933.

The 1920-21 crisis had deep effects, but it did not alter the general conditions of the period. Through this crisis, the economic subjection, the foundation for which had been laid since 1886, was completed. Moreover, in 1923, conditions of sugar trade had become stable to such an extent that in the following years investments were made in the industry, partly so as to be able to produce more efficiently and profitably during periods of low prices.

1926-1958. The total recovery of European industry, the beginning of radical protectionism in large capitalist countries, and the competition among groups of sugar producers which began to appear since 1925-26, had an effect on the economic situation of Cuba. A new crisis cycle began. As a matter of fact, Cuban sugar had reached its maximum possibility for development when it covered 50%, more or less, of United States consumption. Excess production had to be placed in other markets which was neither feasible nor stable, thus revealing the nature of a subjected, single-product economy. Sugar exports and production became stagnant and, from 1927 on, began to decrease, marking the beginning of a reduction stage in the economy; reductions of exports, production, prices, and, especially, investments. The general depression of capitalism (1929-32) worsened Cuba's own structural, economic crisis. Latifundia continued and its retarding consequences deepened.

24.2. *Crisis*

24.2.1. The end of the First World War (Armistice of November 11, 1918) put a sudden stop to capitalist speculation. This was the apparent cause of the initial depression which submerged Cuba, because of its subjected economy, into severe dislocations which would not be overcome until the triumph of the Revolution. This long crisis consisted of two stages. The first stage, from 1920 to 1925, was a sudden deflationary process, evidently connected with an identical phenomenon taking place in the United States, marked by a series of fluctuations in economic activities during those five years. At first, though the main event consisted of a sudden drop in sugar prices, the drive towards the expansion of the sugar industry continued because many of the entrepreneurs expected to overcome the crisis by building more efficient industrial plants. Consequently, the pace of sugar investments was maintained until 1925.

The second stage, from 1926 to 1929, marked by decreasing sugar prices and exports, brought about a decrease in imports and general economic activities in the country, amounting to a relative stabilization under these depressed conditions. This second stage continued and became a part of the general depression of the capitalist system extending from 1929 to 1933, the most acute one in its whole history.

Generally, the process of the Cuban economic breakdown taking place in 1920 and 1921 has been treated as if it were a simple temporary disturbance, with the principal attention focused on the following period, that is, 1926 to 1932. However, the history of Cuba since the Republic was established does not offer more significant events revealing the weakness of our economic structure than those marking the crisis of 1920-21. They reveal the great consequences of the close bonds existing between the Cuban economy and that of the United States due to exclusive sugar production and trade. It is no accident that following this crisis the feeling that economic subjection was the main evil affecting the Cuban nation remained as the fundamental force of the Cuban people's political activity. Since that moment, the anti-imperialist feeling became well defined. That is the reason we can speak of the fixing of a new national conscience beginning in 1923.

The crisis broke out in 1920. Inasmuch as the European countries began to reconstruct their economies and were unable to satisfy their normal demands for sugar consumption, the United States undertook, during the years 1918 and 1919, the extraordinary purchases of this product, thereby continuing in the easy role of middleman which it had been playing throughout the War. Due to the fact that all price and consumption controls had been removed since the beginning of 1919 the price of sugar started to rise in the United States market and importations were made from countries which had a higher production cost than Cuba, but which could comfortably sell their product within the existing price levels, as in the case of Argentina. On the other hand, the limited but sustained price rise in the United States since 1916 had favored the expansion of the domestic beet sugar industry. Consequently, Cuba was suddenly faced with a number of competitors which, under so-called normal conditions in capitalist trade, could have neither sold their product nor increased their production.

The price rise continued throughout 1919 and the beginning of 1920, going as high as 22 cents a pound in New York (May 19, 1920). The following month prices began a steady decline dropping to three cents a pound by the end of the year. The price levels remained at this low and even lower levels until January, 1922.

It should be understood that large sugar investments had been made during the preceding years and, especially in 1919 and even in 1920, the banks had followed an adventurous policy of short-term financing based on temporary sugar prices. For this reason, by the middle of 1920, when prices began to decline, there were some $80 million in short-term loans, especially in sugar financing based on market quotations of ten cents a pound or over. Naturally, those debts could not be met by the mills because the price of sugar in the international market had fallen to a level below ten cents a pound.

Towards the end of 1920, the economic interests which had derived great profits from sugar speculation suddenly found themselves the victims of their own operations, and began to play up the crisis as a grave national problem. All kinds of projects were undertaken, aimed at saving the sugar enterprises and the banks. One of these projects, supported by President Menocal, prepared by one Merchant, of the *Banco Nacional,* and one Marimón, of the *Banco Español,* consisted of a bond issue guaranteed by the 1921 sugar crop. These bonds in practice were to have currency value. The matter was publicly debated and, as in other similar occasions, those interest groups appealed to the Cubans' patriotism in order "to keep the Republic from bankruptcy". A meeting was called for October 16. This public discussion sounded the alarm for the other branches of the economy as well as for bank depositors who until then had not been seriously concerned because the press and the propaganda carried out by the main sectors of the economy involved in the crisis (sugar mills and banks) had tried to convince the Cuban people that it was only a passing disturbance. The scheduled meeting never took place because beginning October 6 a bank panic broke out comparable only to that of 1857.

The panic took the form of bank runs on checking and savings accounts. Since banks at the time operated without governmental regulations and had invested freely in sugar operations, they were unable to face the wholesale withdrawal of funds. The *Banco Mercantil Americano de La Habana* requested a few hours' time to secure the funds for paying its creditors. But the measure was of no avail because short-term loans could not be collected normally.

On October 7 and 8 other important banks were also rushed by their creditors. It was impossible to refund the depositors' money and many banks had to suspend payment. The government, belatedly trying to avoid the unavoidable, decreed a bank moratorium on October 10, 1920. It must be said that had Cuban banking not been so completely subjected to United States policy it would have been able to face the panic successfully. The crisis would not have been avoided, but some of its effects would have been lessened. It should be emphasized that foreign banks in Cuba had, during the bonanza years, invested depositor's funds in diverse operations abroad leaving their Cuban branches without minimally adequate reserves. Moreover, Cuban banks connected with foreign banks were suddenly faced with curtailed credits and placed in an extremely difficult position to meet both the depositors' demands and the delay in collecting their short-term loans.

This was the opportunity for foreign banks to eliminate the Cuban banks which had arisen as the result of speculation.

The October 10, 1920, moratorium had suspended the payment of debts until December 1, providing for immediate payment of 10% of deposits and establishing a commission to enforce the provisions of this law. But, as usual, the law had its loopholes intended to benefit big business and the holders of large checking accounts. In the first place, checks drawn in favor of the State were paid in full. Naturally, large taxpayers circumvented the 10% provision of the law under the pretext of paying debts to the State. Moreover, checks were allowed in so-called compensation operations. An example of this was an operation where a checking account holder issued a check in favor of a creditor who in turn deposited the check in his own checking account and simultaneously, using the funds thus provided, issued a check in payment of his own debt to the bank. This check could be immediately collected by the bank, thus reducing the amount of funds available for the payment to holders of small checking and savings accounts.

An attempt was made to rectify this situation through another decree on October 22, but without prohibiting the "compensation operations" described above which favored the large bank debtors and the banks themselves. The moratorium had to be extended beyond its expiration date to January 31, 1921.

While the moratorium was in force, United States interests began to take an active part in that whole economic and political process. General Enoch H. Crowder, who had previously been in the country on official missions, returned to Cuba on January 6, 1921. He immediately revealed the economic purpose of his visit, favoring those who sought to obtain a loan from the United States He also stated that Cuba was in need of a Central Bank, the controlling part of whose stockholders should be United States citizens in order to have additional "guarantee".

The United States State Department protested the moratorium and demanded that President Menocal not allow any criticism of the National City Bank and the Royal Bank of Canada. Menocal, always willing to comply, took strong measures to silence any criticism of foreign capitalists.

As a matter of fact, the criticism was not simply expressions of discontent on the part of Cuban interests affected by the crisis. Everybody knew that the foreign banks had operated with the funds provided by Cuban depositors, using them not only to take over our economy but also to invest, especially in the New York stock market, for loans to large corporations, purchasing of State securities, and other similar operations.

In the month of February, the Sugar Finance Commission was created. This organization controlled the sale and the price of sugar as well as the payment to the mills on the basis of average prices. However, since the Cuban government was unable to control the country's economy, and as a matter of fact did not expect to do so, the sugar mills owned by United States refineries remained outside the control of the Commission. Moreover, during the period before the Commission was to begin functioning, many operations were made which contributed to weaken the Commission's work. These included sham sales, covered by false bills of sale, of sugar which was thus freed from the contemplated control.

Consequently, without the financial support of the foreign banks' home offices, and in a situation of progressively falling prices, and with ineffective legislation, the crisis worsened in depth and scope. By March, the Cuban banks, one after another, went into bankruptcy. This stage ended in May, when most of them closed, with the exception of United States and British banks established in Cuba.

In the month of May an event of a personal nature took place which was greatly discussed in Cuba: the suicide of José López Rodríguez ("Pote"), who is worthy of mention because he had taken over the bulk of the *Banco Nacional* stock utilizing many millions of pesos of the depositors' funds to deal in sugar operations. Days before, "Pote" had entered into a financial deal whereby he could turn over the greater part of his enterprises to a group of stockholders while still retaining his bookstore businesses with which he had started his meteoric financial career. A magnate's suicide together with the bankruptcy of several mill owners and sugar speculators who had been accused of fraud and embezzlement, but who, in general, had been acquitted, added to the widespread alarm which was completely justified.

The crisis brought about a salary reduction, since the employers believed, as usual, that the workers should be the first to pay for it. However, the cost of living, which had trebled since 1912, causing the great wave of strikes of 1918 and 1919, had not substantially decreased, thus creating discontent among the workers and low income sectors of the population. As a matter of fact, the cost of living did not go down until 1925.

There were protests over the situation; for example, the 1921 rent reduction campaign, not to mention a series of strikes throughout this period of crisis, reaching a climax in the years 1923 and 1924.

It is believed that the worst period of the crisis was over beginning January, 1922. When sugar prices began to recover, without reaching any important levels, since the quotation of five cents a pound was not again reached until 1923, measures were taken in the United States which increased the effects of the crisis: import duties on Cuban sugar were raised from 1 cent to 1.80 cents per pound. That measure would benefit the United States sugar industry as well as other sugar exporting areas, but it deeply affected Cuba which consequently had to absorb the tariff difference by reducing the sales price. As a result, the people of Cuba would bear the brunt of the crisis, while United States bankers and capitalists continued amassing funds to be invested in new sugar operations.

Other sectors of the Cuban economy also felt the weight of the crisis: domestic trade, small industries, and farmers. Many of them went out of business due to the impossibility of obtaining credit, since the foreign banks' traditional policy of lending money on short terms applied only to sugar and tobacco industries and not to other sectors of production. It is well known that bank failures caused the bankruptcy of many small savings account holders. The national bourgeoisie not in the sugar industry, as well as the petty bourgeoisie, suffered a severe blow.

24.2.2. The great depression of 1929-33. The degree of foreign domination advanced to such an extent that the Cuban economy could not take any course other than that charted by the changes occurring in the United States economy which was no longer especially interested in sugar or, at the moment, in other products or basic commodities from Cuba. This was the stage of United States protectionism coinciding with the reactionary government of Herbert Hoover. Cuba had to curtail its production because the United States reduced its imports. Abandoned to her fate, Cuba could not rapidly compensate for the reduction of her sugar production, falling prey to a deep depression some of whose characteristics we shall now describe.

A) *Reduction of foreign trade,* especially sugar exports and, consequently, of imports. Taking the 1919-1923 exports as an index with a value of 100, the 1932 exports came to only 18%. Inasmuch as sugar exports to the United States were the basis of Cuba's deformed economy, it is important to take into account the effect of the crisis and the repercussions the United States protectionist policy had on the participation of the Cuban product in that nation's market. While in the period 1922-1926 Cuba supplied 52.2% of the sugar imported into the United States and 49.4% in 1927-1930, in 1933 it sold only 25.3%. This shows to what extent the national income had been reduced.

B) *Reduction of sugar production* beginning in 1926-1927, which was broken by the 1928-1929 unrestricted sugar harvest, to be resumed until 1933. The sugar production of 1932-1933 was only 50% of that of 1922.

C) As a result, *the number of sugar mills in operation was gradually decreased.* In 1926, 176 mills were in operation and only 135 in 1933.

D) *Reduction of the harvest duration.* Beginning with the 1925-1926 harvest, the working days in sugar mills were progressively reduced due to curtailed production. Consequently, the sugar harvests, which used to last no less than 120 days, were cut to around 90 days and in 1933 to a low of 66 days. As a result, absolute unemployment produced by decreased sugar production was compounded by relative unemployment due to the reduction of working days in the harvest. The authors of the work entitled *Problemas de la nueva Cuba* (New York, 1935) estimated the number of permanently unemployed heads of families in Cuba at the time at 250,000, representing approximately one million persons in an extreme state of poverty out of a total population of 3,900,000.

E) *Income reduction.* A link in the chain of events leading down to the depression was the fall of incomes to unforeseen levels during the years immediately preceding the crisis. According to the above-mentioned work, *Problemas de la nueva Cuba,* the 1933-1934 per capita income was $90.00 a year. Estimates made at the time placed 60% of the population of Cuba in the bracket with incomes below $300 a year, the remaining 40% being distributed between a large group with incomes which could be considered as "middle", and a small group with very high incomes.

As usual in all periods of depression, the ruling classes tried to make the working population bear the brunt of the crisis. Wages were reduced to generally lower levels than those existing in

1909-1910. This was especially the case in rural zones including the sugar mills. Agricultural workers were paid $0.20 or less per 100 arrobas of sugar cane cut and loaded which meant, at best, a daily income of $0.50 during the harvest period. In the mills, the daily wage average did not go over $0.90. No dead season or pre-grinding repair work was done, not even to the reduced extent customary in previous and succeeding years.

The average urban wages were about $1.00 a day. In various sectors of the urban proletariat, wages during the period 1929-1933 amounted to 50% or 70% of those in 1923. [2]

24.2.3. The process of the restrictive sugar policy may be summarized as follows.

1925 marked the beginning of the sugar overproduction crisis with the resultant drop in prices. Early in 1926 some groups considered sugar crop reductions as a means of maintaining high prices through an artificial shortage of the product. This is the same old trick of capitalist speculators known as "bulling the market". Thus, on May 3, 1926, the *Verdeja Act* was passed whereby the 1926-1927 sugar harvest was cut 10%, putting an end to new cane planting. It also set January 1 as the date for the beginning of the sugar harvest. This reduction of Cuban sugar production (4.5 million tons) was to be proportionately applied to each sugar mill and, in turn, to each plantation. But other large producers, especially those of Europe, and Java, far from curtailing, increased their production, keeping stocks very high. As a result, prices remained very low. Sugar prices rallied slightly in 1926, but started a new downward trend in 1927.

As a result, on October 4, 1927, the *Sugar Defense Law* was passed creating the National Commission for Sugar Defense. This Commission was to advise the government regarding pre-crop estimates, market surveys, sales, and matters related to sugar trade. The law also created the Sugar Export Corporation, with sugar mill owners as stockholders, which would handle the quota system and documents having to do with sales, and would in general control the sale of sugar outside Cuban and United States markets, that is, it would have the exclusive control of sales in the so-called world market. Moreover, the sugar crop was cut to four million tons.

The duration of the sugar harvest was cut from 136 to 87 days. Production agreements were reached with Germany, Czechoslovakia, and Poland, and 300,000 tons of sugar destined to the United States were withheld due to the glutting of the market in that country and as another effort to raise prices. As a matter of fact, the mechanism established, leaving the United States sugar mills in Cuba outside the sales control, did not have any positive results. The 1928-1929 sugar crop was completely unrestricted and was known as a "free crop".

The failure of the 1927 policy and, of course, that of the free crops produced a new change materializing in 1929 as the *Sole Vendor Law,* which not only centralized and controlled sales, but also sought an agreement with the United States beet sugar producers, lobbied for United States legislation "favorable" to Cuban sugar, and paved the way for the establishment of the Sugar Export Cooperative Agency, with sugar mill owners as stockholders and favoring a rigid system of sales. This agency had to be discontinued in April, 1930, when it became evident that bulling the market was of no avail.

By that time arose the idea of an international agreement, a disguised sugar production cartel that would guarantee the reduction of crops in all sugar-exporting countries. Before actually initiating this policy, Cuba freed its sugar, coinciding with a similar measure by other great exporters, flooding the markets and causing prices to drop to the lowest levels.

On October 24, 1929, a great economic panic broke out in the United States, marking the beginning of the highest degree of the depression that lasted until 1933.

This served only to worsen the Cuban situation. Another specific factor in worsening the Cuban crisis was the Hawley-Smoot tariff which raised the import duty on Cuban sugar from 1.76 cents to 2.02 cents. It was at this point that the highly-praised Chadbourne plan made its appearance.

Thomas L. Chadbourne was, as in similar cases throughout the period of the United States-controlled Republic, the unavoidable New York lawyer possessing the magic formula to solve all problems, naturally at the expense of Cuba. He was closely connected with Cuban sugar interests and was instrumental in initiating the formula proposed by Cuban groups close to Machado, specifically the Falla Gutiérrez family. The plan consisted in obtaining an international agreement restricting production in sugar exporting countries. That year the situation had changed because the countries that had increased their production and had not entered into any restrictive agreements, now, at a time when depression had stricken the principal capitalist countries, found themselves in a deep crisis that forced them to reconsider their position. By then the production of a number of basic commodities, such as coffee, had been restricted going as far as to commit the unspeakable crime of destroying unsold stocks.

Step by step, an agreement was forged with several European countries leading to the signing in Brussels on May 9, 1931, of the International Sugar Trade Agreement. Under this pact, fixed quotas were allotted to the signatories for a period of five years setting a price of 2 cents per pound for the sale of sugar so that, when the price rose over this minimum, exportable surpluses would be increased. As a result of this agreement, Cuba's production was reduced to a little over three million tons.

The Chadbourne plan did not solve the problem because under the conditions of an increasingly glutted market and a worldwide unemployment and low income crisis, far from increasing, the sale of sugar decreased. As a result, throughout 1932 and part of 1933 Cuba had the lowest levels —in some cases absolute lowest levels— of production, exports, and sugar prices.

As can be seen, during these years the Cuban sugar policy (we shall describe it thus even though it is well known that it was controlled by foreign interests), swayed back and forth proving that the resources of traditional economic policy were not capable of solving or even lessening either the periodic crisis of the capitalist system or the structural crisis of the Cuban economy.

After Machado's fall in the year 1933 when a slight improvement in the market was observed, sugar policy was changed as the result of the United States government's decisions, especially the Costigan-Jones Act which will be dealt with in a succeeding chapter. [3]

24.2.4. Perhaps the most highly-praised aspect of Dictator Machado's economic policy was the customs tariff revision which was believed to have the power of generating and propitiating an accelerated economic development. The stifled national bourgeoisie was in need of new fields, but faced by the depression and the increasing people's unrest, it lacked the strength to carry out adequately this nationalist policy. A customs tariff reform commission was created in 1926 and the new tariffs went into effect in October, 1927. Doubtlessly, the concept of such a reform represented an innovation in the economic policy followed by the various Cuban governments because it aimed at conforming to more realistic political concepts. However, the reform limited itself to a reclassification of traditional items and to an increase in customs duty on imported products that could be manufactured in Cuba. This *protection* was not strong enough to protect national production. As a matter of fact, the protection covered many items imported from Europe and other areas without affecting United States products, precisely those whose entry into Cuba impeded adequate economic development. In other words, the special (preferential) concessions granted United States products were maintained without any appreciable change. For this reason the reform worsened Cuba's dependency on the United States economy.

Naturally, this policy was carried out under the auspices of the furious protectionism then reigning in the United States; that is, the United States economic policy allowed Cuba to apply these insufficient and partial measures. Of course, the international economic picture in general, rather than the tariffs, was the driving force propitiating the development in Cuba of certain products, such as that of eggs, poultry, beef, shoes, and milk products, the importation of which declined.

This "development" was preceded by the disappearance of small and middle industries. According to data published by the National Commission of Statistics and Economic Reforms —though not considered as an industrial census —there was between 1925 and 1927 an elimination of work centers reaching, in some branches of production, 40% or more in shoes, furniture, cement blocks, hats, and leather-tanning, and from 20% to 30% in soft drinks, sausages, soap, candles, and tiles, of the national production.

This phenomenon not only reflected the crisis, but also a certain degree of concentration, since many of the plants opened as the result of the general situation and special legislation were stronger than the ones that had disappeared. Moreover, the new enterprises did not pay better wages, but rather took advantage of the situation of unemployment the better to compete in the national market.

It should be emphasized that a large part of the investment funds came from highly-placed officials in Machado's government as well as from his associates in graft.

Machado's praisers of the time attributed the fact that Cuba had begun to do without or reduced some imported items to the dictator's wise economic policy. But we know that the general international circumstances were decisive in this connection. We shall see later how the new United States policy towards Cuba, on the one hand (Costigan-Jones Act), kept sugar exports at the lowest levels and, on the other hand (1934 trade agreement), controlled the Cuban market, bringing about a crisis in a considerable part of Cuba's industrial production which had had a limited development during the years 1925 and 1932

BIBLIOGRAPHY

1. Pino Santos, Oscar. *El imperialismo en la economía de Cuba,* Havana, 1960.
2. *Problemas de la nueva Cuba,* New York, 1935.
3. Guerra, Ramiro. *La industria azucarera de Cuba,* Havana, 1940; especially chap. V.

CHAPTER XXV

SITUATION OF THE WORKING CLASS

25.1. *From 1898 to 1915*

25.1.1. Continuation of colonialism after 1898. 25.1.2. West Indian migratory workers. 25.1.3. Wages and the cost of living.

25.2. *The rise of popular struggle (1915 - 1933)*

25.2.1. The revolutionary struggle against the high cost of living, 1915-20. The standard of living from 1929-32. 25.2.2. The people's organizations in the struggle.

25.1. *From 1898 to 1915*

25.1.1. The developments described in Chapter XXIV meant that after 1898 Cuba's colonial status was perpetuated and, indeed, intensified. The subordination of all aspects of Cuban life to the interests of a great power could only bring an aggravation of colonial conditions. Moreover, the government of occupation followed a policy of support to colonialist groups who had previously defended Spanish rule and who now became partisans of United States colonialism. These were joined by those groups who had arisen during the revolution but who could not conceive nor desire, much less put into effect, a true liberation of the nation.

As a matter of fact, conditions changed for the colonialist groups (the sugar mill owners, the importers, etc.), since the massive investments of United States capital, which we have described in Chapter XXIII, favored the opportunities of the capitalist entrepreneurs. For the salaried middle class, the urban working class and the poor farmers and agricultural workers, however, living conditions did not change. So much so that from late 1898 on, the majority of the men who had fought to liberate Cuba lived in the greatest misery, seeking work even for a single meal. Gonzalo de Quesada's letters, collected under the title "Correspondence File of Gonzalo de Quesada", are full of eloquent references to this situation. Another testimonial to these conditions is contained in the manifesto of the General Strike Committee of September, 1899, which states clearly that the economic situation of the working people in Cuba was the same as that which had prevailed before 1895, and added that apparently everything had come out just as though the "master of us all", José Martí, had never spoken. [1]

In the long run, the wages of the army of liberation were paid at the expense of the misery of the Cuban people. Neither the occupation government nor the subsequent republican governments made any serious attempts to solve the basic problems of the people. The policy of Tomás Estrada Palma's government, based on "austerity", implied the preservation of the lowest possible living standards for the people. The State did nothing to stimulate the rehabilitation of the rural areas and confined itself to rendering only the most minimal public services. In the meantime, the landowners, mill owners, corporation lawyers, and exporters and importers went on taking advantage of the growing economic relations with the United States. These groups did not suffer from austerity, nor did the money changers, usurers and others who went about buying up the certificates issued for payment to the army of liberation, at discounts which frequently amounted to 40 or 50 percent. [2]

25.1.2. In addition to all this, the practices of the great sugar entrepreneurs also contributed deliberately to keeping down the people's standard of living, since the importation of migratory workers (Haitians and Jamaicans) caused the lowering of the wage level to rock bottom in the country's principal industry.

This immigration, encouraged by the great enterprises, was supplemented with another from Europe and Asia, particularly from countries where conditions of rural life were exceptionally bad. Therefore, until about 1925, waves of Spanish, Chinese and Turkish immigrants, to mention only the major groups, poured into the country. After 1925, immigration practically ceased because of the country's profound economic crisis. In 1927, even the importation of migratory workers ended, since poverty and unemployment were rife. Thousands of these, however, remained and made their homes in Cuba.[3]

25.1.3. An historical study of the Republic shows that the working class was in a state of constant agitation and that partial strikes and even general strikes on a local scale were very numerous after 1902. The famous "apprentices' strike" of 1902 and the "money strike" of 1907 reflect the living conditions of the period and represent two of the greatest efforts made by the Cuban working class to better its lot. But relief did not materialize. The economic activity brought on by massive United States investments simply caused a progressive rise in the cost of living, which the First World War greatly aggravated.

The proceedings of the Workers' Congress of 1914 contain a series of data which are very valuable for a study of the Cuban people's living conditions at the time. The reports of Ramón Rivera, who had been an active member of the Cuban Revolutionary Party in exile during the war of 1895, of Julián González, Manuel Valera, and Juan Valdés, as well as those of the "Society for Resistance" of the "La Corona" Cigar Factory workers, reveal that the wages of even the best paid workers did not cover their basic necessities and those of their families. One of the delegates remarked that in Cuba the press, politicians, and professionals spoke about crisis only when the economic situation threatened the landowners, sugar mill owners, or other dominant economic groups, but remained completely unconcerned so long as only the workers suffered.

25.2. *The rise of popular struggle (1915-1933)*

25.2.1. In the course of the World War, this situation became sufficiently exacerbated not only to make for the continuation of the struggles of the working class in protest against the high cost of living, but to cause it to increase.

Mercantile profiteering with scarce commodities and the failure of the "Subsistence Commission", which committed the most flagrant offences against the public good, generated a wave of general strikes between 1917 and 1919, whose precipitating cause was always the high cost of living. Despite the propaganda touting an economic "boom", wages did not keep pace with prices. The cost of living continued climbing throughout the bonanza period known as "the dance of the millions", that is, until 1921. While the 1920-21 crisis brought on an economic recession and started a downward curve in the people's income, it had no effect on the cost of living which remained very high until 1927-29. This can be easily understood: industrial and commercial entrepreneurs tried to make the population bear the brunt of the crisis reducing salaries and keeping staple items at a high price.

By the time the cost of living went down, in 1929, an extremely low standard of living had already been established owing to the deep general depression of capitalism and the Cuban crisis itself. As seen in Chapter XXIV, the standard of living went down to rock bottom. Thousands of Cubans worked exclusively for their meals. However, even during the worst years of the crisis, the foreign sugar companies reaped profits of from $6 to $8 million annually. Naturally, signs of the people's discontent became increasingly evident, leading to the renewal of the great general struggles of the people of Cuba beginning in 1923. This was the year when the people's income was drastically reduced owing to the beginning, after 1920-21, of the structural crisis of the semi-colonial economy.

In 1923 a series of events took place pointing to a profound change in the national conscience: on the one hand, a strong students movement, led by Julio A. Mella, and a feminist movement, both of which revealed revolutionary positions inspired by socialism; on the other hand, the continued labor struggles lasting until 1925, especially in the railroad sector. The Yankee policy of intervention, personified in Cuba by General Crowder, and the subservience of the corrupt Cuban government, stimulated the anti-imperialist awareness.

The foreign monopolies and the Cuba ruling groups decided to curb the growing wave of protest. Hence, the installation of Machado's dictatorship (1925), which appeared to be a "nationalist" government. Though Machado tried from the beginning to stop the revolutionary movement through brutal methods, he was unsuccessful.

25.2.2. The organization of the National Confederation of Cuban Workers (CNOC), the founding and penetration within the masses of the Communist Party of Cuba, the organization of the first national trade unions, such as the National Sugar Workers Union (SNOIA), and the struggles waged by these organizations from 1929 on, are important elements in the picture of the crisis suffered by the Cuban people

The progressive economic depression continued to create the conditions for stepping up the revolutionary movement. Moreover, Machado's continued efforts to perpetuate himself in power aroused the hatred of a large number of the bourgeoisie and petty bourgeoisie.

A succession of strikes marked that period. Workers in the shoe, textile, hat, and other industries joined the struggle against hunger and repression. The first major battle against the dictatorship took place in March, 1930: the general strike led by Rubén Martínez Villena with the participation of 200,000 workers.

Immediate political aims merged with defensive action of the working class, so that the struggle against Machado became at the same time a struggle against the bourgeois parties, conspicuous among which was the ABC, a clandestine reactionary organization replacing the discredited opposition parties.

The revolutionary clandestine press (*Bandera Roja,* of the Communist Party; *Mella,* of the Anti-Imperialist League, and *Línea,* of the Students' Left Wing) circulated throughout the country, and the organizations established closer ties with the broad masses. Many people's demonstrations proved the futility of repression, as on the occasion of the funeral of a young communist, Mirto Milián, in Santa Clara (January, 1933). Moreover, outbreaks took place in rural zones and towns, which were symptomatic of the spread of the revolutionary movement. At this time the so-called "mediation" of United States Ambassador Welles began. Machado was no longer of any value to the foreign bankers and monopolies. Therefore, a formula was being sought to substitute him and, at the same time, stop the popular protest. However, on August 3, 1933, Machado was overthrown by a nationwide strike.

The struggle went on. In September, 1933, a wave of strikes in the sugar mills served as a pretext for the new rulers, sprung from the September 4 military coup, to crush the revolt of the working class, especially at the Senado sugar mill (Camagüey), the Mabay sugar mill (Oriente), and other mills (Las Villas), where workers' "soviets" had been established. Repression increased, especially after 1934. Of course, Batista was the main instrument for the repression of the people.

However, a stage had begun when the various governments were forced to respect the people's social gains, while continuing the most brutal persecution of the workers movement, including the use of every possible demagogic method. Batista himself launched, in 1936, a much-vaunted Three Year Plan, pretending to be interested in the economic development of the country.

The conservative groups tried to take advantage of Machado's downfall and the re-establishment of repression, beginning in 1934, to curb the people's unrest. However, the workers organizations not only became consolidated, but gained even greater support in spite of the efforts of bourgeois parties, such as the ABC and the PRC.

When the 1940 Constituent election was called, the great central labor organization, the CTC, was coming into being. This organization would be the instrument for the defense of labor and social gains obtained during the period just reviewed. In the new stage beginning at this point, repression would be combined with the bribing of corrupt labor leaders and the division of the movement.

BIBLIOGRAPHY

1. *Archivo de Gonzalo de Quesada, Epistolario*, 2 vols. Havana, 1948-1951.
Rivero Muñiz, José. *El movimiento obrero durante la primera intervención*, Santa Clara, 1961.
Rivero Muñiz, José. *El primer partido socialista cubano*, Santa Clara, 1962.
2. Catá, Alvaro. *De guerra a guerra*, Havana, 1906.
3. Martí, Carlos. *Films cubanos.* Oriente y Occidente. Barcelona (especially chaps. XV, XIX, XXIX and XXXIII).

CHAPTER XXVI

THE PERMANENT CRISIS (1934-1958)

26.1. *Characteristics*

26.1.1. In preceding chapters we have outlined the characteristics of the subservient Cuban economy, from 1886 until 1929-33, stressing its increasing subjection to United States capital.

The general crisis of 1929-1933 disguised the Cuban economy's own crisis. The economy of Cuba emerged from that commotion in the worst condition in its whole history because the degree of foreign domination was so great there was no possible solution for the drop in sugar exports.

Why do we take the year 1934 as the beginning of that period? There are several reasons for this:

1st It was the year when supposedly the great general capitalist depression had passed while Cuba did not emerge from her own crisis.

2nd It was the year when the national reactionary forces and their foreign supporters stopped the popular movement sprung from the struggle against Machado.

3rd It was the year when a trade agreement with the United States was signed, consolidating the predominance of that country's exports in the Cuban market.

4th It was the year when the United States Congress passed the Costigan-Jones law subjecting U.S. importations of Cuban sugar to a system of limiting quotas.

Let us analyze the situation. The weakness in the economic structure had produced a crisis, originating the popular movements beginning in 1923 and coming to a climax in 1933 with the overthrow of Machado. The people aspired to create new socio-political conditions. But national reaction headed by the ABC party, inspired by the United States embassy, united with the worst politicians in Cuba's history, stopped and repressed that movement. Batista's dictatorship served only to establish permanently Cuba's policy of subjection, thus crushing the beginnings of a great liberation movement encompassing not only the working people and sections of the peasantry, but also the middle class, in which a most extraordinary fighter, Antonio Guiteras, was outstanding. United States policy-makers understood that there was a deep restlessness and granted, through the treaty of 1934, the repeal of the Platt Amendment, because it no longer was necessary to secure the economic domination of Cuba.

Future administrations served the foreign interests without the Platt Amendment, sometimes through the application of pressure, sometimes by corruption and demagogy, or both at once. That submission served to stop and frustrate the vigorous conscience of economic development the crisis was forging in the Cuban people, which was opposed by the groups connected with foreign capital and United States exporters, fearful of losing or suffering a reduction of their sales in Cuba. An efficient development of the Cuban economy would have demanded a revision or a scrapping of the "reciprocal" trade; it would have stimulated national production of articles previously imported, and would have lessened Cuba's dependency in respect to sugar, this being equivalent to reducing her dependency on the United States.

26.1.2. By then United States policy with respect to Cuba was very well defined. The 1934 trade agreement only served to worsen the frustrating character of the 1903 reciprocity trade pact. In the first place, because the margin of preference granted by Cuba to United States products increased; secondly, because the number of United States articles that benefited by preferential entry into Cuba was considerably augmented. The logical consequence of these two facts was that, since 1934, it became more difficult for European industry to compete in the Cuban market. Finally, the supposed concession by the United States in exchange for increased preferential treatment of their products, which was a reduction of import duty on sugar, was of no effect, because sugar purchases by the United States were then subject to limiting quotas fixed by the Costigan-Jones Act.

We should remember that under the 1903 trade agreement Cuban sugar was subject to a lower import duty than that from other countries. That reduction made it possible for Cuban sugar —the product of United States capital —to displace sugar from other countries paying higher tariffs, that is, it favored a progressive increase in exports of Cuban sugar to the United States. Towards 1914 sugar from countries subject to high import duties no longer entered the United States. This meant that Cuban sugar had reached its highest expansion in that market at the expense of other suppliers (European and others). The deep crisis of the Cuban economy was already present in that fact. But this crisis could not be immediately appreciated because of the start of the First World War. After the end of the war, restrictions on the export of Cuban sugar to the United States, and on production, began. That is, the period of permanent crisis had begun.

Capitalist development in the United States brought about a growth in beet and cane sugar production in its own territory. Hence, a policy of reduction of Cuban sugar imports was initiated. This policy was favored by protectionist elements coming into power in 1924. Logically, with the reduction of Cuban sugar imports, a disastrous economic crisis resulted in the island, whose single-product economy had been formed by these same imperialist economic interests.

How were imports reduced through the Costigan-Jones Act of 1934? That law called for the importation by the United States of an amount of sugar to be based on a percentage of total consumption. In arriving at that percentage, the years of highest sugar export were not taken into consideration. Those years were the ones prior to 1929. Instead, the period after 1929 was taken as the base. This meant that instead of fixing the percentage at 40%-50% of consumption, the result was only 28%-30%, that is, the percentage of Cuban sugar participation in the United States market was artificially and definitely reduced.[1]

It was claimed that as a result of this change the imperialists were keeping Cuba from being the victim of the great fluctuations in export and production characteristic of the sugar business. From then on, instead of fluctuations there would be a permanent depression.

26.1.3. That depression, and extreme poverty, within the demagogy of the benefits granted by foreign capital, was worsened by the fact that, in spite of the bankruptcy of sugar exports, cane latifundia remained intact, with the result that living conditions of the rural population continued at the lowest levels.

If, on the one hand, sugar production became stationary or even decreased, and on the other hand, new industries were not created or, if created they did not bring enough employment, then there was no solution to the crisis. But there was a still graver problem. This was the fact that since 1925 the population was growing at an accelerated rate, worsening the employment deficit, that is, increasing permanent unemployment which, at the same time, was aggravated by shorter sugar harvests. Living conditions for the people became progressively more difficult. For this reason, the figures on per capita national income prepared after 1950 are almost useless, since the alleged increase in income is the result of manipulating large numbers. As a matter of fact, the income increase of the big capitalist groups and of the middle class, dependent on the large companies or on political positions, distorted the results, disguising the real situation of the Cuban people.[2]

This new imperialist policy was accompanied by a very active propaganda on the need to create other industries. It is curious that, when domination devices had been operated to the full, the Yankee economists and officials should be the ones to speak of non-sugar development. Of course, by then no new investments were made in the sugar business. On the contrary, the imperialists complained of the "unprofitable" sugar industry. Consequently, from then on they would show interest in investing in other businesses yielding higher incomes, under pretense of helping to achieve a more harmonious development of the Cuban economy. For example, the economic report of Stacy May, published by the Chase Manhattan Bank, mentioned the development of cattle-raising for exporting fresh or frozen beef. But that was only a reflection of the Rockefeller financial group's interest. Also, the Truslow mission "discovered" the need of a diversified development of the Cuban economy. In this way they created the conditions for the acceptance of the new, more profitable (for the entrepreneurs) investments, taking advantage of the awareness of economic development growing within the Cuban people.

What were the new investments? Let us take a few examples: the expansion of the "Dime Stores", the opening of Sears, Roebuck & Co. These retail businesses, linked to great industries, served as channels to sell United States exports in Cuba Also, there were investments in the electric power monopoly, thus transforming this public utility into one of the most active means of extracting wealth from the nation. There were some governmental and mixed investments in the mining industry, intended to guarantee the supply of strategic minerals to the United States. Finally, there were investments in cattle-raising, a business offering profitable export possibilities similar to those of sugar prior to 1932.

Now then, these investments were not made with "fresh" capital, in "new" dollars, but with the profits made on previously-invested capital. We must not lose sight of the fact that the huge investments made until 1925 had produced profits which were much higher than the amount of invested capital.

Now, this phenomenon would be repeated on an even greater scale with respect to the new investments. From 1946 to 1956, the net income of United States enterprises in Cuba amounted to some 700 million dollars. This is equivalent to the amount of capital invested then. Of this net profit, some 100 million dollars were reinvested, the rest going into the pockets of United States entrepreneurs. Therefore, the "aid" to the "new" development of Cuba was extended with dollars produced by the Cuban people.

26.2. *Events up to 1958*

26.2.1. All of this policy represented changes in United States capitalism. In the first place, it represented its new role as administrator of the capitalist structure after the Second World War. In this stage, new forms of domination of foreign countries were created. Also, the policy of the government in Washington represented more truly than before 1940 the interests of the great monopolies. It was not in vain that the posts of secretaries in the Cabinet were occupied by the highest executives of such corporations as General Motors, Pan American Airways, and others. The interests of the capitalist groups now appeared under the guise of official and even international institutions (Import-Export Bank, World Bank, International Monetary Fund, General Agreement on Trade and Tariffs, etc.).

This new appearance was revealed particularly with respect to loans. Formerly, the loans granted by great New York bankers (Speyer, Morgan, etc.) constituted one of the more aggressive aspects of the United States policy of penetration into Latin America, serving as a pretext for and support of military intervention in the Dominican Republic, Haiti, and Nicaragua But the bankers complained of the unprofitableness of those operations after the 1929-32 crisis. The firm "Jimmy" Speyer, a good friend of "Teddy" Roosevelt, who in turn was, as we all know, a "good friend" of Cuba, had a bad experience with the $35 million loan made in 1904 to pay the Cuban Liberation Army. Speyer was able to recover, in principal and interest, only 63 million dollars! Results such as this are not very encouraging to a United States banker. From then on, together with the New Deal and the good neighbour policy, measures were taken to safeguard those operations adequately. Consequently, agencies and organizations were created through which bankers would lend funds. However, since these are official and international institutions, privileges and exceptional guarantees were obtained, making sure no losses would be sustained. Besides, since loans were now granted for the purpose of buying United States products, the principal and profits from the operation would be trebled and quadrupled. That is, the financial policy following the Second World War became an instrument for the further exploitation of the peoples.

An example of that policy in Cuba was the $120 million loan granted by the Import-Export Bank to the Prío Socarrás government. This loan was accompanied by all kinds of conditions and "guarantees", down to minor bureaucratic details.

Also, the demagogic use of development awareness was evinced in Cuba's support of the General Agreement on Trade and Tariffs (G.A.T.T.). This organization was created at the end of the Second World War as a means of fighting international commerce fetters. That was its outward appearance. But the purpose of the G.A.T.T. was to remove all protectionist principles established in the capitalist world so that United States commercial power could easily penetrate into all nations, developed as well as underdeveloped. A particular aim was to break up the preferential system set up in the British Commonwealth. The various Cuban governments supported the Agreement and stayed in it despite the fact that that path made it very difficult to protect any national industrial development. This multilateral trade agreement did not annul the United States quota system that constituted an obstacle to an increase in our sugar exports; and it left intact the preferential treatment granted to United States products to the detriment of industrial goods from other countries, and, of course, also to the detriment of the general development of Cuba. Every time Cuba granted a product from another nation an import preference similar to that enjoyed by a United States article, she was automatically obliged, under this unilateral pact, to grant additional customs advantages to other U.S. commodities, as compensation. Thus, benefits of the Cuban preferential system were automatically extended to any United States product without the need to revise, alter or modify in any way the bilateral treaties subscribed to by Cuba and the United States.

All this clearly reveals that United States policy after the Second World War deepened Cuba's dependence, contributing to make the crisis of the semicolonial economy permanent and insoluble within the mechanism of the capitalist world.

26.2.2. Those organizations also served to support corrupt governments, as was the case with that of Prío Socarrás whose policy of persecution of united labor leaders was rewarded by the sending to Cuba of the World Bank's Truslow mission, thus lending his administration a certain prestige. The Truslow mission, after much general talk on the need to develop new industries, recommended a whole plan based on reactionary labor policy, which was initiated during Prío Socarrás' own government and continued by Batista's dictatorship: dismissal with pay, employers' federation, etc.[3]

As far as the national economic policy is concerned, it sought to find support in the development awareness. The Batista Three Year Plan of 1936 was the first clear example of this tendency. The 1955 economic and social development plan was an expanded reproduction of that first demagogic effort. The other administrations, under guise of economic development, created some protected monopoly enterprises, such as textile plants and rice growing. These enterprises permitted some people who had become wealthy as a result of political graft to transform themselves into "respectable" capitalists concerned with resolving the problem of underdevelopment. This development, when understood in the traditional way, is none other than an instrument for the creation of a bourgeoisie. This is clearly revealed in Batista's social and development plan, through which the dictator sought to create a capitalist group who in turn would support him. It has been estimated that of the $500 million Cuba held in foreign exchange in 1952, over $200 million were sent abroad, representing profits and graft.[4]

The ever-increasing siphoning off of Cuban wealth and the constantly mounting graft by the national oligarchy, the squandering of national treasury foreign exchange holdings which in 1959, at the triumph of the Revolution, were well under $100 million, the consolidation of sugar latifundia and the expansion of latifundist structure through the creation of large cattle ranches and rice plantations, the persecution of the revolutionary movement in general and of unified and radical elements of the labor movements, the delivery of the trade unions into the hands of a sold-out bureaucratic group, and the dictatorship constituted the general characteristics of the Cuban economy from 1934 to 1959. These objective conditions, worsened by mounting unemployment and the consequent lowering of the general standard of living of the Cuban people, generated and unleashed the Revolution, with which we shall deal in the next chapter.

26.3. *The people's riposte*

26.3.1. The people of Cuba stood up in the face of continuing and worsening colonial conditions. Demagogy and repression were of no avail. In 1936 a great battle was fought — the March general strike, which was betrayed by traditional bourgeois political parties. The working class marched on. In the future, it channeled its action towards the formation of national trade unions, culminating in the constitution of the Confederation of Cuban Workers (CTC). As already stated, this organization was, during the period from 1939 to 1946, a decisive factor in the defense of the people's interests. An important activity in this stage was the struggle against inflation during the Second World War, together with work by the Communist Party —then called People's Socialist Party, taking advantange of the weak conditions of legality granted by the constitution of 1940— contributing to enrich the political awareness of the working class.

The continuous deepening of that political awareness, as the impossibility of a change within the conditions of the semicolonial system became evident, produced a hounding persecution of the socialist movement and the delivery of the CTC to the agents of the bourgeois political parties, as was the case during the government of Prío Socarrás (1948-1952). The March 10, 1952 military coup that began the second Batista dictatorship was the final note in the reactionary efforts to do away with the social gains obtained by the people since 1933.

The difficult task of setting up a workers' underground movement, now confronting all the reform-seeking political parties, was then begun. The formation of committees for the defense of workers' demands was intended to fight clandestinely against the Truslow mission plan. The great struggle for the 1955 sugar differential wage payment plan, and the great national mobilization against repression and for political amnesty represented a new upsurge in the general protest movement against the dictatorship.

Within the picture of that sharpening people's struggle, there arose a group of young men and women, headed by Fidel Castro, who stormed the Moncada garrison in Santiago de Cuba on July 26, 1953, thus pointing out the new path of armed struggle. From then on, the revolutionary forces progressively rallied round the "victory-through-arms" watchword. When Fidel Castro and his followers landed in Oriente (December 2, 1956), the struggle became expanded as the result of the formation, in the Sierra Maestra Mountains, of a revolutionary army made up mostly of elements from the peasantry and the rural section of the people. Progressively, broad sections of the population were incorporated into the revolutionary fighting. Thousands of Cubans were mobilized by two general strikes (August,

1957 and April, 1958) in spite of brutal repression by the dictatorship. These strikes were, under the existing circumstances, great demonstrations of the revolutionary spirit of the Cuban people, serving to create an awareness of unity in support of the revolutionary program of the Sierra Maestra.

United people's groups were then formed with the participation of members of the 26th of July Movement, the Students' Directorate, the People's Socialist Party, and unaffiliated elements.

The power of the dictatorship was broken by the great military victories of the Rebel Army during the year 1958. Armed struggle spread throughout the nation (northern part of Oriente, Las Villas, and Pinar del Río). During the night hours of December 31, 1958, Batista fled the country. A group of bourgeois politicians attempted to take over the government in Havana, thus trying to impede the full vicory of the Rebel Army headed by Fidel Castro. But a general strike called on January 1, thwarted the scheme. A few days later, the victorious Rebel Army entered Havana and the revolutionary government was established. Though the Revolution then limited itself to carrying out bourgeois-democratic transformations, its most authentic leaders aspired to radically changing conditions in the nation. Irrespective of the economic measures taken, these leaders, with an extraordinarily clear vision of the problems, not only began to change the institutions of the traditional government, but dissolved the old mercenary army, thus destroying the principal instrument of anti-popular reaction.

BIBLIOGRAPHY

1. Guerra, Ramiro. *Op. cit.* chap. XXIV.
2. Pino Santos, Oscar. *Op. cit.*
3. Truslow mission. *Report on Cuba,* 3 vols., Havana, 1951.
4. Cepero Bonilla, Raúl. *Política azucarera 1952 - 1958.* Mexico (published in Havana).

Part VI

THE REVOLUTION

CHAPTER XXVII

TRANSITION TO A SOCIALIST ECONOMY

27.1. *Basic transformation*

27.1.1. Initial program of the Revolutionary Government: the bourgeois-democratic stage. Recovery of embezzled assets, Agrarian Reform. The role of the industrial and commercial bourgeoisie. 27.1.2. The stage of nationalization of foreign assets. The Urban Reform. 27.1.3. General nationalization of industry and commerce.

27.2. *Building socialism*

27.2.1. Basic organs of socialization. 27.2.2. Transformation of the State apparatus. 27.2.3. National economic plans. 27.2.4. Second Agrarian Reform and changes in agricultural organization. 27.2.5 Long-range plans and the role of sugar production. 27.2.6. The situation in 1965.

27.1. *Basic transformations*

27.1.1. Those transformations that took place between January 1, 1959, and the later months of 1961 represent a process of establishment of the social or socialized property. Given the colonial conditions in Cuba, with which we have dealt in previous chapters, the Revolution could not be anything but a profound transformation of the traditional economic, social and political system. The depth and seriousness of the problems faced by the nation and the people demanded substantial and solid solutions. Underdevelopment meant, on the one hand, a very low standard of living, since the yearly per capita income ranged between 250 and 300 pesos and, on the other hand, a permanent and extraordinarily high level of unemployment progressively aggravated by the population increase and the growing need of improving the welfare of the masses. Trade concentration in a highly exportable commodity and in a highly developed market (the United States) were the most visible manifestations of underdevelopment and were, at the same time, the most important obstacles to a harmonious development of the country's production. There was only one way to rectify these basic deficiencies of the economic structure: a revolution which in the economic, social and political aspects would free the stagnant or chained productive forces and, above all, would free the creative forces of the Cuban people, rallying them in support of a powerful program to transform the country.

The decision regarding the way to initiate the transformation of the country was essentially a political one and the experience we have gained since January 1, 1959, proves that in every case the Revolutionary Government made the correct decisions, breaking the vicious circle in which economic underdevelopment found itself. Every new phase of the process initiated in 1959 raised the need to take ever more intense and drastic measures. Consequently, the struggle against underdevelopment deepened the awareness that the political aspect could not be stopped halfway. Every new measure taken revealed the need of complementary measures to extend and strengthen it and guarantee the possibility of a more complete and vigorous economic development because if the growth of the economy were not based on a rapid expansion there was the risk of not fully solving the problems or of excessively postponing their solution. The consensus of opinion is that nowadays an underdeveloped country cannot expect to be able to reproduce the historical development of Great Britain or the United States, that is, that the "model" of capitalist development cannot be repeated again under present historical conditions. The presence of highly developed countries in today's world, like the above-mentioned ones, tends to prevent the independent development of new countries, unless in these countries the State, as a genuine representative of the nation's will, control and carry out the development program, backed by the resolute support of the whole people. On the other hand, there are now in the world countries like the Soviet Union, the People's Republic of China, Czechoslovakia, etc., whose recent history has proved that there are sure ways for self-development without interfering with the independent development of other countries and which, in fact, can be of help to them.

It was therefore necessary that the political decisions coincide with practical formulas to solve Cuba's underdevelopment, that is, that the Revolutionary Government assume the role of representative and, at the same time, of advance guard or leader of the national and people's awareness favoring a vigorous economic development and the breaking of all ties, links and fetters imposed by more developed economies which prevented the free development of the country's productive forces.

The process leading to the new and basic economic structure in our country can be divided into three stages:

First stage: *recovery of embezzled assets and the Law of Agrarian Reform.* The most important political measure taken by the Revolutionary Government in the economic field immediately after assuming power was the *recovery of assets embezzled* by the functionaries, authorities and other officials of the dictatorship. Its significance is clear. Private enterprise was indissolubly linked to the government, on which, in one sense, it depended, and to which, in another sense, it set guidelines; therefore the process of recovery of embezzled assets quickly reached enterprises that apparently had not been connected with the dictatorial regime but which evidently were a product of fraudulent deals with it or had cooperated with it taking advantage of its ties with the government in their own interest. Ever since Machado's dictatorship there had been the opinion that it was necessary to punish corrupt rulers and their accomplices, taking from them what they, in turn, had taken from the nation.

Even though it is not possible to exactly determine in terms of capital or production the importance of the private enterprises and businesses recovered by the nation in 1959, they represented a very important amount of property and capital. It would suffice to remember the construction sector of industry to realize the extent of the impact of the recovery of embezzled assets on the traditional economic structure.

The private sector reacted against the measure even though from the political and ethical points of view it was not objectionable; it reacted that way because of the realization that the recovery of assets would place in the hands of the State a wealth that could serve as the basis to initiate a development program that would reduce its own economic importance to a secondary role. The enemies of progress thought that the measure weakened the base of the "principle" of private ownersnip of the means of production. This explains why the recovery of assets was considered by the internal and external enemies of the Revolution as proof that Cuba was taking the socialist road to solve the country's basic economic problems.

During the second half of 1959 a business recession took place together with numerous statements made by business associations and individual entrepreneurs about investment "insecurity", the absence of a "climate for investments" and other similar concepts which were essentially nothing more than a cloak to cover one thing: the preservation of the so-called "freedom of enterprise" which in Cuba meant the preservation of colonial conditions. It was also said that is was necessary to make a distinction between the accomplices of the dictatorship and those who had contributed capital to the recovered enterprises, thus seeking to establish a distinction which would hide the fact that private enterprise as a whole was an ally of traditional government even though specifically it was not an accomplice in the minor activities of the dictatorship.

The Revolutionary Government acquired enterprises, properties, capitals which it immediately put to work in the solution of national problems, as was the case with building equipment. Yet this stage was characterized by the impossibility of immediately organizing those assets so as to put them at the service of a dynamic development plan. In the first place, the assets consisted of rather isolated enterprises which, as a whole, did not constitute basic sectors or units capable of generating a sufficiently powerful development drive.

On the other hand, big sectors —banking, for instance— were still in private hands and with their characteristic anarchy and resistance to accept the new leading role of the Revolutionary State, prevented the nationalized industries and enterprises from uniting properly to initiate a development plan.

When in January 1959 the revolutionary power was established in the nation, it was necessary that the political decisions made an immediate contribution to lay the foundations for economic development with the means at its disposal within the economic structure prevailing at that moment. That is, there were few State mechanisms available and, therefore, the first steps had to be taken carefully.

The Revolutionary Government and all those who had objectively examined Cuba's economic evolution up to 1958 realized the necessity of starting the march towards development with measures aimed at setting off the process but which, of course, could not be considered as anything but preliminary measures of a limited scope.

Really, the first measures of the Revolutionary Government to start its transforming actions in the first half of 1959 could be grouped under the denomination of *redistribution of income*. The substantial salary increases in several industries, the reduction in public utility service rates (March, 1959) and house rent equivalent to a decrease in the cost of living, represent different aspects of the same policy of *income redistribution* intended to create the necessary internal conditions to set off development.

It was imperative to break the vicious circle of underdevelopment. With income redistribution a new correlation was established between the links of the underdevelopment chain. There is no question but that the political decision was correct in this case. Of course, the traditional businessmen class, their ideologists, and their dependents objected to income redistribution measures, saying that the salary increases represented a curtailment of business profits, and put "in danger" the business ability to invest and reinvest. Really, this attitude tried to conceal an opposition to economic development. Traditionally, Cuba had gone through stages in which the high profits had been based on extremely low salaries, and yet only a very small proportion of the capital accumulated then was devoted to the establishment of new industries or to enlarge and improve the industries already in existence. This means that the poverty of the people was not the inevitable base of development, as the ruling groups pretended in a veiled way, but simply a means to keep profits at a high level. To sum up, the possibility of development did not lie in the policy of maintaining high business profits but in a more general policy which the Cuban businessmen class had not wanted, or been able to carry on, due to its subjection to foreign capital. This policy which included a reorganization of the foreign trade structure and the eradication of the prevalent latifundia was carried out by the Revolution.

Some of the measures taken aimed at a specific redistribution, as in the case of salary increases per production sectors, and others at a general redistribution, as in the case of rate decreases in some public services and house rent.

The income of the poorest sectors of the population did not rise noticeably since the landless and jobless rural masses were practically not benefited by these measures. This situation began to change with the Agrarian Reform Law (May 17, 1959). The elimination of land-leasing and the expropriation of latifundia represented the foundation for the building of a new structure in agricultural production.

The resistance of the land-owning bourgeoisie was not late in coming even though this measure was supported by a powerful national movement which reflected the enthusiasm the great majority felt for it. Some sectors of the industrial bourgeoisie momentarily took advantage of the effects of the agrarian reform which caused consumption of domestic products to grow extraordinarily.

The consumption increase of the lowest income groups was immediately felt. Towards the end of 1959 a strong pressure on the national production and on the stock of imported articles was felt. Naturally, the Revolutionary Government imposed a strict control on foreign exchange which could serve also as an instrument for the selection of imports and the restriction of those considered undesirable. Towards the year's end it was evident that national industry, in spite of the passive resistance of numerous businessmen, was operating at a growing pace. The considerable consumption increase in the rural zones was reflected in the sales volume of the People's Stores, which had been opened recently.

This marked the beginning of a new series of objections to the economic policy. It was said that inflation represented an imminent menace to economic development. Obviously, there were inflationary pressures, but it was overlooked that, income redistribution excepted (already weakened by the end of 1959), the rest of the Revolutionary Government's measures represented compensatory means to check that tendency (reduction of high incomes, elimination of luxury or undesirable products, and investments in enterprises engaged in basic production).

As agriculture and industry fell more and more under the control of the State, each invested peso represented more and more a means of production or a finished product. By the middle of 1960 the inflationary pressures had decreased. Once more a correct policy had been applied and the discouraging forecasts had been proved wrong.

Up to this point, detractors to the contrary, the Revolution had not exceeded the scope of a bourgeois-democratic transformation of radical character. However, since July of 1959 the attacks and aggressions by imperialist interests, who considered themselves affected by the income redistribution and the Agrarian Reform, began. Cancelling the "aid" program, public hearings in the United States Senate with counter-revolutionary witnesses, Fifth Consultative Meeting of Foreign Affairs Ministers, in Chile, to discuss the "Caribbean tension", was a formula devised by the United States to condemn the Cuban Revolution. In October began the attacks and bombardments with planes taking off from United States bases. Thus, the internal and external aggression became a stimulus for the more radical elements of the Revolution, who were acquiring a conscience and objectives of their own during the implementation of the Agrarian Reform.

27.1.2. Second stage: *nationalization of foreign capital.* The stages we are dealing with cannot be thought of as jumps, but rather as moments in which the leadership of the Revolution took action in concrete, specific measures. Therefore, in what we call the second stage it is worth noticing the continuation of the process started in the first. The enmity of the businessmen emerged immediately under very different —sometimes very sophisticated— forms of opposition to the revolutionary orientation. These men, who did not see with clarity the recovery of assets, began to decrease or disrupt production in their own firms and sometimes they even abandoned or paralyzed them. Sometimes on the pretext of not having raw materials (among other reasons, because they had not applied either in time or due form for import permits); in some cases, as they said, for lack of operating capital or because their accounts receivable were not collected with sufficient speed to allow them to keep going; and finally, accusing the workers of a perverse unwillingness to work. By the end of 1959 and early 1960 the objective of the reactionary offensive became evident, to paralyze the country's economy.

The Revolutionary Government dealt with that resistance by means of several measures which had one objective: to keep all work centers operating and, beside, to open those factories which had closed shortly before January 1st, 1959, or soon afterwards. This was accomplished through interventions by reason of conflicts between the workers and the employers. We must call attention to the fact that the industries implied were not the biggest nor the basic ones but rather the medium-sized industries or work centers. Because of their size and economic role the nationalization of those enterprises (even though they represented an important acquisition) did not put at the disposal of the State —as in the case of recovered industries— a volume of capital and production means capable of generating a quick economic development.

The increased standard of living and the encouragement to development brought about by income redistribution laid the foundations for the establishment of a new economic organization in the country.

Income redistribution was a temporary measure which, by no means, could be applied indefinitely. According to results produced, it was possible to advance and deepen the process of economic reorganization and, therefore, it was necessary to control and check it. But it had to be substituted by more solid measures. This was the problem faced in 1960.

The Cuban people, especially the workers, realized the need of measures to stimulate the country's investment capacity. This resulted in a voluntary 4% salary contribution to create an industrialization fund and in some sectors, like that of sugar, the labor unions themselves actively supported a policy of freezing salaries.

The attempt to paralyze production gained strength in the early months of 1960. An attempt was also aimed at depriving the country of its means of defense. This became evident with the sabotage of the ship *La Coubre* in Havana when it was unloading a shipment of arms acquired from Belgium by the Revolutionary Government. In June, it was necessary to intervene in the old refineries (Texaco, Esso and Shell) which deliberately were exhausting the stock of fuels essential to transportation and production On July 6, Washington announced a 700,000-ton cut in the Cuban sugar quota. The only possible answer to these economic aggressions was the one given by the Revolutionary Government when it confiscated United States enterprises. This was intended not only as a way to compensate for the damages that the quota reduction momentarily might have caused to the country but also as a means to establish an equity in the relations between the country that invested and the one in which the investments were made; in fact, the more reliable estimates showed that in the last 25 years the foreign capital invested in Cuba had reproduced itself many times and had been exported to the United States as profits; so, in fact, the confiscation of those firms was nothing more than the establishment of true equality in the relations between the two countries.

So, on the fifth of July a law was passed authorizing the President of the Republic and the Prime Minister to nationalize enterprises through resolutions; the next day, 26 big foreign enterprises were nationalized.

The nationalization of foreign capital, concretely, United States capital, put in the hands of the Revolutionary Government well-equipped, basic industries; suffice is to mention the two big public utilities monopolies (electric power and telephone) and numerous sugar mills.

It was then possible to start the planning of economic development since the Revolution now had industries which, once at the service of the other industries, would be important centers or points of support.

Yet a great part of the industries owned by nationals, as well as industries of United States capital not nationalized, remained outside the process because the first nationalization movement was based exclusively on the principle of compensation for economic aggression. This stage of the process ran through the first half of 1960.

27.1.3. Third stage: *general nationalization of industry.* As we know, the second stage met increasing resistance from the business class who adopted an attitude of allowing the gradual deterioration of the financial conditions of their enterprises. For that reason, the Government continued intervening in industries which had to be managed by the Revolutionary Government and put to work in the solution of national problems.

On the other hand, imperialism took another step in its collective aggression policy when on July 24 the Ministers of Foreign Affairs held in Costa Rica the Seventh Consultative Meeting, from which the Cuban delegation walked out. Now, besides seeking internal economic paralysis, suddenly reducing the sugar exports, withdrawing credits for the importation of merchandise, and preventing the arming of the Cuban people, imperialism started a general blockade, implementing through its Latin American puppets the policy of breaking relations, and trying to get the capitalist countries of Europe not to trade with Cuba. On one hand, the Cuban people's answer was not late in coming: it approved the First Declaration of Havana; on the other hand, the USSR, symbolizing socialist solidarity with the national liberation movements, offered and provided Cuba with essential raw materials, like oil, to keep production going, and purchased substantial amounts of sugar and other products.

This situation lasted until November of 1960, when the big industrial and commercial enterprises —national and United States— remaining in private hands were nationalized. On September 17, the banks were nationalized, and on October 13, 382 big industrial, commercial and public service enterprises were nationalized. Evidently, an awareness and experience existed that the economic development plan had to be carried out in a general way, that is, embracing all the basic sectors of the economic structure. It was realized that as long as some of those sectors were in private hands it was not possible to arrange a harmonious plan for development. Besides, banking and private industry in Cuba, as in any capitalist country, were characterized by their anarchy, that is, they were out to make money without taking into consideration the needs of the nation's masses.

When nationalization of basic sectors of the Cuban economy was about to be carried out, the banks reduced credits for basic productive activities while enlarging those intended for nonbasic activities which, in some cases, were even undesirable. The big industrialists were concerned only with the maintenance of a conveniently high level of profits and did not reinvest. That is, they were interested neither in enlarging production to satisfy the growing market nor in creating jobs. And this was all the more necessary because by the beginning of 1960 the positive effects of income increases and the expansion of the domestic market were felt as a result of the implementation of the Agrarian Reform Law. After this fundamental step, which defined the Revolution as something that surpassed the bourgeois-democratic "model", there remained a strong capitalist sector, made up of the owners of urban real estate, which was a disturbing influence on development plans. The Urban Reform Law, passed on October 14, 1960, sought to eliminate that group within a period of five years. At the end of that period a great part of the tenants would become the owners of their houses. Another group would become owners after a longer period and still another would have to pay only 10% of their salaries as house rent.

The nationalization of the most important sectors of the economy —in October 1960— added to the awareness of the Cuban people with respect to the road to be followed; now the success of the revolutionary program had to be based on the proper distribution of the resources between consumption and investment. At this moment the income redistribution policy —already weakened by the freezing of salaries and the voluntary 4 per cent. contribution— had to cease and give place to a policy of adequate utilization of the resources with a view to gradually raising the standard of living on the basis of a substantial production growth. In short, the success of all economic development plans depended on the correct allocation of a growing proportion of the resources to capital investments.

Nationalization, on the other hand, means that when the State receives practically all the benefits previously received by the business sector it can follow the policy of raising the nation's living standard under the form of services to the whole working population. Thus, the previous policy of income redistribution was substituted by a policy of growing availability of public services, which is a proper way to supplement income, particularly in the low income brackets.

27.2. *Building socialism*

27.2.1. Basic organs of socialization. In October of 1960, some facts showed the failure of the threats, aggressions, and policy of blockade and isolation carried out by imperialism. Yet the Yankee monopolies and their political representatives believed they could smash the Revolution by strengthening those measures contrary to all principles of international coexistence. Accordingly, on October 16, a general embargo was imposed on products of trade with Cuba. Besides, on December 16, it was decided to withdraw the Cuban sugar quota for the first six months of 1961. The sugar trade with Cuba was not permanently cancelled it seems, because it was expected that the aggression then being prepared —and once carried out— would defeat the Revolution within the first six months of 1961.

Of course, with the nationalization implemented in October 1960, a basic step was taken that allowed the State to plan the economy, carry out the plan, and reorganize completely the administration to put it at the service of that plan. On the other hand, with the nationalization of the whole sugar industry and the transformation of banking into a social service, two basic elements came to help development. It was now possible to plan the modernization of the sugar industry to make it more efficient and make sure that no industrial installations or lands were left idle. This was not possible under the private ownership system. Besides, when the financial resources of the nation are under the control of the banks they can be directed towards the promotion of the country's basic production.

But, of course, that nationalization could not be a simple change in the administration or ownership of the enterprises. A development program and economic planning presuppose that all industries and production centers be integrated in such a way that one helps the other and that the productivity of all be directed, in a general way, to national funds intended for new investments and to improving the standard of living of the whole population. Once the expropriation of the big businesses was accomplished and the objectives and nature of the plan were set, new managing bodies and operating methods were needed in industry and commerce. Those new bodies were already being developed in agriculture through the implementation of the Agrarian Reform Law (INRA, Zones of Agricultural Development, People's Farms, Sugar Cooperatives and others); regarding other sectors, only in the Industrialization Department of INRA —where the concept of consolidated enterprises was developed— the beginnings of the new organization were established. The grouping or *consolidation* of national industries —in which the workers' participation is fundamental —conformed to the need of integration. If each nationalized industry were not integrated to the rest in its branch, and with all other industries in the country, there would be a possibility that the differences in efficiency and productivity would go on indefinitely. On the other hand, through integration it was possible to transfer to other industries or put at their service capital resources, production means, and labor that would have remained idle in a private enterprise and which could be fully utilized now. This was something that could not be even dreamed of under a private ownership system and would be very difficult to achieve under a system without centralized integration of industries.

In fact, once the nationalization and integration were accomplished, it was possible to speak not of State ownership but of social or socialized ownership. State ownership can be found in capitalist countries, but of a very different nature from the one existing in Cuba at that moment because, *firstly,* in capitalist countries the State enterprises behave just like private ones; and, *secondly,* the production or services rendered are not aimed at activating development in other branches of production or at improving the standard of living of the nation's masses. Property can be considered as socialized when it is an integral and indissoluble part of the general development plan and supports the two fundamental aims of the Revolutionary Government; a very powerful economic growth and a parallel improvement of the standard of living of the population. Within the consolidated enterprises there arose the need for the workers and the whole population to participate in the preparation of plans, to watch production, and to lead in the administrative policy and measures; that is, the workers must be active participants in the new organization through a series of mechanisms and functions which are in the hands of the workers in all work centers, for instance, the production assembly, production council, and emulation. They are new organs, some of them temporary —as is usual in every process— which help to socialize the nationalized assets. These organs and mechanisms marked the beginning of social ownership.

The growing capacity of the new Cuban State —born of the revolutionary transformation— to provide the nation with the daily necessities is clearly reflected in the establishment of numerous rural towns, in the elimination of chronic unemployment, the multiplication of educational facilities and in the extension of health services to zones that up to 1958 did not enjoy any of the basic elements necessary to the welfare of the population.

27.2.2. The year 1961 marks not only the final moments in the first stage of imperialist aggression but also the beginning of socialist construction. On January 3, Washington broke diplomatic and consular relations with Cuba; on March 31 the sugar quota was cancelled for the whole year. The stage having thus been set, air attacks were carried out on the 15 and 17 of April against several airports, and a mercenary army made up of Cuban counter-revolutionaries, trained, equipped and protected by the U.S. Armed Forces, landed at Girón Beach. The Cuban people, as one, got ready to fight and defeated the invaders in less than three days. On April 16, at the funeral of the air attacks victims, the Revolution, through Major Fidel Castro, was publicly declared to be a socialist one and the decision to face with growing determination the imperialist aggressions was proclaimed to the whole world.

After the nationalization of the country's basic economy it was necessary to keep creating the material base for the fulfillment of development plans. On the one hand it was necessary to provide for the training of cadres, and this required the eradication of illiteracy. The literacy campaign, when more than a hundred thousand Cubans of all ages were mobilized and went to the rural zones and mountains, was a complete success. On the other hand, the State apparatus demanded important institutional changes; the ministries of Industries, Foreign Trade, and Domestic Trade were created; the national banks, the Ministry of Finances and the Central Planning Board were reorganized; the local and provincial JUCEI (Boards of Coordination, Execution and Inspection) came into being. The basic structure of those organizations conformed to the principles of centralization and mobilization of resources demanded by socialist planning. This meant that the foundations of a socialist State had been laid, which, in the political plane, was reflected by the beginning of the integration of all revolutionary forces with the end of organizing the United Party of the Cuban Socialist Revolution. At the same time the National Association of Small Farmers (ANAP) was born.

The new State organization put an end to the second stage, since it introduced the basic order in the operating aspects of the economy which, by the logic of the process started in January 1959, had not been able to adopt permanent form and methods. Of course, this organization, even though different from the inherited State apparatus, still had elements unsuitable for future tasks. But, at any rate, as it developed later, the ideological remnants and practices of capitalism could be eliminated by ordinary administrative means, by the growing awareness of the workers and of the whole population, and by the leading presence of the Party.

In fact, the subsequent creation of the National Institute of Water Resources, the Ministry of the Sugar Industry, and the reorganization of the ministries of Transport, Construction and Labor as well as of the universities, and the establishment of the Academy of Sciences, were all part of that complementary work which demands a constant adjustment of the institutional forms to the experience acquired by the Revolution.

27.2.3. Once the big enterprises were nationalized, the creation of an administrative structure more closely fitted to the principles of socialism made it possible to initiate in 1961 the preparation of the First National Economic Plan whose discussion at national level was started at the mass assembly held on October 20. The discussion went on later at the production unit level, that is, with the participation of the workers and the enterprises.

This national plan, which for the first time integrated the whole economy around the investments intended for development, was based on the transformations accomplished up to that moment. On the one hand, according to the 1960 labor census, unemployment had been reduced to 8.9% of the labor force; on the other hand, the basic industrial equipment was fully at the service of production objectives; besides, diversification and mechanization of agriculture had been started; some plans were being developed to give technical training to the workers. The plan gave rise to discussions about several problems, such as financing, value, operative centralization, which reflected a careful search for practical and technical methods, both correct and genuinely socialist.

Naturally, through the execution of the plan during 1962 it was possible to acquire a deeper knowledge of the real situation of the country's productive resources, laying the foundations for a more adequate preparation of subsequent plans, whose main characteristics would be the efforts to adjust foreign trade to national production goals, to improve quality and to raise productivity. The results can be seen in the 1964 plan.

27.2.4. During 1962 and 1963 significant changes were made in the organization of agricultural production. In the plenary meeting held at its first anniversary, ANAP defined itself as a mass organization of peasants, thus eliminating the managerial tendencies born within it as expression of a stage of the Revolution's general development. Besides, at the Congress of Sugar Cooperatives (August 17, 1962), Major Fidel Castro explained why those cooperatives should become Farms —as it happened— since they were made up of agricultural workers for whom the participation in the ownership and profits derived from the operation of the farm, even in a cooperative way, was a social regression. More than a hundred thousand peasant families had become owners of the land they tilled, but agricultural workers were not demanding and did not need ownership of the land but rather year-round work, good salaries and efficient public services (health, education, etc.).

The specific problems of sugar production were raised in concrete form for the first time the following year; lack of manpower, role of the private sugar planter; and, as a result, the mechanization in the cutting and loading of cane, the massive mobilization of voluntary workers during the sugar crop, the introduction of economic incentives for private farmers as well as the strengthening of the regional and provincial directive organs were also discussed.

The Revolution then showed a great ability to take advantage of experience when it corrected the errors made in 1961 and 1962. On the other hand, it came out stronger from the so-called Caribbean Crisis, provoked by capitalism's desperate attempt to blockade Cuba completely (October, 1962). In the face of the second stage of aggression, which would be carried out not by mercenary forces but by the regular United States armed forces —with the support of mercenary bands operating in the countryside— the Cuban people did not weaken; on the contrary they got ready to fight to the end for their freedom and well-being.

The extermination of groups of bandits armed by imperialism, which had tried to undermine the Revolution, had as a corollary the Second Agrarian Reform (October 3, 1963) eliminating the landowners of more than five *caballerías* (67 hectares), whose negative attitude regarding agricultural development and their support to the counter-revolutionary bandits constituted the last resource of capitalism. That measure deepened the worker-peasant alliance and favored production as well as the distribution of crops.

27.2.5. As a result of the changes made during 1961, 1962 and 1963, and of the victory of the people over the blockade which did not win general support in Latin America or the capitalist world, the Revolution entered into a maturing stage which in 1964 was characterized by production growth and the preparation of a Long-Term Plan for 1965-70.

On the other hand, the long-term establishment of mutual-benefit economic relations with the countries of the socialist camp guaranteed the sale of sugar —starting in 1960 and enlarged in 1963— under conditions that made it possible to plan the country's economic development.

The long-term plan, prepared in 1964, anticipates a 10,000,000-ton sugar production for 1970, as well as the start of mechanization in the sugar harvest and the improvement of plantations on the basis of high-yield cane and more scientific methods of cultivation. But other goals were being incorporated into the plan, for instance, cattle development through massive artificial insemination, enlargement and replanting of coffee plantations, the maintenance of a high degree of agricultural diversification, and the continuation of the reforestation project. Or course, the long-term plan acknowledges sugar production as the driving force that can push ahead future development.

The 1964-65 sugar production of more than 6,000,000 tons not only reflects the growing organizing ability and resources but also guarantees the fulfillment of the goals set for 1970.

27.2.6. The success of the sugar harvest and the visible accomplishments in the agricultural plan mark the year 1965. In the first place, monthly egg production went above 60,000,000. On the other hand, fruit distribution —unrationed— to the urban population, together with the unrationed sale of some vegetables, reflects an extraordinary production and organization level and marks the first successes of the economic plans.

In general, 1965 should in the future be considered as the expression of a higher and wider socialist development, that is, as a significant proof that under the conditions of a country like Cuba it is possible to achieve a quick and harmonious development of the whole economy.

Since 1960, the situation is characterized by the resolute struggle of the Cuban people. Some foreign governments which act as representatives of the monopolies or are subjected to them —headed by the United States —have carried on a ceaseless political, military and economic aggression against Cuba. They have avowed that they can not allow the success of the Cuban Revolution to become bigger and stronger. Yet their efforts have been defeated by the Cuban people's determination. Socialism is invincible in Cuba.

The solidarity of the other socialist countries has played an extraordinary role in the whole process while the improved organizing ability of the workers, quick technical training, growing productivity, awareness and adjustment of institutional procedures to planning needs are positive facts which guarantee an unerring march towards socialism. The inevitable experimentation is not, as the enemies of the Cuban people would say, a proof of weakness; on the contrary, the road to socialism is full of daily experiments, whose fruits, when immediately utilized, become a powerful creative force. The future success of socialism is not based on the freezing or crystallization of the revolutionary power but on the awareness and determination of the people and their leaders, on constant improvement and the training of the revolutionary forces.

New factors are pushing development ahead. We are entering the stage of administrative decentralization, technical revolution, science promotion, and growth of the Cuban Communist Party. We are on the road to socialism.

The people and their leaders know where they are going and what they want. Therefore, all difficulties brought about by the enemies and the heroic struggle itself will be overcome.

On the occasion of hurricane Flora our Prime Minister said some thing that will always hold true:

> "Today we are working for nobody but ourselves. Human labor is the creator of all wealth. Labor is stronger than nature. With our labor we will emerge victorious from this trial".

BIBLIOGRAPHY

There is no general reference work on the Revolution. However, materials for the study of the process can be found in the series entitled *Obra Revolucionaria* published in Havana since 1960, in which the main documents, and especially speeches of leaders of the Revolutionary Government, constituting basic study material, are periodically reproduced.

El camino verdadero. Speech by Fidel Castro on February 24 1960. Havana, 1960.

La liberación económica de Cuba. People's University, first period, No. 1, Havana, June, 1969.

SPEECH BY FIDEL CASTRO ON JUNE 24, 1960. *Obra Revolucionaria.* No. 12, June 25, 1960. (Summary of Sugar History in Relation to the United States).

SPEECH BY FIDEL CASTRO ON AUGUST 6, 1960. *Obra Revolucionaria,* No. 17, August 9, 1960. (Nationalization policy).

SPEECH BY FIDEL CASTRO ON OCTOBER 15, 1960. *Obra Revolucionaria,* No. 27, October 7, 1960. (Nationalization).
August 9, 1960. (Nationalization policy).

Nuestra Industria, monthly magazine of the Ministry of Industry, Havana, beginning in February, 1961.

ALFREDO MENÉNDEZ. "Balance de la Zafra de 1961. Primera Zafra del Pueblo." *Cuba Socialista,* No. 1, September, 1961.

OSVALDO DORTICÓS. "La Revolución Cubana en su cuarto aniversario." *Cuba Socialista,* No. 17, January, 1963.

REGINO BOTI. "El Plan de Desarrollo Económico de 1962." *Cuba Socialista,* No. 4, December, 1961.

MAJOR *Che* GUEVARA. *El Papel de la Ayuda Exterior en el Desarrollo de Cuba,* Havana, 1961 (MINFAR).

REGINO BOTI. "El Plan de la Economía Nacional de Cuba para 1963." *Cuba Socialista,* No. 20, April, 1963.

CARLOS RAFAEL RODRÍGUEZ. "Cuatro Años de Reforma Agraria." *Cuba Socialista,* No. 21, May, 1963.

ALFREDO MENÉNDEZ. "Algunas Experiencias de la Zafra de 1963." *Cuba Socialista,* No. 23, July, 1963.

CARLOS RAFAEL RODRÍGUEZ. "El nuevo camino de la agricultura cubana." *Cuba Socialista,* No. 27, November, 1963.

RAÚL LEÓN. "La planificación del comercio exterior." *Cuba Socialista,* No. 28, December, 1963.

ALBÁN LATASTE. "1964. Año de la Economía." *Cuba Socialista.* No. 30, February, 1964.

MARCELO FERNÁNDEZ FONT. "Desarrollo y funciones de la Banca Socialista de Cuba." *Cuba Socialista,* No. 30, February, 1964.

MAJOR *Che* GUEVARA. "La Banca, el Crédito y el Socialismo," *Cuba Socialista,* No. 31, May, 1964.

MAJOR *Che* GUEVARA. "Posición de Cuba en la Conferencia Mundial de Comercio y Desarrollo." *Cuba Socialista,* No. 33, May, 1964.

ALBERTO MARTÍNEZ. "El plan de la economía nacional para 1964." *Cuba Socialista*, No. 31, May, 1964.

Printed in Section No. 274.05.00 of the
Consolidated Enterprise of Graphic Arts.
Havana, Cuba. Free Territory of America.